The Care and Keeping
of Cultural Facilities

The Care and Keeping of Cultural Facilities

A Best Practice Guidebook for Museum Facility Management

Angela Person-Harm and Judie Cooper

ROWMAN & LITTLEFIELD
Lanham • Boulder • New York • Toronto • Plymouth, UK

Published by Rowman & Littlefield
4501 Forbes Boulevard, Suite 200, Lanham, Maryland 20706
www.rowman.com

10 Thornbury Road, Plymouth PL6 7PP, United Kingdom

British Library Cataloguing in Publication Information Available

Library of Congress Cataloging-in-Publication Data

Person-Harm, Angela.
  The care and keeping of cultural facilities : a best practice guidebook for museum facility management / Angela Person-Harm and Judie Cooper.
    pages cm
  Includes bibliographical references and index.
  ISBN 978-0-7591-2359-5 (cloth : alk. paper)—ISBN 978-0-7591-2360-1 (pbk. : alk. paper)— ISBN 978-0-7591-2361-8 (electronic)
  1. Museums—Management—Handbooks, manuals, etc. 2. Facility management—Handbooks, manuals, etc. 3. Public institutions—Management—Handbooks, manuals, etc. 4. Museums—Planning—Handbooks, manuals, etc. I. Cooper, Judie. II. Title.
  AM121.P473 2014
  069.068—dc23
                                                                    2013045395

Printed in the United States of America

CONTENTS

CONTENTS

LIST OF TABLES AND BOXES

Tables

Boxes

FOREWORD

When you are the custodian of irreplaceable artifacts that define our history, our cultural heritage, and the natural world, and you host millions of visitors each year, the responsibility can keep you awake at night. The challenges have come without warning due to earthquake, by steady onslaught through a snowstorm, and by storm surge from a hurricane. Though they may seem less dramatic, the daily concerns involved in maintaining public spaces and preserving collections ranging from artistic and historic treasures to scientific specimens are just as important. Those who protect and maintain the facilities of our nation's cultural institutions have to prepare equally for the mundane and the disastrous.

From benchmarking to best practices, and from energy efficiency to artifact preservation, *The Care and Keeping of Cultural Facilities* shows the way. Judie Cooper and Angela Person-Harm have crafted a book that is both a guide for those new to the field, as well as a reference for experienced professionals. Judie has honed her skills at the Smithsonian's Office of Facilities Management and Reliability (OFMR) since 1978, and has worked in departments across the Smithsonian Institution. In her current role as a facility management analyst, she takes responsibility for best practices, policy documentation, employee training, and benchmarking. She has been involved in outreach programs for students, other members of the museum community, and the general public.

Angela, too, came through the Smithsonian in 2009 as an intern in facilities management when she was finishing her master's degree in museum studies at the University of Oklahoma. In 2010, she returned to the Smithsonian as a visiting student while at work on her dissertation at Oklahoma. She and Judie coauthored an article that documented many challenges for museum facilities managers. That article was published in the *Facility Management Journal* and became the beginning point for this book.

During my years as president of Georgia Tech and more recently as secretary of the Smithsonian, I learned that today's large, complex organizations need first-class facilities staff to run smoothly. When I look around me, I am mindful of the words of the sculptor Constantin Brancusi, who said, "Architecture is inhabited sculpture." Make no mistake—caring for that architecture is as important as its creation. The artistry of those who maintain facilities remains long after their architects have moved on to new projects.

At universities like Georgia Tech and institutions like the Smithsonian, the facilities base is a mix of the old and the new. Many of the existing buildings at the Smithsonian are particularly complicated because of their historic nature. Whether a project involves renovation or new construction, today the design has to incorporate the latest concepts in technology and sustainability. It must serve the expectations of the users and the public and take advantage of the latest in energy conservation and water reuse. As a result, buildings are more sophisticated than ever and call for advanced skill sets to operate and maintain them. And the work must be done more efficiently in this time of constrained budgets.

At the Smithsonian, a number of our buildings date from the mid-to-late 1800s. The Castle, which houses my office and much of our administration, is the oldest Smithsonian building and opened in 1855. Our Victorian-style Arts and Industries building opened in 1881, but was closed in 2004 and was in limbo until 2011, when we began needed renovations. It is on schedule to reopen in 2014 with exhibitions celebrating American ingenuity. Indeed, the project itself has been an exercise in ingenuity. We have had to respect the original architectural concepts while incorporating innovative technology into the design. Blast-resistant windows contain nanoparticles that filter the light coming in while allowing a clear view from inside. Cisterns will be employed around the building to capture, store, and reuse water. All of these ideas came from our professionals and will lead to a building that will serve the public for another century.

My appreciation of the critical work performed by facilities staff goes back to my days as a graduate student at the University of California, Berkeley, where I studied civil engineering and became interested in the causes and effects of earthquakes. In Northern California, earthquakes are a way of life, but even here on the East Coast we are not immune to them. On August 23, 2011, an earthquake put everyone on notice that even the nation's capital is vulnerable. The Washington, DC, area felt the shockwaves of a 5.8 earthquake from its epicenter in Mineral, Virginia. Approximately one-third of the U. S. population felt the effects, including people in New York City who ran from their buildings when it hit.

Damage was widespread through Virginia and Washington, DC, with significant economic impact. The Washington Monument has been closed for two years, and the Washington National Cathedral sustained damage to its central tower and its flying buttresses. Damage to Smithsonian buildings and our collections was contained but will ultimately cost upward of $20 million to repair. To compound the problems caused by the earthquake, our facilities team had to deal with a double whammy as Hurricane Irene arrived just four days later.

During Irene's assault on the East Coast, leaks occurred in some of our museums as a result of newly opened cracks from the earthquake. But the Smithsonian Disaster Management Program, implemented immediately, obviated further damage. Our staff prepared for the worst while working around the clock. In New York City, officers at our National Museum of the American Indian George Gustav Heye Center and the Cooper-Hewitt, National Design Museum sheltered in place for two days to give protection coverage until relief could report for duty. OFMR crews filled and moved over 1,000 bags of sand—around 20 tons' worth—to prevent flooding in buildings that were susceptible to storm surge. While the conditions were not as severe as expected, our staff demonstrated how prepared they were for any contingency.

Preserving cultural facilities demands knowledge, skill, and the flexibility to deal with the unexpected. *The Care and Keeping of Cultural Facilities* offers a wealth of wisdom culled from experiences here at the Smithsonian and other institutions around the world. New facilities management professionals and seasoned veterans alike will benefit from reading this wonderful resource.

G. Wayne Clough
Secretary of the Smithsonian
December 2013

ACKNOWLEDGMENTS

This book grew out of some interesting conversations about facility management practices in museums and cultural institutions. Over time, we talked with many facility managers in museums, zoos, libraries, science centers, and art galleries and kept returning to one theme: facility management of a cultural facility is different from that of commercial, residential, retail, or other environments. Cultural facilities are places that create environments that ultimately support learning and interest, conservation and research, and, to be managed well, they require particular expertise.

After a number of discussions, we decided to act on our observations and write an article about managing cultural facilities. The article was published in the International Facility Management Association's *Facility Management Journal* (January–February 2011). The article was well received, and it led to an invitation from the American Alliance of Museums (AAM) to speak at their 2011 conference about the challenges that museum executives face when managing the built environment. Following the AAM conference, we set out to conduct a literature review of cultural facility management best practices and discovered that there was a reason for all of this interest and excitement: a guidebook that specifically addressed cultural facility management had yet to be written. We felt we had no other choice but to set out planning a text that would begin to address the range of issues related to managing cultural institution facilities.

One of the benefits of working with facility managers is that the community shares information and supports each other. The networking and knowledge sharing in the facility management community certainly benefit the professionals as well as the cultural facilities. A number of facility managers and professionals shared their time and insights for this project through interviews, behind-the-scenes tours, questionnaires, and networking.

We want to thank our colleagues who helped so much with the creation of this book, especially John Bixler (Smithsonian Institution), Daniel Davies (Smithsonian Institution), Alan Dirican (Baltimore Museum of Art), Stephanie Erickess (Seattle Public Library), Roger Hankins (Smithsonian Institution), Christy Jellets (Atlanta Botanical Garden, now with Girl Scouts of America), Loren Plotner (Smithsonian Institution), Thomas Reavey (Smithsonian Institution), Lee Richardson (Experience Music Project), Angel Rodriguez (Smithsonian Institution), and David Samec (National Gallery of Art). We also would like to thank the members of the Museums/Cultural Institutions Council of the International Facility Management Association for their support.

We would like to thank the dozens of individuals, organizations, and institutions who were willing to share their photographs, stories, and information, which appear in the info boxes and tables found in this text. We would also like to express our appreciation to Rowman & Littlefield for seeing the potential of this book and for their enthusiastic support throughout the writing and publishing process—especially Marissa Parks, Charles Harmon, and Robert Hayunga, who worked with us as the book took shape.

Special thanks are due to those who have championed this project. At the Smithsonian Institution, our thanks go to Nancy Bechtol and Kendra Gastright for their support and encouragement from start to finish. Judie would like to convey her thanks to and deepest appreciation for Angela Person-Harm. The opportunity to work with a professional of Angela's caliber on this project (and others) has been her pleasure. She would also like to thank her parents, John and Virginia Cooper, for their encouragement and support; her brother Jim for his sage facilities advice from the design/build and project management perspective; and her daughter, Kaylie, for being a keen observer of the built environment in the many cultural facilities they visited over the years.

Angela would like to thank Judie Cooper for advocating for this project at every turn, for imparting her countless insights into the field of cultural facility management, and for sharing her truly contagious passion for this critical discipline. She would also like to thank her husband, Nickolas Harm, who dedicated many hours to carefully editing the manuscript, and her daughter, Nora, for being the perfect companion on their many visits to museums over the past several years.

Finally, we must thank the many practitioners, scholars, and organizations that went before us, documenting the range of best practices in cultural facility management that we cite in this text. Without their enthusiasm for the field of facility management and their meticulous care for cultural institutions, this text would not be possible.

Angela Person-Harm
Judie Cooper

AN INTRODUCTION TO MUSEUM AND CULTURAL INSTITUTION FACILITY MANAGEMENT

For centuries, cultural facilities have been among the most important places of gathering, scholarship, and historical significance the world over. Counted among these facilities are museums, performing arts centers, libraries, archives, historical sites, art institutes, theatres, zoos, and botanical gardens, to name a few. Many of these facilities are hundreds—even thousands—of years old. Regardless of age, each cultural facility has unique requirements when it comes to maintaining its structural and aesthetic integrity, serving its staff and visitors, educating the public, and, in many cases, keeping its collections safe and sound for perpetuity. Because of these unique requirements, the individuals who manage cultural facilities play a very important role in achieving each of their institutions' missions.

Facility management (FM) of cultural institutions integrates "people, place, process and technology" (IFMA 2012). Take a minute to consider the people, places, processes, and technologies that must be integrated in your cultural institution on a daily basis as means for meeting the institution's mission. Who are the unique people served by your cultural institution facility? What type of place is it? And what is unique about this place? Consider a range of elements, from concrete details, like its climate and architecture, to more intangible features, like its character. Now, consider the processes facilitated within your museum, like special events, exhibitions, conservation, and pest management; the list surely goes on. How does technology, like building automation systems, help keep art and artifacts safe and sound in your museum? By integrating these four elements—people, place, process, and technology—facility managers can ensure that operations, maintenance, capital improvements, and support activities are performed in the manner that best supports the mission and strategic goals of the cultural institution.

Facility managers in cultural institutions—regardless of whether there is only one member of facility management or a whole FM team—must constantly balance their facilities' preservation needs against their institutional mandate to educate visitors by opening their doors to share facilities and artifacts. Artifacts, zoo animals, and botanical collections are often in their most well-preserved and healthiest states when they are kept away from throngs of people and, instead, held in very particular environmental conditions. For this reason, facility managers are tasked with the tough challenge of keeping these things safe and sound amid the high traffic that often accompanies exhibitions, performances, and special events (Merritt 2005).

This chapter describes how several prominent types of cultural institutions—including museums, zoos, and botanical gardens—have evolved to their current levels of sophistication, as well as some distinct challenges faced by their facility managers. Additionally, this chapter touches on issues that cultural facility managers face as they are tasked with serving special events, implementing new technologies, and meeting growing storage and conservation needs.

The Evolution of Museums

The word *museum* has had a number of definitions that have evolved over time. During classical times, the Greeks used the term to refer to a temple dedicated to the nine Muses who oversaw the vitality of the fields of astronomy, dance, comedy, history, oratory, tragedy, poetry, the epic, and music. Macedonian general Ptolemy Soter founded one of the most prominent early museums—the Mouseion of Alexandria—in the third century BC. This museum held statues of prominent intellectuals, natural history samples, botanical and zoological parks, and scientific instruments. Perhaps more importantly, it was used as a place of study for important scholars of the day (Alexander and Alexander 2008).

Grand museums, like the Mouseion of Alexandria, vanished from record for some time, though it has been recorded that the Roman elite were active collectors of art and artifacts. Then, during the Middle Ages, religious relics and other curiosities were assembled within churches and abbeys (Burcaw 1997). At this time, the word *museum* was used primarily to refer to places of study in which scholars gathered. By the 1800s, the term had evolved to mean a building in which collections were held for preservation, display, and research purposes (von Naredi-Rainer and Hilger 2004).

Leading up to this, wealthy individuals collected interesting or entertaining items in what were termed curiosity cabinets or *Wunderkammers*. In addition, many wealthy individuals began amassing large art collections—some royal art collections became so large that dedicated buildings were built for the sole purpose of storing this additional art. So, it followed that many of the great European art museums were founded as a result of royal art collecting, when royals began opening their collections for limited public viewing.

Museum-style public viewing of collections has been traced back to the public viewing of Abbot Boisot's private collection following his death, at the Abbey of Saint Vincent in Besançon, France, in 1764. Nearly 50 years later, the British Museum began hosting up to thirty visitors per day. These visitors were required to apply, in advance, for admission to the museum. Around the same time, the royal French government started to allow select members of the public to visit the Palais de Luxembourg's picture gallery. By the late 1700s, plans to make the royal collection in the Louvre available to the public began to coalesce, and, following the French Revolution, this vision became a reality. Though art museums gained popularity throughout this time, natural science collections were not put on display for the purpose of educating the public until the 1850s.

Today, many museums draw tens of thousands of visitors—sometimes millions of visitors—each year. Table 1.1 shows the attendance for the ten most-visited art museums in the world in 2012, while table 1.2 shows the attendance for different types of museums in the United States in 2009. Many of these museums occupy buildings that were not originally constructed for the

Table 1.1. Most-Visited Art Museums in the World, 2012

Rank	Art Museum	2012 Attendance
1	Musée du Louvre, Paris	9,720,260
2	Metropolitan Museum of Art, New York	6,115,881
3	British Museum, London	5,575,946
4	Tate Modern, London	5,304,710
5	National Gallery, London	5,163,902
6	Vatican Museums, Vatican City	5,064,546
7	National Palace Museum, Taipei	4,360,815
8	National Gallery of Art, Washington, DC	4,200,000
9	Centre Pompidou, Paris	3,800,000
10	Musée d'Orsay, Paris	3,600,000

Source: "Top 100 Art Museum Attendance: The Top 10, 2012." Available from www.theartnewspaper.com/attfig/attfig12.pdf.

Table 1.2.   Median Annual Attendance for Different Types of Museums in the United States, 2009

Type of Museum	Attendance
Art museum	44,878
Children's or youth museum	130,870
General museum	58,500
Historic house or site	11,700
History museum or historical society	10,000
Living collections	208,574
Natural history or anthropology museum	58,176
Science or technology center or museum	357,103
Specialized museum	22,000

Source: AAM (2009).

purpose of controlling environmental conditions to exacting preservation standards while also accommodating large crowds. Because many museum buildings were built 50 or more years ago, they require updating in terms of their mechanical, roofing, and electrical systems. In addition, bringing these antiquated buildings up to the appropriate technological and safety standards can be a daily challenge for these buildings' facility managers. Juggling the expenses that go along with these updates on an often-limited museum budget is an additional challenge. In tandem with modernizing mechanical systems, there is currently increasing pressure on museum facilities to "green" themselves. Museum members, visitors, and trustees are increasingly expecting their local museums to operate sustainably through such efforts as recycling initiatives, green transportation, and, in some cases, Leadership in Energy and Environmental Design (LEED) accreditation of facilities. See box 1.1 for an example of a unique challenge faced by a facility manager at the National Museum of American History in Washington, DC.

The Evolution of Zoos

While museums originated with the private collections of royals and other elites, the beginnings of zoological parks can be traced back to humans' early attempts to domesticate animals. For example, humans raised pigeons as long ago as 4500 BC in the region now known as Iraq, and elephants had been domesticated in India by 2500 BC. By 1000 BC, Wen Wang, a Chinese ruler, had built a 1,500-acre zoo, which he called Ling-Yo, the Garden of Intelligence. Around this same time (1000 BC), King Solomon, an early zoologist, paved the way for many generations of royal animal keepers, in-

BOX 1.1.

THE NATIONAL MUSEUM OF AMERICAN HISTORY: AN EMERGENCY OF PRESIDENTIAL PROPORTIONS

Angel Rodriguez, a facility manager at the Smithsonian Institution's National Museum of American History in Washington, DC, describes the importance of being a creative cultural institution facility manager:

> One of my most challenging experiences at the National Museum of American History occurred on May 16, 2011, when a pipe broke on the 4th floor and leaked into a large lighting panel. The lighting panel filled with between 150 and 200 gallons of water, causing it to fall. Luckily, nobody was standing under this panel, which probably weighed between 1,250 to 1,600 pounds when filled with water. The engineers could not secure the water where the pipe had broken, because the supply valve was damaged, and we could not cut the water off at just that spot. They resorted to turning the water off to the entire museum in order to stop the leak. The museum was still open to the public and this meant trouble for the bathrooms. Well, the museum closed an hour early that day, because the toilets did not flush, and it was not a good scene.
>
> Let me tell you that, just as the engineers were getting materials ready to make repairs, we were notified that President Obama and his daughters were coming to the museum for an unscheduled tour of the Lincoln exhibition. Under this pressure, we attached a plastic hose to the broken pipe, ran it to a sink and were able to turn the water back on to the museum so we could clean at least one bathroom and have it ready for the president's 7:00 p.m. tour. After the president left that evening, we secured the water again, installed new valves and repaired the broken pipe. One of the things that I learned was that you have to be very creative in these emergency situations.

Source: Rodriguez (2012).

cluding Semiramis and King Nebuchadnezzar of Babylonia, who also held collections of animals.

Developing collections of living animals became common in Greece by the seventh century BC, and, three centuries later, animals lived in captivity in nearly all of the Greek city-states. Alexander the Great provided Greek zoos with a plethora of specimens that had been captured during his military conquests. Initially, these zoos served merely as public spectacles, rather than as places of scientific research and discovery. During Aristotle's lifetime

(384–322 BC), zoos became common sites of research in Greece. Meanwhile, Romans divided their animal collections into two groups—those used in arena spectacles and others held in private zoos and aviaries.

With the fall of the Roman Empire, zoos found themselves in a state of decline. By the eighth century AD, however, the emperor Charlemagne revived the tradition of royal animal collections. By the 1300s, Philip VI had amassed a menagerie at the Louvre in Paris, and members of the House of Bourbon had their own living collections at Versailles. In the early 1500s, explorer Hernán Cortés documented a zoo so large in Mexico that it required a staff of 300 to keep its collection of birds, mammals, and reptiles.

Contemporary zookeeping can be traced to the mid-1700s in Vienna, where the Imperial Menagerie—which remains in operation to this day—was founded at the Schönbrunn Palace. By 1775, a zoo had been founded in a park in Madrid, and the Jardin des Plantes was founded in Paris nearly 20 years later. This trend found its way to London in 1828, with the founding of the Zoological Society of London's collection in Regent's Park.

The mid-1800s saw the rapid expansion of zoos, with openings the world over. As a result, there are now more than 40 zoos that are 100 years old or older. Following World War II, zoos again saw growth, and today there are more than 1,000 zoos in the world ("Zoos"). As with museums, many zoo facilities were constructed long ago and require updating. In addition, zoo facilities require constant evaluation of animal enclosures to ensure the safety of animals, zookeeping staff, and the visiting public. To achieve accreditation from the Association of Zoos and Aquariums (AZA), it is important that zoo facilities are carefully maintained to rigorous AZA standards. See box 1.2 for an example of how one facility management organization supports a zoological park in Washington, DC.

The Evolution of Botanical Gardens

Just as early zoological collections can be traced back to China, early botanical gardens also originated in ancient China, as well as near the Mediterranean Sea. Such gardens were used to grow fruit trees, vegetables, and herbs to supplement the local diet, as well as to make medicine.

With the advent of the printing press, information about plants was made more widely available in publications called "herbals." The herbalists who published these informational manuscripts were instrumental in the

BOX 1.2.

THE NATIONAL ZOOLOGICAL PARK: FACING UNIQUE CHALLENGES

Discovering new capabilities is something that Smithsonian Institution Facility Manager Dan Davies's team has grown accustomed to. Davies manages one of the Smithsonian's eight operational divisions, or zones, the Upper Northwest Zone (UNWZ). This zone includes both the National Zoological Park in Washington, DC, and the Smithsonian Conservation Biology Institute in Front Royal, Virginia. The National Zoo has over 100 buildings and structures and is occupied by over 2,000 animals, many of them members of endangered species.

In addition to maintaining their facilities, the UNWZ Zoo team takes on a variety of roles related to animal welfare throughout the zoo. For example, anytime that an animal needs to be moved to another location, all crate handling is done by Davies's staff. Davies commented on the nature of working with the zoo's sensitive living collections, saying, "Handling the animal crates requires an understanding . . . those involved must not get excited or nervous." The zoo's facilities team often partners with curatorial staff to solve unique problems. Together, they recently engineered, designed, and fabricated a crate with an integrated life-support sling system that could accommodate a 5,000-pound hippopotamus on its cross-country voyage from the National Zoo to its new home in Milwaukee.

Source: Davies (2010). Reprinted with permission of the International Facility Management Association's *Facility Management Journal.*

founding of better developed botanical gardens. By the late 1500s, there were five botanical gardens in Europe—the first in Italy, in Pisa (1543) and Padua (1545). Initially, these gardens were planted to serve medical school research and training.

By the 1800s, Jean Gesner, a Swiss botanist and physician, recorded that there were over 1,600 botanical gardens in all of Europe. At this time, the discipline of botany had begun to take root, and prominent botanists began to oversee botanical gardens. Present-day botanical gardens are often less devoted to medical teaching and more focused on plant culture, as well as on displaying ornamental plants. Botanical gardens present their visitors with a vivid opportunity to learn about specific plants and their growing needs. It is common for these gardens to offer instructional sessions about various gardening strategies.

In contrast to parks, which are often planted with a pleasurable landscape in mind, botanical gardens seek to arrange their plant collections with respect to plant type and, many times, geographic origin. These gardens range in size from several hectares up to nearly a thousand hectares. In addition to outdoor gardens, botanical gardens frequently have greenhouses that grow plants susceptible to seasonal variance. Botanical gardens with very large collections may also require storage facilities for plants susceptible to freezing temperatures or for others that require shady conditions.

In addition to living plant collections, botanical gardens often have collections of herbaria, which are dried plant specimens that have been mounted to sheets of paper. These specimens are used for reference when naming unfamiliar plants. Botanical gardens frequently have research facilities and libraries that accompany their herbaria, as well as classrooms ("Botanical Gardens").

Like museums, botanical gardens can earn accreditation from the American Association Alliance (AAM). In order to qualify for this accreditation, institutions must meet rigorous facilities standards. Because of their variety of structures, expansive grounds, and frequent special events, botanical gardens present a dynamic array of ongoing challenges to their facility managers.

Museums, zoos, and botanical gardens represent only a portion of cultural facilities worldwide. That said, many of the challenges they share—providing exacting environments for collections, serving visitors, maintaining often aged facilities, and meeting meticulous accreditation standards for facilities—provide us with a representative snapshot of cultural institution facility management. See box 1.3 for an example of how the facility management organization at the Atlanta Botanical Garden supports special events each year.

Trends in Cultural Facilities

Facility managers must work to support their organization's core mission by strategically operating facilities to achieve efficiency, safety, and an ideal work environment (IFMA 2009). As facilities evolve over time, facility managers must think on their feet to keep up with current trends while continuing to achieve these high standards.

BOX 1.3.

THE ATLANTA BOTANICAL GARDEN: ON THE MOVE

At the Atlanta Botanical Garden, Facility Operations Manager Christy Jellets and her staff not only are responsible for security, special events setup, and regular maintenance but also are on duty for exhibit installation, lighting, electrical work, and coordination with art handlers.

The Botanical Garden hosted an exhibition of large-scale Henry Moore sculpture in 2009, which happened to coincide with the grand opening of a new building, and the facilities staff faced a number of distinct challenges. Among these challenges were move-in deadlines and accommodating very large member previews—over 19,000 guests in a single day—which became a bit overwhelming. Even so, Jellets says, "Working with the art handlers from England who travel with the pieces was incredibly educational and rewarding."

Jellets's staff also handles special event setup, staffing, and cleanup for a number of high-occupancy special events. Some of the larger events they serve include the annual Garden of Eden Ball for 500 people; the Concerts in the Garden series, which draws 2,200 people per night; and the Garden Lights Holiday Nights event, which can draw over 6,000 people per night. At times, it can be challenging for staff to remain jovial for the duration of each event, but ensuring that staff members are invested in the Botanical Gardens' mission helps!

Source: Jellets (2012).

Currently, updating and expansion of cultural facilities are being driven by a number of variables. For example, while 25 years has been noted as the standard life cycle of a museum facility, many museum buildings are much older than this and have deteriorating roofs as well as deteriorating electrical, plumbing, and heating and cooling systems. In addition, many of these facilities are in need of Americans with Disabilities Act (ADA) compliance updates, as well as improved storage for their collections.

Presently, there are several different lines of thought when it comes to constructing or renovating a museum—the building itself can be seen either as a work of art or purely as a container in which collections, exhibitions, and programs are held (Crimm et al. 2009). From the facility manager's perspective, this is an important division. The more intricately or elaborately designed the museum building becomes, the more difficult it can be to budget for and perform maintenance work on throughout the life of the facility. For example, the Experience Music Project Museum (EMP) in Seattle, designed by internationally renowned architect Frank Gehry, has a central space that rises an extravagant 72 feet high. The museum had to invest in a specialized boom lift to reach this height to be able to perform regular maintenance (Richardson 2012).

Cultural facilities are also choosing to pursue sustainable practices. Aside from the inherent environmental benefits, doing so often achieves cost savings for the organization and pleases potential donors who may place a premium on environmental preservation. From the facility manager's perspective, when his or her cultural institution chooses to "go green," he or she has a lot of important work to do to fulfill this mandate. Examples of this work include everything from implementing a recycling program to a total overhaul of the facility's mechanical systems.

Because of space constraints in prime locations, many museums are choosing to build and operate off-site storage—and some are even building satellite museum facilities. Additionally, museums are now placing more emphasis on accommodating the needs of visitors through their new construction projects. By catering to visitors' needs, museums can extend the amount of time each visitor spends within their walls. Additional space is now being allocated for orientation, eating, shopping, learning, studying, and lounging. Flexible-use space is also being sought as a way to better facilitate special events, a wider variety of exhibitions, and larger groups of people (Crimm et al. 2009). For an example of a museum that caters to visitors, see box 1.4.

Summary

Cultural institutions like museums, botanical gardens, and zoos have rich histories that date back centuries or more. These institutions, originally designed to care for their collections, have become more complex over time, as educational and research components have been added to their operational mandates. As these institutions have developed and become increasingly more complex, so have the requirements of their facility management. Facility managers frequently perform mission-related functions, including preparing facilities for accreditation visits, facilitating special events, and working with conservators to maintain exacting environmental conditions for preservation.

BOX I.4.

THE SCIENCE MUSEUM OF MINNESOTA

Above: The atrium at the Science Museum of Minnesota.

The Science Museum of Minnesota's facility, completed in 1999, incorporates a wide variety of spaces that exist to serve visitors, including its Omnitheater, a public science education center, and dedicated areas for teacher education and its school outreach program. The Science Museum of Minnesota facility hosts over 1 million people per year.

Photo source: Reproduced with permission from the Science Museum of Minnesota, www.smm.org.

Today, cultural facility managers are an important part of their organizations, and they work every day to keep operations running smoothly, to keep collections and visitors safe, and to accommodate future needs. Current trends in cultural facilities include greater environmental sustainability, increased flexibility of space, more off-site storage, as well as elaborate architectural design. Each one of these trends represents an area in which the cultural institution's facility manager serves as a valuable resource, in terms of both planning and execution.

CHAPTER TWO
AN OVERVIEW OF CULTURAL FACILITY MANAGEMENT

We are making these sweeping changes and improvements to our facilities because they will enrich the experiences people have at the Smithsonian—those of us who work in these historic buildings, and our visitors who come to us to learn and be inspired. Better facilities will open new possibilities for our research and scholarship, enliven our exhibitions, and create a more welcoming face for our visitors, so we can serve as a better steward of natural resources, tell more compelling stories, and protect our precious collections for future generations.

—Dr. G. Wayne Clough (2011), 12th secretary of the
Smithsonian Institution and president emeritus
of the Georgia Institute of Technology

As Smithsonian Institution Secretary Wayne Clough emphasizes above, museum and cultural institution facilities have a significant impact on visitors' experiences as well as on the staff's ability to conduct research and keep collections safe and sound. For this reason, it is necessary to cultivate dynamic facilities that are capable of meeting the museum's mandate through innovative design and careful management.

Cultivating such dynamic museum facilities is frequently challenging for museum and cultural institution directors and facility managers alike, due to a number of unique challenges and constraints. Common challenges include aging buildings and infrastructure, uncertain funding, and the wide variety of needs that each facility must meet. From meeting environmental requirements for artwork to identifying specific cleaning methods required for zoological applications, from hosting elaborate special events to keeping heavily used restrooms spotless, cultural institution facility managers are kept on their toes. Despite this wide array of challenges, museum and cultural institution facility managers consistently find ways to meet and exceed expectations by thinking on their feet, networking with facility managers from other cultural institutions, pursuing facilities best-practice training, and recruiting the best possible staff for their facility management teams.

This chapter provides a brief history of facility management, describing how facility managers transitioned from information technology managers to their current role as stewards of the built environment. In addition, this chapter discusses several requirements of cultural facility managers, as well as the key customers served by these managers.

A Brief History of Facility Management

Though people have cared for their buildings for centuries upon centuries, facility management, as a formalized profession, did not begin to gel until the 1960s, when computers became more commonplace in offices with large staffs. When constraints were placed upon energy use in the 1970s and the need for efficiency became greater, facility managers were employed to help reduce costs and increase efficiency. Since then, as technology in the built environment has continued to develop, the need for facility managers to manage workplace environments has increased over the past 40 years.

Ross Perot, founder of Electronic Data Systems—and several-time American presidential hopeful—actually coined the term *facilities management* in the 1960s. During the 1960s, facility management personnel were employed to manage information technology and network infrastructures in booming office buildings around the country. As modular furniture became more popular, facility managers also began taking responsibility for its care and arrangement. Driven by manufacturers like Herman Miller, whose furniture systems could be rather complex, a group of knowledgeable experts in space planning convened in Ann Arbor, Michigan, in the late 1970s to discuss "strategic organizational planning" (Wiggins 2010, p. 2). This group formed the Facility Management Institute (FMI), and one of its members—Dave Armstrong—has since been dubbed the "father" of facility management.

In the 1980s, the profession began to evolve from furniture arranging and space planning into more sophisticated work that engaged facilities' infrastructures holistically. By the turn of the twenty-first century, facility

BOX 2.1.

THE INTERNATIONAL FACILITY MANAGEMENT ASSOCIATION'S (IFMA) ELEVEN CORE COMPETENCIES OF FACILITY MANAGERS

In 2009, IFMA utilized a global job task analysis (GJTA) to define the eleven core competencies of contemporary facility managers. These integral core competencies are as follows:

1. *Communication*: Communication plans and processes for both internal and external stakeholders
2. *Emergency Preparedness and Business Continuity*: Emergency and risk management plans and procedures
3. *Environmental Stewardship and Sustainability*: Sustainable management of built and natural environments
4. *Finance and Business*: Strategic plans, budgets, financial analyses, and procurement
5. *Human Factors*: Healthful and safe environment, security, and FM employee development
6. *Leadership and Strategy*: Strategic planning; organize, staff, and lead organization
7. *Operations and Maintenance*: Building operations and maintenance, and occupant services
8. *Project Management*: Oversight and management of all projects and related contracts
9. *Quality*: Best practices, process improvements, audits, and measurements
10. *Real Estate and Property Management*: Real estate planning, acquisition, and disposition
11. *Technology*: Facility management technology and workplace management systems

Source: "What is FM: Definition of Facility Management." Available at www. ifma.org/resources/what-is-fm/default.htm. Reprinted with permission of IFMA.

management had grown to encompass issues including business continuity, risk management, security, and energy efficiency. Today, the International Facility Management Association (IFMA) defines eleven core competencies for facility managers (see box 2.1). These present-day facility managers frequently strive to take on the role of "champion of the user or occupier of buildings" (Wiggins 2010, p. 12). This allows the facility manager to dovetail the facility management strategic plan with the overall strategic plan of the customer and provide better services in the long run. See box 2.2 for sample mission, vision, and values statements from the Smithsonian Institution's facility management organization's strategic plan.

The Cultural Facility Manager

Museums and cultural institutions, regardless of size, present unique challenges to those tending and mending their facilities. From housing precious collections to hosting thousands of guests, maintaining the invaluable and often fragile nature of these important environments requires a team of well-trained individuals who are just as comfortable with problem solving as part of an integrated team as they are with troubleshooting on their own. See box 2.3 for a description of how these challenges are met at the Baltimore Museum of Art.

The term *facility management* (FM) does not merely apply to the people who clean buildings, nor simply to the people who repair buildings. Instead, there are a broad array of facility management activities and responsibilities, including, but not limited to, disaster recovery, institutional safety, special event preparation, space planning, sustainability initiatives, and aiding in collection conservation. These activities have a generous impact on each museum—how the museum operates, how its money is allocated, as well as how its mission is met.

Within museums, a viable facility management program must assume that the facility in which the museum is located is entitled to the same exacting care and attention as the museum's precious collections. That is to say, to a facility manager, the museum's physical space is just as important and significant as the collections are to their conservators.

Facility management encompasses many elements and processes that aid an organization in its efforts to perform the work that it intends to accomplish. Facility managers are able to do this by taking a strategic view of their facilities and ensuring that these facilities are operated in the most

BOX 2.2.

SAMPLE CULTURAL INSTITUTION FACILITY MANAGEMENT MISSION, VISION, AND VALUES STATEMENTS

Thoughtful mission, vision, and values statements that are closely aligned with a facilities department's strategic plan provide team members with a sense of purpose, cohesion, and direction. The following carefully crafted mission, vision, and values statements, reprinted with permission from the Smithsonian Institution's facilities department, the Office of Facilities Management and Reliability (OFMR), were written in 2013, when OFMR wrote its *2013–2017 Strategic Plan*. Note how the OFMR mission statement relates directly to the preservation of collections.

Mission

The OFMR provides world-class services through a dedicated and professional workforce that is committed to managing resources wisely and preserving the integrity of our facilities by providing a safe and appropriate environment for people and collections.

Vision

We manage our cultural facilities in safe, effective, efficient, and sustainable ways.

Values

Excellence: Developing the skills and talents of our team members to accomplish our vital work

Leadership: Fostering an environment that rewards creativity and supports innovative ideas

Integrity: Personally dedicated to supporting the Smithsonian's mission

Teamwork: Succeeding together through mutual respect and support

Effectiveness: Delivering the right service in the right place at the right time

Reproduced with permission of the Smithsonian Institution Office of Facilities Management and Reliability.

BOX 2.3.

PUTTING CUSTOMERS FIRST AT THE BALTIMORE MUSEUM OF ART

Alan Dirican is the deputy director for operations and capital planning at the Baltimore Museum of Art in Baltimore, Maryland. He shares these thoughts on what makes facility management of a museum unique:

"Prior to the Baltimore Museum of Art, I worked in the hospitality industry—prior to that, I worked in the Merchant Marines. In facilities management, we are in a service field; everyone is our customer. In museums, obviously the product is the artwork and collections, and you also serve the visitors. Museums present a unique set of challenges different than other buildings and fields. In that sense we do everything to make sure that we are good custodians of the collections. If we do our job right, the collections will last centuries. We work hand-in-hand with conservation and other departments to ensure that the temperature and humidity are at the right levels. In hotels, you want to make sure the building is clean and safe, maintained at a reasonable temperature, and has hot water, for example. But, in the museums, the conditions are so much more strict—you have to maintain very strict temperatures and humidity year around, while often contending with the building's age, condition, and equipment.

"In addition to that, in the museum, you want to make sure that you serve the visitors—not just the art work. The museums are now looking to create a memorable, pleasant experience and provoke the thought process, deepen their understanding and connection with the art work and assure repeat visitorship. We want to make sure that they want to come back here. Another difference is that museums are almost all non-profit, whereas many other fields are not. With non-profits, you want to make sure you balance your sheet and don't go into debt, but profit is not the biggest factor. We don't have shareholders—we have the whole public to answer to—tax dollars, contributions, grants, and so forth. There is an incredible pressure, because resources are so tight in the non-profit world. When resources are stretched, you must constantly reinvent yourself to be more productive, innovative, and collaborative. You think about where you can save and then turn that into a better product."

Source: Dirican (2012). Photo courtesy of the Baltimore Museum of Art.

cost-efficient manner. In addition, cultural facility managers make sure that everyone and everything in these facilities—everyone who works in them, everyone who attends events in them, everyone who supports those events, and everyone who visits—are safe and not in any danger of an unanticipated problem or situation.

Functions of Cultural Institution Facility Management

It is really important, even for those who are not members of the facilities team, to familiarize themselves with the building in which they work. Consider a cultural institution facility for a moment. Do you know:

- the number of restrooms,
- the square footage cleaned per cleaning staff member,
- the number of windows,
- the annual energy cost,
- the type of roofing system,

- the type of heating and cooling system,

- the age and condition of its mechanical equipment,

- how space is allocated,

- the wear and tear of special events on the facility,

- when and how garbage and recycling are picked up,

- whether the loading dock is easily accessible,

- what type of light bulbs the facility uses,

- whether its cleaning supplies are environmentally friendly,

- the number of space heaters and refrigerators in the facility,

- the annual maintenance costs,

- the annual energy cost,

- the number and value of assets,

- what its capital improvement plan looks like,

- whether it is fully ADA compliant,

- whether there is a comprehensive pest management plan in place, and

- who is responsible for safety and disaster management and business continuity?

This list of questions serves to get us started in thinking about the responsibilities, costs, and concerns related to cultural institution facilities. No matter one's role within the museum environment, it is important to have an understanding of facility-related issues. Staff should understand how the facility supports a museum's mission and how it affects the museum's bottom line, as well as how they, as users, affect the facility's performance. Something as simple as choosing to shut down computers before leaving work or turning off lights when leaving a room, for example, can have a considerable impact on a museum's energy use. For museum administrators, this understanding of facilities can help them to budget, staff, and plan more capably.

Today, in cultural facilities, facility managers assist with a wide variety of functions that support their organizations' broader missions. These functions range from setting up for large special events, like the Atlanta Botanical Garden's Garden of Eden Ball, to researching suppliers for a new water filtration system, preparing the museum for a presidential visit, and cleaning gum out of the carpet—a common problem at the National Air and Space Museum. In addition, guest safety is a primary concern for cultural institution facility managers—these managers must constantly be on the lookout for ways to reduce risk to the many guests who pass through their doors each day.

In museums, specifically, the basic requirements for facilities management operation have been described in terms of six primary responsibilities:

1. Supply and sustain the built environment needed to maintain organizational operations within the space.

2. Supply and sustain the utility services required for organizational operations within the space.

3. Supply housekeeping services that support organizational operations within the space.

4. Supply a healthy and safe environment for all people utilizing the space.

5. Supply a physically secure environment for both people and assets within the space.

6. Supply integrated pest management services appropriate to the space. (Quoted from Wilcox 1995)

Whether a museum or cultural institution has a formalized FM team or employees with additional nonfacilities duties who fulfill the FM role, managing the institution's facilities remains critical to achieving the organization's mission. A survey by the American Alliance of Museums (Merritt 2005) suggests that most museums do not have a dedicated, full-time maintenance worker until the operating budget exceeds $400,000 or the facilities exceed 20,000 square feet. Museums do not tend to hire even a part-time maintenance worker until their budget exceeds $125,000 or the facilities exceed 8,000 square feet. This suggests that it is important that all museum staff members, especially those in smaller institutions, have an understanding of basic FM principles.

Those responsible for cultural institution facilities—whether full-time, part-time, or on an as-needed basis—must provide space and utilities, and ensure the levels of cleanliness, safety, and security that are necessary for the institution to capably fulfill its mandate to collections, employees, and visitors. Regardless of the size of the museum or cultural institution, those who manage facilities face similar challenges. From keeping public restrooms clean to setting up for pristine special events, cultural facility managers oversee a broad range of activities each day. Each of these activities ensures that the facilities continue to serve the needs of their customers over time.

Providing this level of service requires an understanding of how complex processes intersect within the museum environment (Merritt 2005)—for example, how to keep collections safe while also allowing the public the opportunity to learn from them, how to balance the need for office space with the needs for exhibition and storage space, and how to clean and maintain public areas of the museum despite being open to the public nearly every day.

Stakeholders in Cultural Institution Facility Management

Managing museum and cultural institution facilities is not only about maintaining healthy buildings. In addition, cultural institution facility managers need to keep in mind the following:

- Visitors have expectations.

- Staff have expectations.

- Collections have requirements.

- Funding agencies and donors set constraints.

At the end of the day, facility managers are responsible for balancing the diverse interests of each of these stakeholders.

As Secretary Clough states at the beginning of this chapter, the Smithsonian Institution works hard to ensure that visitor experiences, staff research, and environmental mandates are supported by world-class facilities. Without an understanding of how these stakeholders' interests fit together, it would not be possible to formulate a mission or strategic plan, or to populate a plan with goals and objectives. While each group of stakeholders differs from institution to institution, there are some commonalities worth discussing. For example, most cultural institutions serve a population of visitors, and these visitors will have basic expectations of the facility that must be met in order to engender repeat visitorship, as well as to maintain a first-rate reputation.

A few examples of these expectations are that the facility makes reasonable Americans with Disabilities Act (ADA) accommodations; keeps its restrooms in clean, working order; provides appropriate signage; and, in this day and age, demonstrates a commitment to sustainability. In addition to having these expectations, stakeholders want to feel welcomed in the space and expect an atmosphere conducive to learning about the collections on display. Ensuring that facility management staff are properly trained to answer questions related to the institution's collections—because these staff members are often approached by curious visitors—can be just as important as ensuring that the facility is in a sparkling, clean condition.

Cultural institution staff and collections count among internal stakeholders. Of course, staff members have requirements that vary, depending upon their responsibilities. What does not vary is that the facility manager is responsible for facilitating each staff member's work by providing a comfortable work environment with adequate space, furniture, supplies, and lighting, as well as a comfortable temperature. In addition, cultural institution facility managers carry a high degree of responsibility for ensuring that museums embody particular characteristics and standards that are necessary to achieve accreditation, whether from the Association of Zoos and Aquariums (see box 2.4 for AZA facilities requirements), the American Alliance of Museums (see box 2.5 for AAM facilities requirements), or another recognized accrediting organization.

Balancing the needs of staff members with the needs of collections can be difficult at times. For example, the ideal temperature and humidity levels for maintaining some museum collections may not be the most comfortable levels for the same facility's staff and visitors. In addition to requiring particular—and stable—environmental conditions, collections necessitate that an integrated pest management (IPM) plan be in place that considers the entire "ecosystem" surrounding collections and how to prevent pests from entry (Genoways and Ireland 2003). It is also very important that cleaning supplies used near artifacts be selected carefully, so that they do not harm

BOX 2.4.

ELEMENTS OF PHYSICAL FACILITIES EXAMINED DURING AN ASSOCIATION OF ZOOS AND AQUARIUMS (AZA) ACCREDITATION REVIEW

The Association of Zoos and Aquariums has a set of standards directed specifically toward zoo facilities for those organizations seeking accreditation. As you can see, the role of facility management within the zoo accreditation process is very important. Facilities elements that are examined during the accreditation visit include the following:

1. Facilities and conditions that exist at the time of the inspection and review
2. Appearance and condition of the buildings and grounds
3. Adequacy of maintenance program
4. Adequacy, appropriateness, and condition of exhibits and holding areas
5. Adequacy of furniture in exhibits
6. Appropriateness of exhibit groupings
7. Adequacy of ventilation in buildings and holding areas
8. Whether the animal facilities meet or exceed all relevant federal and state requirements
9. Whether all service areas have sufficient space for safety
10. Program of water quality monitoring for all animals, including written records

Source: "AZA Guide to Accreditation of Zoological Parks and Aquariums, 2013 edition." Association of Zoos and Aquariums (2013, p. 34). Available at www .aza.org/uploadedFiles/Accreditation/Guide%20to%20Accreditation.pdf.

the collections. It is also crucial that FM staff work with the institution's conservators to establish a framework for collections housekeeping and environmental conditions.

Because most cultural institutions are nonprofit entities that rely on outside donors, grant agencies, and—frequently—federal, state, or local taxpayers for funding, they must look for ways to meet the needs and requirements of these funding parties while acknowledging that resources are limited. It is possible, for example, that a donor will push for an addition to the museum

BOX 2.5.

THE FACILITY MANAGER'S ROLE IN MUSEUM EXCELLENCE: THE AMERICAN ALLIANCE OF MUSEUMS' (AAM) FACILITIES AND RISK MANAGEMENT CHARACTERISTICS

The AAM has identified characteristics of excellence for museums related directly to facilities and risk management. The museum's facility manager carries a high degree of responsibility for ensuring that his or her museum embodies these characteristics in order to achieve AAM accreditation. Key characteristics related to facilities include whether

- The museum allocates its space and uses its facilities to meet the needs of the collections, audience, and staff (Characteristic 7.1).
- The museum has appropriate measures to ensure the safety and security of people, its collections and/or objects, and the facilities it owns or uses (Characteristic 7.2).
- The museum has an effective program for the care and long-term maintenance of its facilities (Characteristic 7.3).
- The museum is clean and well maintained, and provides for the visitors' needs (Characteristic 7.4).

Source: AAM (2012).

building without an understanding of the added annual maintenance costs associated with increasing the square footage. Educating this donor on the compounded lifecycle costs of a new addition—especially additional maintenance and operations costs—will help with planning and budgeting for a realistic solution to the community's and facility's needs over time.

One additional group of stakeholders in the museum and cultural institution environment is made up of the vendors who work within these institutions. Many museums host caterers, have outside vendors operating museum cafés, and also have vendors who operate museum shops. It is important that the expectations on both sides—those of the vendor and those of the museum or cultural institution—are well defined prior to formalizing the partnership.

It is just as important to provide vendors with the facilities necessary for them to do their jobs well as it is to provide adequate facilities for museum staff. Providing the necessary facilities will help ensure that these vendors reflect well on the institution. Even so, vendor activities should not interfere with the institution's greater mission and vision. For example, at a popular museum in Washington, DC, one fast-food vendor's kids' meal cartons frequently litter the host museum's facility and grounds, reflecting poorly on the institution. Reworking the vendor agreement such that the vendor is responsible for controlling litter specific to its consumers may be one way to curb this problem.

The cultural institution facility manager has an important duty to each of these stakeholders to prepare, practice, and implement a comprehensive disaster management plan, as well as to ensure a safe environment on a day-to-day basis. This will ensure that both the people and collections within the cultural institution are well taken care of in the event of an emergency. Because cultural institution facility managers must serve a diverse array of constituents, it is important for these managers to take time to understand the requirements unique to their respective institutions. To understand and meet these needs, facility managers must have excellent leadership and managerial skills (Fried 2005).

Summary

Since the 1960s, the FM profession has emerged as an important part of any organization that is serious about safety, long-term planning, and serving staff as well as outside customers. Within cultural facilities, FM is no less important. Key stakeholders, including visitors, staff, collections, and funding agencies, must be served in ways that meet each of their unique needs over time. By seeking visitor feedback, working closely with staff members from throughout the museum, and participating in senior leadership meetings, the facility manager is able to respond to stakeholders' concerns while meeting their needs and helping them plan for the future.

CULTURAL FACILITY STRATEGIC PLANNING

Cultural facilities contribute to society, creativity, humanism, learning, personal development and enjoyment. There is no corporate profit to the activities and services, or to the facilities management work. I love learning and I love reading; I value personal interactions, dialogue and community building—and this is what libraries are all about!

—Stephanie Erickess (2012), facilities manager, Seattle Public Library

Managing cultural facilities requires leadership that understands the importance of strategic planning and effective communication and that has an ability to earn the buy-in of staff, administrators, and, in some cases, donors. Integral to earning this buy-in is a capacity to clearly tie a facilities operation to the mission of its organization as a whole. This means making the value of well-managed facilities—and the means to achieving them—clear to administrators. In addition, cultural facilities personnel must understand that they are not simply maintaining a facility but also helping to preserve cultural heritage. It is a facility manager's duty to educate staff to this effect through clear communication of the facility's organizational goals and mission.

Leadership in Cultural Facilities

There are at least as many leadership strategies as there are distinct organizations to lead. The strategy that works best is wholly dependent upon the leader, the workforce, and the organizational culture of a particular situation.

Though there are many ways to approach leadership in a cultural facility environment, several key knowledge areas and proficiencies have been identified as common to nearly every successful facility manager.

For example, Cotts et al. (2010) identify six principles as being broadly applicable to facility management (FM) leadership. First, a facility manager must meet the needs of both external and internal constituents by reconciling business-oriented (external) and technical (internal) requirements. Second, a facility manager must serve in an "activist" capacity, making sure that organizational leaders know why it is important to allocate resources to the management of their facilities. Third, a facility manager must cultivate a facility management team capable of accomplishing the technical tasks necessary to achieve the organization's mission. Fourth, a facility manager should "manage by walking around" and continually assess a facility's performance, while being sure to hire capable team members. Fifth, a facility manager should hold his or her team to a high standard of service, so that customers come to expect a quality experience. Finally, a facility manager needs to be able to balance the needs of today with the needs of the future—he or she should "be reactive without being reactionary" (Cotts et al. 2010, pp. 61–62). Taking a look at how these principles relate to cultural facilities, in particular, is helpful to understanding effective leadership strategies in these unique circumstances.

Bridging the demands of varying constituencies—or stakeholders—in a cultural institution environment means constantly balancing customer requests, perceived needs, and future plans against budgetary constraints and staff competencies. It can be a messy process at times; as Dan Davies, facility manager at the National Zoological Park in Washington, DC, points out, success relies upon making careful choices. Davies describes his approach:

> One of the biggest challenges is that it's all about choices—most of the time you can choose to accommodate customer requests. All of our interactions with the customers are about finding a balance that is representative of where priorities should be. At the zoo, we have to be able to go with the flow, because it's flowing and the animals have different ideas about what our priorities should be. Then, add to that funding pressures and political pressure. (2011)

Key to Davies' balancing act is communicating with customers on a regular basis to ensure they have an understanding of how the zoo's facilities team can serve their needs, as well as an understanding of the other requests and duties that the facilities team is concurrently responsible for fulfilling.

The facilities activism that Cotts et al. refer to is particularly important in cultural facilities, which tend to have challenging budgetary circumstances. It can be easy for facilities' concerns to get lost in the shuffle, and, over time, continually putting facilities on the backburner can add up to an overwhelming backlog in maintenance. As an example, in 2007, the Smithsonian Institution revealed that its maintenance backlog totaled $2.5 billion, largely due to the age of many of its facilities (Crimm et al. 2009). To overcome this backlog, Smithsonian facility managers have been working hard to educate museum administration about the importance of sound maintenance and operations planning and procedures. In addition, they have been implementing new strategies, like reliability-centered maintenance (RCM), to perform their work as efficiently as possible. It seems that educating the administration is paying off—in 2011, Secretary Clough, who leads the Smithsonian, published the article "The Top Ten Reasons I Get Excited about Facilities" on the organizational website. This explicit support from the organization's leader likely would not have come without strong facility activism by the facility managers. See box 3.1 for additional examples of how the facility management organization at the Smithsonian Institution "keeps the show on the road."

Because facility managers often supervise a broad array of employees—from administrative assistants to painters, electricians, and cleaning staff—integrating such a diverse workforce to achieve an overarching mission can be a challenge. At the National Gallery of Art, Chief of Facilities Management David Samec strives to do this by clearly communicating the Gallery's mission at each town hall meeting. In addition, Samec starts each meeting by describing "here's where we are, and here's where we're going," so that all staff have a sense of purpose as they complete daily tasks, which, in turn, sets the tone for quality service.

Of course, hiring well is important to any organization and no less important in cultural institution facility management, where priceless artifacts and collections are kept safe within facilities each day. Despite challenges that may come with nonprofit status, having a compelling mission tied to educating the public and caring for fragile collections can help with building a committed staff. Christy Jellets, facility operations manager at the Atlanta Botanical Garden, believes that being associated with a cultural institution "absolutely helps with retention" at the Gardens.

Common among these leadership principles is clear communication of the organizational mission to staff, as well as educating cultural facility

BOX 3.1.

KEEPING THE SHOW ON THE ROAD AT THE SMITHSONIAN INSTITUTION

Smithsonian Institution Office of Facilities Management and Reliability (OFMR) Director Nancy Bechtol credits the presence of her in-house maintenance and operations staff for their ability to "keep the show on the road" amidst an often challenging environment composed of both ongoing preventive maintenance and active corrective maintenance related to the presence of aged facilities constructed over a century ago and the inherent wear and tear of such high traffic levels.

By engaging in this multifaceted maintenance system, the OFMR team makes unmistakable contributions to the Smithsonian's overarching mission to support "the increase and diffusion of knowledge."

The OFMR's support of the Smithsonian's mission is further reinforced by the myriad roles it plays that extend beyond the preventive and corrective maintenance services it provides the organization. For example, over the years OFMR staff has found themselves transporting endangered animals at the National Zoo, staffing elaborate special events, and putting the final touches on significant Smithsonian exhibitions.

Bechtol recalled one particular instance in which a Smithsonian donor took a final walk-through prior to the opening of an exhibition he was sponsoring. "The donor felt that his name appeared too small on the exhibition sign and asked that it be enlarged." With fewer than twenty-four hours before the exhibit opened to the public, the existing elegant signage had to be resourcefully edited so that a larger iteration of the donor's name appeared—without drawing attention to the fact that the new name was a last-minute change.

"These are the sorts of things that keep us [OFMR] networking with other Smithsonian offices, like the Office of Exhibits Central [OEC]," said Bechtol. By working all night, OFMR staff—who have their own large-format, high-quality plotter—helped OEC finalize the exhibition signage to both the donor's and curators' satisfaction. Such challenging, time-sensitive situations allow OFMR staff to be constantly meeting new people and discovering new capabilities.

Source: Person and Cooper (2011). Reprinted with permission of the International Facility Management Association's *Facility Management Journal.*

administrators as to the ways that facility management can, and does, support the organization's mission. Taking the time to communicate a cultural institution's mission to its facility management staff helps ensure that each decision that they make—and each task that they carry out—supports the mission.

Long-Term Strategic Planning in Cultural Facilities

Every successful organization, regardless of size, should have a strategic plan that is dynamic and adaptable to changing circumstances and realities. Every five years, the Smithsonian Office of Facilities Management and Reliability (OFMR) develops a comprehensive strategic plan that aligns with the larger Smithsonian Institution strategic plan. Doing so ensures that the future direction of OFMR is consistent with the future vision of the Smithsonian. When drafting this strategic plan, OFMR envisions the plan working as a guiding document that staff will refer to frequently. This requires that the strategic plan be written in a format that is engaging, clear, and relevant to both facilities staff and Smithsonian staff at large. See box 3.2 for sample goals and objectives from OFMR's 2013–2017 strategic plan.

In preparation for the strategic planning process, any organization first must gain an understanding of the varied processes available for developing strategic plans. There are as many ways to develop a strategic plan as there are strategic plans, and no one way is necessarily more correct than another. A good starting point is to review several strategic planning guides and determine which manual fits with the personality of the facility in question. It is critical that a strategic plan strikes the right balance between providing information and inspiring growth, so facilities staff and customers have a clear idea of their FM organization's goals and strategies over the coming years.

When developing a strategic plan for a cultural facility, be careful to avoid common traps, including:

- not allowing enough time for a clear plan to be mapped out and written,
- trying to write the plan in a vacuum,
- having a plan that is too vague (or one that is too specific),
- identifying goals that may not be realistic or achievable, and

BOX 3.2.

A SAMPLE STRATEGIC PLAN: THE 2013–2017 SMITHSONIAN INSTITUTION STRATEGIC PLAN FOR FACILITIES

The Smithsonian Institution's Office of Facilities Management and Reliability (OFMR) collaboratively constructed a strategic plan with four primary goals. These simple, easy-to-remember goals are each further described—and made quantifiable—through several objectives. In turn, the objectives are described and assigned ownership through discrete strategies and tactics. The OFMR plan's four goals and accompanying objectives are as follows:

Goal 1: Care for Smithsonian
- Objective 1A: Operate Facilities Consistent with the OFMR Vision
- Objective 1B: Maintain Facilities Consistent with the OFMR Vision
- Objective 1C: Support Smithsonian Facilities, Staff, and Collections

Goal 2: Support Workforce Excellence
- Objective 2A: Ensure a Safe and Healthy Workforce
- Objective 2B: Excel in Human Capital Management
- Objective 2C: Cultivate a Professional Workforce

Goal 3: Value All Stakeholders
- Objective 3A: Ensure Stakeholder's Interests Are Met
- Objective 3B: Cultivate a Culture of Service and Support
- Objective 3C: Collaborate with OFEO (OFMR's Parent Organization) for Integrated Facilities Support

Goal 4: Advance Organizational Best Practices
- Objective 4A: Research and Identify Industry Best Practices
- Objective 4B: Develop Operating Standards

Source: Office of Facilities Management and Reliability (OFMR), Smithsonian Institution (2013). Reproduced with permission of the Smithsonian Institution Office of Facilities Management and Reliability.

- being overconfident about what can be accomplished or, alternatively, not confident enough in terms of what you can accomplish given your resources. (Cooper and Person 2012)

In addition to keeping these common traps in mind, it is also important to make sure that a 360-degree perspective is taken throughout the strategic planning process. This means that those constructing a strategic plan must seek feedback from the entire spectrum of stakeholders—which, for cultural facilities, is often a large and diverse group.

It is essential to bear in mind that staff at every level within an organization—both inside and outside of facility management—have important insights related to its facilities program. Some of these perspectives may carry with them criticisms, advice, and other commentary, and it can, at times, be difficult not to take these perspectives personally. Even so, compiling such a broad array of viewpoints can spark discussions that become essential to the strategic planning process as a whole (Lord and Markert 2007).

At its most basic level, it is possible to break a strategic planning process into ten steps, which are described in further detail in Lord and Markert's *The Manual of Strategic Planning for Museums* (2007). An outside consultant, or a capable internal manager, frequently leads the first three of these steps: an environmental scan, external assessment, and internal assessment. An environmental scan works to identify current trends that affect an organization, as well as to spur discussion about challenges and opportunities that are anticipated over the next several years.

An external assessment can be an important step that allows the organization to understand how it is viewed by "outsiders." In the case of cultural institution facilities, those interviewed as part of the external assessment could include visitors, facility managers at other cultural institutions, and FM industry experts. For an internal assessment, it is important to collect opinions from staff at all levels, including those who work in both the facilities and nonfacilities parts of the cultural institution.

After data are collected, this information can be assessed by a steering committee that is responsible for the overall planning process. This assessment works to identify critical issues that must be addressed in order for the organization to achieve greater success. These issues are often organized thematically into a document that can then be circulated to those who will attend a strategic planning retreat later on.

Having identified the critical issues makes it possible to begin comparing or benchmarking against other similar institutions that have faced comparable challenges. Ultimately, this comparison can help an organization understand ways similar challenges have been overcome. Facility-related data from other institutions can be obtained in several ways. For example, the International Association of Museum Facility Administrators (IAMFA) conducts a thorough annual benchmarking exercise that provides up-to-date information about many current museum facilities practices. In addition, the American Alliance of Museums' *Covering Your Assets* (Merritt 2005) provides statistics related to FM practices in museums in the United States.

After benchmarking, the steering committee might consider holding a retreat that "establishes the optimal future . . . and the changes required to achieve it" (Lord and Markert 2007, p. 37). The director of the facilities department may prepare a draft of the strategic plan prior to the retreat or, alternatively, wait until after the retreat before writing a draft. The retreat might be held as an opportunity for the steering committee to address:

- the mission, vision, and values statements of the facilities organization, and whether they are up-to-date;

- the ranking of critical issues according to importance; and

- the strategic directions necessary to tackle these issues.

If there is time during the retreat, it is possible to move on to establishing goals, which are the long-range visionary statements that will help move the facilities organization in the desired direction over several years. These goals are normally identified by the steering group.

After defining the goals, it is time for management and staff to come together to determine the objectives, or short-term measurable outcomes, that support these goals. If necessary, specific tasks that support each objective can be written into the plan as well. (See box 3.3 for descriptions of goals, objectives, and tasks.) After establishing the plan's goals and objectives, the management team can begin constructing an implementation plan. This plan arranges the goals into a logical order, assigning implementation to appropriate teams within the facilities department and making sure that each goal is allocated the funding necessary to succeed.

One final step to consider is evaluation. This step is often forgotten, because strategic plans are frequently set aside following completion and not

BOX 3.3.

WHAT IS THE DIFFERENCE BETWEEN A GOAL, AN OBJECTIVE, AND A TASK?

Goals can be thought of as long-range, qualitative outcomes.
Objectives can be seen as short-term, quantitative—or measurable—outcomes.
Tasks are particular steps that must be implemented in order to achieve an objective.

Source: Lord and Markert (2007, p. 38).

referred to often enough as guiding documents. If facility managers make concrete plans to evaluate progress toward achieving the goals and objectives within a strategic plan, it is more likely that the plan will make a positive impact on the organization (Lord and Markert 2007).

The ten steps toward developing a strategic plan that are outlined in this chapter are representative of only one of the many prospective strategic planning processes that are available for museums and cultural institutions to consider. As mentioned earlier, it is important for each institution to consider its unique organizational culture when determining how best to formulate its plan.

Facilities as a Part of the Institutional Strategic Plan

In addition to coordinating strategic planning for the facilities organization, a facility manager can also play a role in helping to determine and implement at least some aspects of the strategic plan for an institution as a whole. Museum facilities exist at the intersection of many museums' three primary functions: the curatorial, administrative, and programming functions. See box 3.4 for a graphic depiction of the relationship between these three functions. Because facilities impact nearly every aspect of a museum's ability to achieve its mission and meet its mandate, it is important for museum and cultural institution administrators to integrate facility managers into institution-wide strategic planning efforts. Doing so will help an

BOX 3.4.

THE INTERRELATEDNESS OF MUSEUM FUNCTIONS: ADMINISTRATIVE, COLLECTIONS AND CURATORIAL, AND PROGRAM AND COMMUNICATION FUNCTIONS

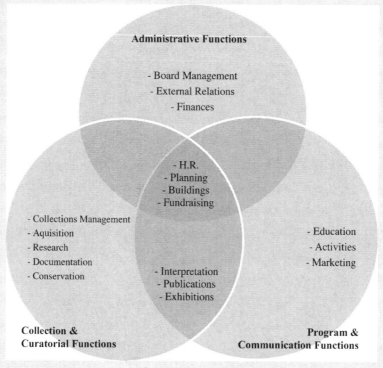

This diagram illustrates several important elements of three primary museum functions—the administrative, collections, and programming functions. Note that buildings, or facilities, fall at the intersection of each of these three functions, serving as one of the key elements that knit together the core museum functions.

Figure source: Lord and Markert (2007, p. 13). *The Manual of Strategic Planning for Museums*. Lanham, MD: AltaMira Press.

institution's strategic planning committee and senior leadership to appreciate major upcoming facilities costs, as well as how facilities can be improved to meet future goals. This also helps facility managers tailor their
own strategic plans to better accommodate the plans of their institutions.

If a strategic planning committee does not automatically include the
facility manager, he or she should not wait for an invitation to join the
group. Oftentimes, because of the behind-the-scenes nature of the work that
facilities managers do, their perspectives are overlooked. For this reason, it is
beneficial for cultural institution FMs to volunteer to join planning groups,
pointing out specific ways that their institutions' facilities are important to
meeting institutional goals in the future.

To illustrate the importance of including facility managers in a museum's strategic planning process, consider how different approaches to
museum leadership impacted one museum facility manager's planning at two
different Washington, DC, museum facilities. This facility manager worked
at several different museums, and he noticed that each museum director
had a distinct leadership style. In turn, each director had a particular way of
viewing the role of facility management. At one of the museums, the facility manager was considered a part of the museum's senior leadership team.
This allowed the services provided by the facilities team to be tailored very
sensitively to the collection's needs and to those of the customers. The other
museum he worked with did not allow the facility manager to participate in
senior leadership meetings. This meant that facility management was not
privy to information about upcoming plans for the museum. In turn, the
facility manager had no way of knowing how to be sensitive to the requirements of this particular museum.

If facility management is not explicitly considered during the museum's
strategic planning process, it can be challenging for the facility manager to
use the museum's plan as a guiding document when making facility management decisions. Ultimately, however, finding ways for the facilities operation
to support the institution's strategic plan is beneficial to staff and visitors
alike. As Stephanie Erickess, facility manager for The Seattle Public Library,
states so plainly,

> We [facility management] actively reinforce the Library's mission. A
> couple of years ago, The Seattle Public Library launched an initiative to de-
> velop a strategic plan for the Library with input from patrons, non-patrons
> and staff. We gathered thousands of pieces of information. This was the

basis for our strategic plan, which is what guides us. The mission is the condensed version of the plan's five major goals. It may seem a challenge to frame facilities work in the context of that, but we haven't found it difficult. We simply translate. We may not be the ones checking out the books, but we are the ones who keep the counters clean and ensure egress, so that library patrons can get their books and access our facilities safely and with enjoyment. As I see it, our facilities work naturally aligns with the agency's mission and strategic plan. (Erickess 2012)

As Erickess points out, there is some translation involved when relating the practical elements of facility management with the often visionary nature of cultural institution strategic plans, but it is not an impossible task. Rather, it is a matter of framing work that facility staff does in terms of how it impacts the overall visitor experience, the staff's work, and the conservation of collections.

Effective Communication Strategies

In addition to strategic planning efforts, effective communication is part of the foundation for organizational success. Clear communication strategies should be used any time a facilities department is sharing information with staff, volunteers, stakeholders, donors, and other organizations. Effective communication should be embedded into all aspects of supervision, leadership, and management.

In cultural institution facility management departments, communication can be pursued in a number of ways and through a variety of events. Having a facilities department host an annual or semiannual "open house," where it exhibits its equipment, supplies, and materials and gives live presentations that demonstrate its staff's technical talents, can be a great way to showcase how the facilities department serves a cultural institution. The complexities of facility management are seldom well understood outside of the FM team, and this annual "open house" provides facility management with the opportunity to share their story while educating their customers.

To further strengthen communication, consider publishing and circulating a newsletter to staff and stakeholders, highlighting many of the unique requirements of facility management–related work. This newsletter can describe upcoming facilities projects and how they may impact the museum, as well as ways in which museum staff can help each project go smoothly. Sharing it over organizational e-mail can simplify distribution.

Publishing an annual report, much like many business enterprises, helps a facility department build an archival record of accomplishments for each year of operations. This document can, in turn, be used as a framework for a presentation to other museum or cultural institution staff members that describes what work the facilities department has done over the past year. This planned communication with those outside the facility department reinforces the value of the facility to the organization and educates staff on the role that the facility plays in achieving the institution's mission.

At the Smithsonian, where the facility management office is organized according to geographic zones, each zone has a monthly "all-hands meeting." During this meeting, zone leaders discuss current initiatives or issues, recognize outstanding facilities employees, and discuss priorities and other information they need to share in order for all staff to know the context of the work they perform. Quarterly, Smithsonian facilities employees from all zones meet for a one-hour presentation, led by the director of facilities. This presentation is a valuable time for sharing organizational successes during the previous three months, for employees to ask questions about the organization, and to reiterate the department's mission.

Another strategy that the Smithsonian employs to ensure effective communication between facilities staff and management are employee surveys. The facilities department surveys its employees periodically— about every eighteen months—in addition to participating in the annual Smithsonian-wide Employee Perspective Survey. This structured feedback from employees became an important part of OFMR's strategic planning process, as the survey results were used to help determine goals and objectives within the plan. In addition to seeking employee feedback, the facilities department should seek customer feedback as well. Having a simple survey on hand to e-mail customers who have recently placed a work order can be an efficient way to gauge how well the facility management branch is meeting the needs of museum staff.

Staff members responsible for bringing new employees onboard must begin clearly communicating with each new employee on—or, ideally, before—his or her first day. Welcoming new employees with a formal orientation to the facilities department provides an opportunity to review facility-specific details, such as general safety, the departmental mission, and other policies, that are likely not covered at the museum's new employee orientation. This provides an opportunity to share the history of the facility department as well as its strategic plan. In addition, this is a good

BOX 3.5.

FIVE AREAS TO CONSIDER FOR EFFECTIVE COMMUNICATION IN YOUR FACILITY MANAGEMENT (FM) ORGANIZATION

1. Communicating information about projects and initiatives to all staff
   - Hold quarterly "Town Hall" meetings with all FM staff to ensure that each member understands the financial picture, progress in ongoing initiatives, and upcoming projects, and—perhaps most importantly—to describe the attendees' general roles toward achieving these initiatives and projects.
   - Hold monthly departmental "All Hands" meetings to break down current and upcoming efforts within your specific department of the FM organization. Be sure to describe the roles that various attendees play in achieving these goals.
2. Communicating with new employees
   Be sure to provide documentation of and take time to personally describe the following:
   - Organizational policies
   - Professional etiquette within your organization
   - Organizational safety standards
   - Other issues such as security credentials, access, attendance processes, and so on
   - On-the-job expectations
3. 360-degree communications
   - The organizational leadership team should take time to assess which sources they derive their information from and to whom they normally relay information.
   - Following the assessment, this team can make an effort to draw from previously overlooked sources of information, as well as to better inform and communicate with those parties identified as underinformed in past circumstances.
4. Communicating with stakeholders
   - Hold an annual "FM Open House" so that stakeholders can learn more about the goings-on within the FM organization. These open houses can be a fun way to demonstrate how your FM team works to serve both stakeholders and their facilities on a daily basis.
   - Circulate an annual report to stakeholders that documents and describes ongoing and upcoming FM efforts in clear language.

- Circulate newsletters to stakeholders that describe specific efforts and strategies that they can help the FM team implement. Examples include "sustainability" and "technology" newsletters.
5. Benchmarking.
  - Contribute data about your facility operation to a benchmarking effort.
  - Learn—and implement—lean, efficient, and productive best practices from similar facilities.

Source: Cooper and Person (2012). "Facilities Best Practices that Don't Have to Break the Bank." Proceedings of the International Facility Management Association's 2012 Facility Fusion Conference in Chicago, IL, April 11–13, 2012.

time to introduce senior leadership staff, host a question-and-answer period, and share important contact information (Cooper and Person 2012). See box 3.5 for a list of ways that a cultural institution facility management organization can begin to effectively communicate with its stakeholders.

Summary

Strategic planning is important for cultural facility managers on two fronts—that of the institution and that of the facilities department. First, it is important for facility managers to ensure participation in organizational strategic planning to see that issues related to the built environment are well represented throughout the museum's strategic planning process. In turn, a facility manager should work to develop a facilities-specific strategic plan that relates broadly to the organization's strategic plan and mission and, specifically, to the facilities department's own mission. Developing a facility management strategic plan that fits hand in glove with the organization's strategic plan helps connect daily facility management tasks, duties, and decision making to the organizational mission in a way that is meaningful to both employees and customers (see box 3.6).

BOX 3.6.

THE HILLWOOD ESTATE, MUSEUM & GARDENS

Above: The well-manicured grounds and beautifully maintained facilities that comprise the Hillwood Estate, Museum & Gardens in Washington, DC, are made possible through careful strategic planning.

Photo Source: Courtesy of Hillwood Estate, Museum & Gardens.

CHAPTER FOUR
MANAGING CULTURAL FACILITY SYSTEMS

> The society which scorns excellence in plumbing as a humble activity and tolerates shoddiness in philosophy because it is an exalted activity will have neither good plumbing nor good philosophy: neither its pipes nor its theories will hold water.
>
> —John W. Gardner (1961), Secretary of Health, Education, and Welfare under President Lyndon Johnson

Cultural institution facility managers face a number of challenges each day, and this chapter begins to address the challenges associated with aligning a museum's systems with the specialized needs of its collections and the comfort of its human occupants. See box 4.1 for a list of several additional challenges commonly faced by cultural facility managers.

This chapter encourages an understanding of why it is crucial for cultural institutions to maintain robust and sensitive facilities systems and processes, such as lighting, integrated pest management, and heating, ventilation, and air conditioning. In addition, it outlines several strategies for measuring, evaluating, and improving these systems. Sustainable facility management practices, including energy and waste audits and benchmarking, are further discussed in chapter 6.

Agents of Deterioration That Affect Museum Collections

In museum and cultural institution facilities, many of the buildings' systems are geared toward cultivating an environment that keeps collections

BOX 4.1.

CHALLENGES FROM THE CULTURAL FACILITY MANAGER'S POINT OF VIEW

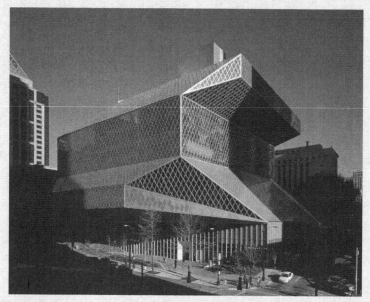

Above: The 11-story, 362,987 square foot Seattle Public Library Central Library facility opened in 2004, and it can hold around 1.45 million books and other materials.

Cultural facility managers have identified these issues as being among the challenges they face:

- Balancing the priorities of people and collections in mixed-use space,
- Bridging the gap between needs and expectations,
- Aging infrastructure,
- Continuous adaptation of spaces in the cultural facility environment,
- Cultural facilities that are often repurposed from other facility types,
- Decisions that are often made about space allocation without consulting the facility manager,
- Design and construction that often do not take into account operations and maintainability in the long term,
- Inadequate artifact storage space and configurations, and
- Planning appropriate responses to emergencies.

Source: International Association of Museum Facility Managers (IAMFA, 2011). Photo courtesy of the Seattle Public Library.

in pristine condition while allowing for the comfort of staff and visitors. To understand the factors that affect collections, we can consider what the U.S. National Park Service (NPS) terms "agents of deterioration." Agents of deterioration are elements that museum staff, including cultural institution facility managers, must monitor and control by implementing and maintaining specialized facility systems. These agents include

- air pollution,

- unnecessary light,

- insufficient temperature control, and

- insufficient relative humidity (RH) control.

Agents of deterioration, like those listed above, act upon an object to cause either chemical or physical damage.

Air pollutants include harmful gases, liquids, or solids found in the air, such as ozone, plasticizers, and dust. These pollutants can cause discoloration or corrosion of many types of objects, especially those that are very reactive or porous. Other agents of deterioration are ultraviolet (UV) radiation and excessive visible light. Light can fade or darken the outermost layer of materials like wood and paint. Insufficient temperature control can have drastic effects on collections objects. In addition, temperatures that are *too high* can promote the disintegration or discoloring of organic materials. Temperatures that are *too low* can cause paints or adhesives to desiccate, or dry out, and become cracked. In addition, fluctuating temperatures can trigger the fracturing or delamination of brittle items.

Relative humidity is also a concern. Relative humidity over 65 percent can dampen objects, causing them to mold or corrode. By contrast, relative humidity that is too low for a given object can cause it to shrink, stiffen, crack, or flake. Fluctuating relative humidity is also hazardous for many objects, for much the same reason that fluctuating temperatures are detrimental—objects may contract and swell during fluctuations in humidity and, in turn, crack or delaminate (Johnson 2006).

Managing Air Pollution

Air pollution affects the well-being of museum collections and building occupants. Pollutants originate both inside and outside of the museum building's envelope. Common pollutants include dirt, grease, soot, ash, sulfur dioxide, hydrogen sulfide, formaldehyde, and ozone, among others. These pollutants can come from ordinary equipment and processes. It is especially important to understand the effect that introducing any new material, product, or piece of equipment to the museum facility may have on the collections. For instance, ozone is released by copy machines, and formaldehyde comes from many common construction materials.

Air pollutants come in both particulate and gaseous forms. Particulate air pollutants include skin cells, dirt, soot, dust, ash, molds, and fibers, to name a few. Particulate air pollutants are detrimental to collections because they can act as catalysts for acid formation from gases, can attract gaseous and moisture pollutants, and can be sources of sulfates and nitrates, which become acidic when they come in contact with moisture. Gaseous air pollutants are substances such as sulfur dioxide, hydrogen sulfide, nitrogen dioxide, formaldehyde, formic and acetic acid, and ozone, among others. In museums, indoor air pollution frequently originates within the building materials themselves. Common building materials that release harmful substances into the air are:

- wood (including plywood and particle board, which can release acids and formaldehyde);

- unsealed concrete (which can release small alkaline particles);

- a number of paints and varnishes (which can release peroxides, organic solvents, and organic acids);

- fabrics and carpeting that have been finished with urea-formaldehyde or wool, which can release sulfur compounds;

- carpet glue, which may release formaldehyde; and

- plastic, which may release plasticizers. (Johnson 2006, pp. 4:44–45)

Because these gaseous and particulate air pollutants may be harmful to collections and unhealthy for human occupants, it is essential to monitor them and take steps to reduce their presence in the museum environment.

Monitoring indoor air for the presence of gaseous pollutants can be accomplished by investing in monitoring devices, as well as through acute observation of the museum environment. Monitoring equipment can be either active or passive. An example of active monitoring equipment is an environmental reactivity monitor (ERM), an electronic monitoring device that detects, nearly immediately, changes in air quality at the level of *parts per billion*. An ERM can be connected to a computer to allow a user to monitor air contaminants in real time. Environmental reactivity coupons (ERCs) are an example of passive monitoring equipment. Environmental reactivity coupons are cards that have exposed strips of metal, like copper or silver. Over a period ranging between 30 and 90 days, these metal strips are placed in a space and allowed to react to environmental pollutants, such as sulfur dioxide, ozone, and nitrogen oxides. At the end of the designated period, the cumulative reactivity rate can be read from the metal strips, allowing for an understanding of the sorts of corrosive pollutants present in the indoor atmosphere (Muller 2011). Each passive monitoring device may be able to detect only one type of pollutant, so it is likely that a museum would need to invest in more than one ERC to monitor its spaces. In addition, these devices may have to be read off-site by specialists, resulting in added costs.

While monitoring equipment is a valuable investment, funds are not always available to purchase this equipment. In this case, there are several monitoring options that require little more than an investment of time and can make an appreciable difference in the environmental quality of a space. For example, storage spaces should be regularly inspected for dust, with special attention given to areas such as open shelving, floors, and the tops of cabinets and tables. The amount of dust that accumulates in between cleanings should be recorded, as should any increase in insect activity that can be attributed to dust accumulation.

Many steps may be taken to improve the environmental quality of a space. Items such as storage cases, cabinets, or shelves that may be made of potentially harmful wood or coated with paints that could off-gas acetic acid or formaldehyde can be identified. It is important to understand a building's air control system and its structural materials. Air intakes should be properly filtered to reduce the introduction of harmful particles. Steps to mitigate possible harm can be taken if a building is built of potentially hazardous materials, such as asbestos. In a facility located in a coastal area, it is important to look for corrosion due to chlorides. This can be observed in rusting of unpainted iron or steel. No matter where a facility is located, it is important to pay attention to the quantity of dust and dirt visitors and museum staff bring into the facility each day. This monitoring will help with planning a number of things—from scheduling cleaning staff to purchasing appropriate entrance flooring to trap and reduce dirt and water tracked into the facility.

While it is nearly impossible to eliminate every bit of air pollution from museum spaces, there are several steps that can be taken to achieve safer conditions for artifacts and occupants in museum facilities. It is important to have a dedicated cleaning staff that is enthusiastic about minimizing the accumulation of dust. Vacuums with high-efficiency particulate air (HEPA) filters that catch tiny dust particles rather than merely kicking dust up, as vacuums without HEPA filters have a tendency to do, can aid the effort. Doors and windows should be sealed well with weather stripping in order to keep out as many pollutants as possible. Sealing doors and windows not only keeps the dust out, but also is an efficient means for helping keep out pests.

It is also helpful, from a space planning perspective, to keep workspaces away from collection storage spaces. This separation will help collections areas to stay cleaner than other, higher traffic work areas that have necessarily less stringent cleaning standards. Installing pollution filters on heating, ventilation, and air conditioning (HVAC) systems may be necessary in areas that have a high incidence of air pollution (see table 4.1 for commonly accepted control levels of indoor gaseous pollutants). These filters are able to remove both particulate and gaseous pollutants from air before they are introduced into the museum spaces. When working with an HVAC engineer to design a filtering system, it is important to select a system that will not produce ozone. In smaller spaces, it is also possible to use a portable air-filtering system with an activated-carbon filter to eliminate particulates, as well as some gaseous pollutants, from the air (Johnson 2006).

Table 4.1. Several Indoor Gaseous Pollutants and Commonly Accepted Control Levels

Gaseous Pollutant	Accepted Control Levels, Parts per Billion (ppb)
Sulfur dioxide	< 0.35 – < 1.0 ppb
Ozone	< 0.94 – < 12.5 ppb
Nitrogen dioxide	< 2.65 ppb
Chlorine	< 1 – < 3 ppb
Hydrogen chloride	< 1 – < 3 ppb
Acetic acid	< 4 ppb
Formaldehyde	< 4 ppb

Source: Muller (Winter 2010–2011). "Air-Quality Standards for Preservation Environments: Considerations for Monitoring and Classification of Gaseous Pollutants." *Papyrus: A publication of the International Association of Museum Facility Administrators* 11(2): 45–50. Available at www.iamfa.org.

Managing Lighting

Lighting in cultural facilities is very important to consider for two primary reasons. First, light is comprised of vibrating particles of radiant energy called photons, which can be very damaging for many works of art and artifacts. For this reason, lighting must be carefully selected in order to lessen this damage. Second, in exhibition spaces, lighting must be selected in order to enhance the viewers' experiences of each object on display. In many cases, this means that lighting must be specified to allow the object to be viewed in the way the artist or craftsperson intended it to be seen, which can be a challenge when preservation is also a concern.

Truth be told, no amount of exposure to light is truly safe for many pieces of art or artifacts. The only exception to this is found among non-light-responsive materials, such as metal, stone, and minerals. By and large, if a work of art or an artifact can be seen, it is being damaged by exposure to light. Examples of pieces that are sensitive to light include silk, newspaper, watercolors, natural history and botanical specimens, and tapestries.

Light is measured and classified on the electromagnetic spectrum according to its wavelength. Smaller wavelengths have higher photon energy levels than do larger wavelengths and are, thus, more damaging (Cuttle 2007). Three types of light on the electromagnetic spectrum are important to consider in the cultural institution environment, because they have the potential to affect collections. In order of increasing wavelength, these types are UV light, the visible spectrum, and infrared (IR) light.

UV and IR light are both nonvisible forms of radiation. UV radiation occurs at wavelengths between 300 and 400 nanometers (nm), where one nanometer is one thousand millionth of a meter. Though ultraviolet radiation contains a high level of energy, humans cannot perceive it. Infrared radiation occurs at wavelengths greater than 760 nm and manifests as heat. Neither ultraviolet radiation nor infrared radiation is necessary for visibility, and both UV and IR can be blocked entirely in order to increase the safety of collection objects.

The visible spectrum occurs at wavelengths between about 400 and 760 nanometers. Visible light is necessary to allow people to see, so it is nearly impossible to eliminate it from the museum and cultural institution environment, with the exception of storage areas. Despite its necessity when viewing objects, visible light is nonetheless damaging for many types of museum collections (Johnson 2006).

Lux and foot-candles are important for cultural facility managers to understand, because conservators use these units to express acceptable light exposure for varying artworks and artifacts in cultural institution settings. The International System of Units (SI) has established the lumen (lm) as the unit that quantifies the amount of visible light emitted by a particular source. In the United States, the foot-candle (fc) is sometimes used in place of the lumen, where one foot-candle is equal to one lumen per square foot ("Optics" 2012). The SI unit for quantifying the density of lumens per square meter on a given surface is expressed in lux (lx), where one lux is equal to one lumen per meter ("Lux" 2012). The lux is sometimes expressed in foot-candles in the United States, where one foot-candle is equivalent to 10.764 lux.

To help classify acceptable exposure levels, the International Organization for Standardization (ISO) has provided a means for rating the light-fastness of different materials. This rating is on a scale from 1 to 8, with 1 being the most responsive to light and 8 being the least responsive to light ("Textile" 2012). For example, an object with an ISO rating of 1 might fade noticeably after exposure to UV-rich light for just 1.5 years, while an object with an ISO rating of 8 might fade noticeably after exposure to UV-rich light for 800 years.

Over time, light causes degradation through photochemical reactions as well as through the radiant heating effect. Photochemical reactions occur when an object is exposed to light that causes its molecular structure to undergo a change. Photons from either UV or visible radiation are capable of inducing these structural changes in a variety of materials. One such change, called photolysis, happens when energy from the photons is strong enough to affect the bonds between the molecules comprising an object. When this happens, generally with exposure to wavelengths of fewer than 300 nm, the molecules split apart. This damaging process can be avoided when UV is filtered out and illumination is managed in accordance with the level of exposure that a particular collection object can safely handle (Cuttle 2007). It is also important to remember the reciprocity law: "Low light levels for extended periods cause as much damage as high light levels for brief periods" (Johnson 2006, p. 4:34). That is to say, damage caused by light accrues over time and is irreversible.

In distinguishing between the types of damage caused by visible light, UV, and IR radiation, we can remember the following:

- visible light can trigger fading or bleaching of colors. This fading can happen over a period of years with exposure to museum lighting or in a short time, such as several hours of exposure of light-sensitive objects to direct sun.

- ultraviolet radiation can trigger weakening, chalking, yellowing, and, possibly, the breakdown of objects.

- infrared radiation can heat the surfaces of collections objects to potentially-damaging high temperatures. (Quoted from Michalski 2011b)

In order to reduce this damage from light, there are two routes to pursue—reducing the amount of light in a space and reducing the overall amount of time that an artifact is exposed to light. Reduced lighting in exhibition spaces, even at very low levels, does not necessarily impede visitors' ability to view the collections. Human eyesight is able to become accustomed to a broad range of lighting conditions; however, it is important to allow enough time for eyes to adjust as people move from bright areas to more muted lighting. This can be accomplished by decreasing lighting at a measured pace as visitors move from space to space.

To aid in efforts to reduce lighting damage, it is important to have a light-monitoring program to track both visible and ultraviolet exposure levels in all spaces that collections will be held. Tracking these levels is meaningless unless there is a standard against which these levels can be evaluated. It is imperative that all parties who have a vested interest in lighting design—from conservators to curators, and from facility managers to lighting designers—work together to establish specific guidelines for each space. These guidelines, in turn, serve as a valuable tool when implementing a program of monitoring and controlling lighting. In addition, these guidelines are an indispensable roadmap for facility managers tasked with executing lighting upgrades to their facilities.

Two types of meters are necessary—one for measuring visible light and one for measuring ultraviolet levels. A visible light meter should be sufficiently sensitive to capture levels as low as 25 to 50 lux with a high degree of accuracy. For measuring UV, available meters provide readings in microwatts per lumen on an analog scale. When using both metering types, it is important to place each meter in a location near the collection object where exposure to artificial and natural light is being measured. If it is a large object, it will be necessary to take more than one reading to document its exposure at different points of its surface area. It is important to ensure that a person performing the metering does not cast shadows that may interfere with the accuracy of the readings and that the meter's sensor is parallel to the object's exterior and directed toward the light source in question. As with any new piece of equipment, it is imperative that anybody who will be operating the light-metering equipment be familiar with the manufacturer's instructions and that it be properly maintained and calibrated on a regular schedule.

When collecting data about visible and UV light, it is important to have a record of the types of fixtures, filters, and ballasts in all spaces that hold collections. It is similarly important to have an understanding of how sunlight moves through these spaces each day and how this movement changes, depending upon the season. Any changes to a given space that affect lighting—even if they are subtle, such as flash photography or taking down draperies for cleaning—should be documented and measured as well. Facilities staff, conservators, and others concerned with the interaction between the environment and the well-being of collections must have a mutual understanding of the significance of documenting baseline conditions and monitoring changes that are made to the space over time.

Once baseline conditions have been documented and communicated to all essential members of the staff, it is time to identify light-sensitive collections objects. Their locations will serve as "monitoring sites" and should be indicated in a floor plan of the space. At regular intervals, each of these sites should be monitored in terms of lux, UV, and temperature and subsequently documented. This documentation can be used to make adjustments to the facility, such as adding or replacing UV filtering film, tracking and adjusting for seasonal changes in natural lighting, and adjusting lighting based on occupancy (Johnson 2006).

To hold visible light within the levels recommended by conservators for the collections objects in each space, a number of techniques can be employed. Stefan Michalski, senior conservation scientist at the Canadian Conservation Institute, advocates to *avoid, block, detect, respond,* and *recover* when it comes to controlling visible light and ultraviolet and infrared radiation.

In part, the first strategy, to avoid, involves putting in place guidelines for allowable light and UV levels, as well as the operation of light sources. The next strategy, to block, involves placing UV filters on any light sources that emit high levels of UV radiation. Windows should be covered with screens, blinds, louvers, or a comparable shading device to block excessive natural light. Areas that display collections should be separated from brighter entrance areas, and the corridors between these two differently lit areas should allow for visitors' eyes to adjust between the two lighting conditions. When the museum is not open, windows and cases should be covered to protect collections from additional exposure. The third strategy, to detect, has, for the most part, already been discussed in this chapter. Detection, as defined by Michalski, involves being on the lookout for indications of radiation damage, as well as using light meters, UV meters, and thermometers to gauge whether visible light, UV, and infrared radiation levels are detrimental to collections.

The final two strategies, to respond and to recover, occur after detection has indicated either that there is damage or that the potential for damage exists due to the present lighting conditions in a particular space. To respond involves determining the causes and likely solutions to issues discovered during detection. Michalski cautions that recovery from visible light, UV, or IR damage is basically impossible but that restoration may be a viable option. During restoration, the damaged portions of an item must be replaced (Michalski 2011b). From the facility manager's perspective, his or her job is to help prevent the need for response or recovery by helping to maintain appropriate lighting conditions.

Other advice for protecting collections from visible light and UV includes implementing a schedule for covering and uncovering windows for portions of the day in order to reduce cumulative exposure to light. Opaque dust covers can be used to cover collections objects that are light sensitive when they are not being viewed by the public, such as when they are being stored or when their exhibition is closed for a portion of the year. Light fixtures can be fitted with filters that effectively reduce the damage caused by incandescent bulbs. The number of fixtures should be minimized and lights should be turned off when the light source is not needed. Motion detectors or timers are especially helpful for reducing exposure to light during times that lighting is not necessary for patrons (Johnson 2006).

The radiant heating effect occurs when the energy from IR radiation—which is not visible but can be emitted from incandescent light sources, such as tungsten halogen lamps—makes surface temperatures increase (Cuttle 2007). In addition to raising the temperature, IR can also lessen the amount of water in porous objects (Johnson 2006). As temperatures increase, the likelihood that heat-sensitive materials will expand increases. In turn, when these IR-emitting lights are turned on and off, day in and day out, these sensitive materials can expand and contract, causing additional damage. The presence of IR cannot be easily measured, but one quick and easy way to assess whether IR is a problem is to hold the back of one's hand near the collection piece of concern and observe whether an increase in heat is felt due to the light source. If so, adjustments can be made accordingly (Cuttle 2007).

If IR is perceived as a threat to collections, its heat buildup can be controlled in part by ensuring spaces that hold collections have sufficient air circulation and window coverings. In addition, ensuring that lights are outside cases and that appropriate filters are on light fixtures will help keep temperatures from rising. It is also important to have a policy for photography in spaces containing collections. The lighting used for photography can cause unnecessary heating, so it is important that the photographers and videographers use heat-absorbing filters. It is also important that the spaces are well ventilated, using fans and/or air conditioning. Anytime that cameras are not in use, their lighting should be turned off. Collection objects should only be placed under the photographer's lighting during the final filming stage—during any rehearsals, a proxy object should be used (Johnson 2006).

Incandescent and fluorescent lamps, high-intensity discharge lamps (HIDs), and white light-emitting diodes (LEDs), as well as daylight, are common lighting options in museums. Among these options, there are a range of factors, such as cost, life span, and light quality, which influence whether a lighting option is a good fit within a particular museum environment. Please see table 4.2 for general information about each of these lighting types, including filtering possibilities

As table 4.2 depicts, LEDs are among the most cost-effective and sustainable lighting options available to museums and cultural institutions. LEDs have been gaining currency in museums throughout the United States over the past several years, as the cost per LED has begun to drop significantly and conservators have become increasingly more confident that LEDs are not significantly damaging to many types of collections. A recent study conducted by the U.S. Department of Energy in three different museums—the Smithsonian American Art Museum, the Getty Conservation Institute, and the Jordan Schnitzer Museum of Art—illustrates that careful vetting of available LED options can yield viable lighting with a character comparable to that of the halogen lights that have previously been more commonly preferred for collections display.

Not only do LEDs save energy, but also they save on maintenance time and costs. Because they need to be replaced infrequently, fewer maintenance personnel hours are dedicated to their replacement. In addition, LEDs produce less heat than do incandescent bulbs, ultimately reducing the amount of cooling that the building's air conditioner must accomplish (Brodrick 2011). It should be noted that LEDs are not without their conservation challenges, as they have been observed to hasten damage to natural yellow dyes (Druzik 2010).

Table 4.2. General Characteristics of Light Sources for Museums

		HIGH INTENSITY DISCHARGE (HID)	FLUORESCENT	
	WHITE LED		Traditional Tubes	Compact
			HIGH EFFICIENCY ELECTRIC LIGHT SOURCES	
VOLTAGE	220 V, 120 V, 12 V, 6V	220 V, 120 V, and higher	220 V, 120 V	220 V, 120 V
COMMON TYPES AND NOMENCLATURE	Retrofits: A19, PAR20, PAR30, PAR38, MR16, small base candelabra lamps. Custom luminaires: track and troffer designs, custom tracks or track adapters. Single lens LEDs for tight locations such as interior of display cases	HID: high intensity discharge; this class includes the following: M: mercury MH: metal halide CMH: ceramic metal halide S or HS: high pressure sodium Xenon Many elaborate shapes and fixtures.	T5, T8, T10, Circline T: tube diameter in multiples of 1/8 in. (3 mm). F18, F20, F40, F96 F: fluorescent, number refers to wattage CW: cool white. WW: warm white. NW: neutral white. CWX: cool white deluxe. WWX: warm white deluxe.	CFT or CFL: compact fluorescent tubes (or "lighting"). Helical shapes most common, also twin and triple-tubes. Many sizes between 5 and 30 Watts, which replace incandescent lamps of x4 wattage.
LIFETIME, HOURS	25,000–50,000 (70% of original intensity). Less if lamp insufficiently ventilated. Most with warranty against premature failure.	3,000–40,000+	10,000–16,000	6,000–15,000
COST (per lamp)	Retrofits: $25–$60 Custom luminaires $100+	Varies widely with size	$5–$20 (varies as CRI)	$10–$20, built in reflector types up to $40
RELAMP COST (per year of 3,000 hours)	Retrofits $1.51–$7 3–5 year warranties standard	Varies widely with size	$1–$6	$2–$20

(continued)

Table 4.2. (continued)

	WHITE LED	HIGH INTENSITY DISCHARGE (HID)	FLUORESCENT Traditional Tubes	Compact
COLOUR TEMPERATURE (CCT)	Any CCT possible. Standard: 2700K, 3000K, 3200K, 4000K, 5600K, 7000K	Mercury, metal halides: warm to cool available. Xenon almost mimics daylight 6500K	"warm white" 2700K "neutral white" 3000K "cool white" 4200K "daylight" 5000-6500K	"warm/soft white" 2700K "bright white" 3500K "cool white" 4100K "daylight" ≥ 5000K
COLOUR RENDERING INDEX (CRI) Excellent 90-100 Good 80-89 Fair 70-79 Poor below 69	Best LEDs over 90 (excellent), some 80-90 (good) but many fair to poor. Check website or packaging for each lamp. Seek warranty against color shift during use.	Best metal halides are over 90 (excellent), some 80-90 (good), but most metal halides, mercury, and sodium lamps are below 69 (poor).	Best fluorescent lamps over 90 (excellent), many 80-90 (good) but some fair to poor.	Most CFL near 85 (good). Most are "triphosphor", the spectrum consists of three peaks, tuned to our eye's three colour receptors.
UV OUTPUT (microW/lm)	Blue exciter LED: no UV emitted Violet exciter LED: unknown	Most high to very high UV	Most 75-150 (low to medium) Some over 150.	Most 100-150 (medium)
UV FILTERING POSSIBILITIES	Unnecessary for blue exciter types. Plastic UV filters could be used on violet exciter type.	Most use a glass UV filter against short wavelength UV, but this is not museum grade. Glass UV filters (Optivex ™) available for some shapes. Plastic UV films must be used at some distance from the heat of the bulb.	Plastic sleeve UV filter available. If they have end caps, ensure they are certified against fire risk (some have ignited). Alternatively place UV filters on fixture diffusers.	Plastic film sleeves or covers must be custom fabricated if desired. Alternatively place UV filters on fixture diffusers.

HIGH EFFICIENCY ELECTRIC LIGHT SOURCES

FIBER OPTIC OR LIGHTPIPE APPLICATION	No sufficiently intense LED lamp available at present (2013) but likely soon.	Small MH or xenon lamps are used in some fibre optic illuminators. Whole rooms of cases have been lit by one powerful lamp in a separate area. This will reduce the risk from heat.	Light pipe shelves can be used in cases.	Not suitable.
MAIN MUSEUM ADVANTAGES	Wide variety of beam widths available. Low-frequency relamping. Low energy consumption. Maintain colour temperature when dimmed. Useful at short distances in display cases. Excellent cost recovery when replacing incandescent lamps.	Useful for lighting large areas, for high ceilings, and for security purposes outdoors. Low-frequency relamping. Low energy consumption.	Low-frequency relamping. Little heat from tube. Low energy consumption.	Very useful at short distances as in display cases. Low frequency relamping. Little heat from tube. Low energy consumption.
MAIN MUSEUM DISADVANTAGES	Initial costs are high, especially for museum quality CRI. The small point source causes glare if not shielded. Many low quality lamps on the market. (Media reports that white LED lamps caused more damage to paintings than other white lamps were incorrect).	Most have terrible CRI. Most slow to start. Intra-batch variation is high. Output can change significantly with aging.	Too bright at short distances. Not easily directed in a beam. Most fixture are unattractive, lighting can be "flat"	Not easily directed in a sharp beam.

(continued)

Table 4.2. (continued)

	LOW EFFICIENCY ELECTRIC LIGHT SOURCES *(Some of these will be phased out in the near future)*		
	INCANDESCENT		*DAYLIGHT*
	Quartz Halogen	*Traditional*	
VOLTAGE	220 V, 120 V, 12 V, 6V	220 V, 120 V	N/A
COMMON TYPES AND NOMENCLATURE	MR16, PAR20, PAR30, PAR36 MR: multiple reflector PAR: parabolic reflector. Number refers to diameter in multiples of 1/8 in. (3 mm.) MR16 types also referred to by three letters, e.g. BAB, EXN, etc. and have bases defined as GU 5.3 (bi-pin, most common) or GU 10 (twist-pin, 220V, high efficiency) Q series: no reflector, number refers to wattage	A19, R30, R40, PAR38, tubular A: common round bulb C: candle. G: globe. T: tubular R: reflector ER: elliptical reflector PAR: parabolic reflector. Number refers to diameter in multiples of 1/8 in. (3 mm.) As of 1996, many R and PAR types no longer available due to energy regulation. All traditional incandescent lamp may be eventually replaced by LEDs or CFLs.	N/A
LIFETIME, HOURS	2,000 typical. Short lifetimes reported for high wattage lamps in some fibre optic systems.	A, R, PAR: 2,000 ER: 5,000+ Long life lamps available: 10,000–20,000	N/A
COST (per lamp)	$5–$25	A: $1–2 R, PAR, ER: $5–$10	Costs "hidden". High initial building cost, larger heating and cooling systems.
RELAMP COST (per year of 3,000 hours)	$8–$40	A: $3 R, PAR, ER: $7–$30	High maintenance costs: energy for heating/cooling, skylight leaks, etc.

COLOUR TEMPERATURE (CCT)	3000K, typical Specialty MR lamps with filters available from 3500K to 5000K	2700-2800K typical Some lamps with blue reflectors or filters will increase CCT to 2900K	Late afternoon: 3000K Noon sunshine: 6000K Blue sky: 9000-12000K Daylight: mix of above, standard is 6500K or "D65"
COLOUR RENDERING INDEX (CRI) Excellent 90-100 Good 80-89 Fair 70-79 Poor below 69	100, excellent. Dichroic reflectors (low heat) may reduce CRI. NOTE: Incandescent lamps and daylight both score 100 by definition of the CRI because both have a smooth "black body" spectrum. i.e. a continuous spectrum between 400 nm and 760 nm. The low colour temperature of traditional incandescent lamps, however, sometimes provokes criticism in museums, especially for paintings created outdoors using blue colours. The increase from 2800K to 3000K with quartz halogen lamps eliminated most such criticism.		100, excellent
UV OUTPUT (microW/lm)	Behind glass: 100-200. Medium Those labeled "UV STOP": 40, low	75, low	300-600 typical, very high
UV FILTERING POSSIBILITIES	Bare quartz bulb emits shortwave UV, blocked by plain glass envelope or safety filter. MR16 behind Optivex glass filters ($10-$50) Low cost plastic filters must be at a distance from the hot bulb.	Not essential, but higher UV-sensitive objects would benefit from a UV filter.	Window glass filters shortwave UV, but not enough for museums. Laminated glass with a middle layer of UV filter available, or self-adhesive plastic films over windows. (Applied films may void the warranty on sealed insulated glass windows.)

(continued)

Table 4.2. (continued)

| | LOW EFFICIENCY ELECTRIC LIGHT SOURCES (Some of these will be phased out in the near future) | | DAYLIGHT |
| | INCANDESCENT | | |
	Quartz Halogen	Traditional	
FIBER OPTIC OR LIGHTPIPE APPLICATION	MR16 commonly used in fibre optic illuminators. Glass or polymer fibres possible and thus some may filter UV and infrared. Illuminator: $200-$500. From 1-10 separate fiber outputs per fixture typical, sometimes more.	Not suitable.	Light pipes have been used for daylight transfer through museums.
MAIN MUSEUM ADVANTAGES	Excellent variety of beam widths and wattages available. Best light spectrum available. Low-voltage lamps can be wired without concern for shock hazard. Very small change in lamp output over its lifetime.	"A" types have very low costs. Fixtures are low cost. Useful in historical house museums to maintain ambience. Historic lamp designs are available.	Feels good. Looks nice. Can provide very high intensity light without high heat content. Can be a net gain in terms of sustainability and energy consumption, but this requires careful design.
MAIN MUSEUM DISADVANTAGES	Bulbs are very hot, bare quartz bulbs can explode. High heat output. Relamping cost can be high. Some low voltage fixtures very expensive. Bare wire designs create fire risks.	Too bright at less than 1.5 m. Highest heat output of any lamp (not suitable inside cases). No narrow spots.	Difficult to control intensity to museum requirements. Varies with the weather and seasons. Windows and their control fittings are expensive to build and to maintain. Usually a net loss in terms of sustainability and energy consumption, due to high heating and cooling loads.

Cultural institutions, like the San Diego Art Institute's Museum of the Living Artist, have begun seeking external support to convert their current lighting systems in part, or in whole, to LEDs. In 2012, the Museum of the Living Artist received $170,000 in the form of an Energy Efficiency and Conservation Block Grant for the conversion of their existing halogen light bulbs to LEDs. The museum saw the conversion not only as an opportunity to switch lighting types, but also as an opportunity to make its lighting more customizable. The new light fixtures are divided into seventeen groups, and each group has a separate control for added customization (Tung 2012).

The information in this section—including the information related to conservation—is essential to understanding and planning for a cultural institution facility's overall lighting program. A facility manager who has a basic understanding of the conservation issues related to lighting—and the vocabulary to discuss these issues—can have more productive and collaborative conversations with lighting engineers, conservators, and exhibition designers. When any changes are made to the facility's lighting program, it is important that members of the museum's staff work together to ensure that the desired viewing conditions are achieved, while maintaining a high level of energy efficiency and maintainability, and conserving collections.

Temperature Considerations

Temperatures at extremes—either too hot or too cold—or temperatures that oscillate between hot and cold can be damaging for museum collections. Higher temperatures mean that the molecules that comprise an object will move faster and spread apart, causing expansion of the object. By contrast, at lower temperatures, molecules move more slowly and ultimately contract. The generally accepted range for temperatures in research, storage, and exhibition spaces is 64–68 degrees Fahrenheit (18–20 degrees Celsius). In general, temperatures should not be allowed above 75 degrees Fahrenheit (24 degrees Celsius).

Poorly regulated temperatures can affect museum collections in several ways. By and large, warmer temperatures are more dangerous for most collections objects than are cooler temperatures. Higher temperatures can increase biological activity, the softening of materials, and instances of chemical reaction. For example, artifacts that contain wax, adhesives, or other soft surfaces may begin to soften when exposed to high temperatures. In addition, both mold and insects may begin to thrive at higher temperatures. Finally, any increase in temperature will typically increase the rate of chemical reactions that affect the collections objects. For some objects, such as film, high temperatures can be disastrous. When temperatures climb in an environment that serves as film storage, cellulose nitrate can become a fire hazard.

One rule of thumb when approaching lower temperatures is that most collections can be exposed to them, as long as the temperatures do not dip below freezing. Some types of collections, such as film, demand cold—even freezing—storage. Maintaining such low temperatures is frequently complicated by the fact that many collections share space with human occupants, who require a particular temperature range in order to be comfortable. While colder temperatures can be safe for collections, fluctuations in temperature should be avoided. Rapid expansion and contraction can harm many collections objects (Johnson 2006). In any case, facility managers and conservators should work together to identify a temperature range that keeps collections safe, while allowing the facility to operate as sustainably as is feasible.

Relative Humidity Considerations

Relative humidity (RH) describes the amount of water vapor that is held in a particular mass of air at a given temperature. Temperature is also an important factor to bear in mind when considering relative humidity, because air at higher temperatures has a greater capacity for holding water vapor than does cooler air. Warmer air molecules move more quickly and diffuse more, which ultimately creates more space for water molecules.

Relative humidity and temperature are inversely related. This means that, in a closed system like a storage case, if the temperature goes up, the relative humidity will drop, and vice versa. Many facility managers choose to turn the thermostat setting down in their facilities when there are no people present in order to save on the cost of heating. This practice should be carefully executed in museum environments, however, because the lower temperature setting will cause an increase in the relative humidity. When the temperature is turned up the next morning, the relative humidity will again drop. This cycle of raising and lowering the relative humidity can be harmful for collections objects held in museum environments. For example, wooden objects can swell and contract, causing deterioration and, eventually, cracking. Other objects that may be harmed by these fluctuations in RH include photographs, paintings, veneered furniture, as well as items that are either laminate or composite in nature.

While variation in relative humidity is potentially hazardous to museum collections, RH that is either too high or too low also puts collections at risk for damage. Water is a key ingredient for many different chemical reactions, and a high degree of relative humidity can provide the water necessary to initiate these reactions, including corrosion of metals. It is also possible for materials like wood or ivory to begin to warp or swell when exposed to an environment with high RH. Adhesives can also soften or become sticky and canvas can begin to slacken due to high RH. A moist environment also encourages mold growth, especially when RH levels exceed 65 percent. While high relative humidity may cause swelling or warping, low relative humidity, by contrast, may cause shrinking or cracking of wood, ivory, photographic emulsions, leather, and other materials. It can also dry out paper and other fibrous materials, as well as adhesives.

In order to maintain relative humidity at levels that do not greatly affect collections or promote mold growth, it is important that RH be monitored on a regular basis. That said, monitoring, in and of itself, is not enough—facility managers must work with curatorial staff to determine what an acceptable RH set point is for a particular collection. Normally, RH should not fluctuate more than 5 percent above or below the RH set point, and it should not be allowed to creep above 65 percent, the point at which mold growth blooms. Climatic conditions particular to certain geographic locations can affect the RH set point that is decided upon for a given facility. For example, in an arid environment, where artifacts may have become acclimated to fairly low RH levels, the set point may need to be lower. This lower RH set point will help keep the artifacts in an environment closer to the RH levels to which they have become accustomed.

Often, museum facilities are managed in a way that allows for drift, in which case the RH set point is unique to a given season. Frequently, when allowing for drift, the RH set point will be higher in the summer and lower during the winter. Over time, allowing for seasonal drift lowers utility costs, as does allowing for mechanical systems to run at reduced intensity, possibly extending their lives. As discussed earlier, it is important that collections not be exposed to variations in RH over short periods of time. When a drift method is employed, the shift in the RH set point must occur over a long period of time—ranging from several weeks to a period of months—to avoid causing the problems inherent to rapid fluctuations in RH (Johnson 2006).

Monitoring Temperature and Relative Humidity

It is very important that temperature and relative humidity be observed and documented throughout storage and exhibition spaces. Monitoring these variables reveals whether collections are provided with safe conditions, brings to light how temperature and RH change from space to space and season to season, and demonstrates areas where control and/or efficiency need improvement.

Prior to purchasing new monitoring equipment, it is helpful for anyone invested in monitoring—museum directors, conservators, and facility managers, for example—to work together to craft an environmental monitoring plan or policy. This plan articulates exactly what data is needed and why it is necessary. In addition, it states where the monitoring equipment should be strategically located, as well as lists the training necessary to operate and maintain the monitoring equipment. The environmental monitoring plan should also include a budget that accounts for the initial purchase, as well as the ongoing maintenance and operation, of the monitoring equipment. During the process of drafting this plan, it is important to keep in mind whether the museum building will be updated in the near future, how much time staff will need to spend working with the equipment, as well as how many monitoring stations are needed to capture the data required for various spaces throughout each building. Finally, it is important to circulate the plan, making sure that all relevant parties are able to access and easily implement its guidelines. As an example, the Royal Air Force Museum (2008) in the United Kingdom posts its "Policy for Monitoring Relative Humidity and Temperature" on its website, making it readily available to all staff members.

Monitoring equipment ranges in cost, complexity, and accuracy. It is important to be sure that a specific device is capable of providing a desired level of accuracy before investing in any particular monitoring device. For example, will the space being monitored house Japanese scrolls, which may be very sensitive to temperature and humidity and, in turn, require a very sensitive monitoring system? Or, instead, does the space hold a geological collection that may be much less sensitive to temperature and humidity and, thus, a less sensitive system will suffice? Asking questions about the space—and what it is meant to accommodate—will help narrow down the options when considering different types of monitoring equipment.

Monitoring equipment registers readings through a variety of means, including chemical, mechanical, and electronic mechanisms:

- *Chemical mechanisms*: Humidity indicator cards provide a simple, nonmechanical way to gauge changes in humidity. These cards work when cobalt salt reacts with ambient humidity, causing a color change that indicates a change in humidity has occurred. Humidity indicator cards provide spot readings and are typically used in microclimates, such as cases or cabinets.

- *Mechanical mechanisms*: Among the mechanical equipment available to monitor temperature and humidity are dial thermohygrometers, thermohygrographs, whirling hygrometers, aspirated hygrometers, and thermometers. Save for the thermohygrographs, which record temperature and humidity on a revolving drum, these mechanical options provide spot readings that must be manually recorded.

- *Electronic mechanisms*: Digital display thermohygrometers and data loggers are electronic means of keeping tabs on temperature and humidity. Data loggers provide continuous monitoring and recording of temperature and humidity data over time, while thermohygrometers with digital displays allow for spot readings that must be recorded manually. Data loggers are particularly useful, because they can be connected to a computer—either by a hardwire connection or over a network—to upload the data that has been collected. This removes the need to manually record data, as is necessary with many other monitoring equipment types.

Once monitoring equipment has been installed, an ongoing observation program should be established so that data can be collected and analyzed. Analysis of this data allows museum staff, including facility management, to work together with engineers to determine how to best achieve the desired RH and temperature range within the built environment.

When analyzing the data collected, bear in mind that it can be influenced by a variety of common circumstances. To ensure accuracy of the monitoring equipment, it should be serviced on a regular schedule, as recommended by the manufacturer. The location of the monitoring equipment is also very important and can affect the accuracy of readings. Easy accessibility of the equipment, lending it to being tampered with by visitors, can lead to inaccurate data. Whether the equipment is located in a room that has external walls, in a location where doors are propped open, in a room with large expanses of windows, or in a place where it will receive direct sunlight for part of the day can also affect the data. In addition, something as simple as wet cleaning of floors in the room the monitoring equipment is located can affect the readings at that time. If special events are held in the same room as the equipment, overcrowding can affect the readings as well.

When installing a new monitoring system or beginning a monitoring program for the first time, it is helpful to begin recording data over a brief period to learn how temperature and humidity fluctuate from day to day and to begin to identify the variables that influence this fluctuation. During this early data-gathering effort, be ready to explore a variety of previously unconsidered or unknown variables that could be contributing to the environmental conditions in each space. When first implementing a monitoring program, it can be helpful to allow temperature and RH set points to be fairly broad, while learning more about what is affecting the temperature and RH. These ranges can then be narrowed over time as adjustments are made and conditions begin to steady (Cassar and Hutchings 2000).

It is very important for facility management and exhibition design personnel to work together to notify one another of changes planned for exhibit spaces. For example, there may be an exhibition design that requires false walls that will partially block vents in the exhibition space. The facility manager should be consulted prior to the installation of these walls, so that he or she can account for this vent being blocked and ensure that appropriate RH and temperature levels can be maintained. If possible, the facility manager and exhibitions team should hold regular meetings, allowing facility work and exhibition plans to be discussed and necessary planning and troubleshooting to occur. This collaboration will help keep the exhibition spaces in good working order and prevent the sorts of last-minute emergencies that result from lack of communication. For an example of how the HVAC system was updated at a cultural institution in Delaware, see box 4.2.

Controlling Temperature and Relative Humidity

As has already been discussed, museum environments with high temperatures and dangerous relative humidity levels present particular challenges to the preservation of collections. For this reason, parameters have been established to encourage temperatures to be between 64 and 68 degrees Fahrenheit and humidity to remain at or near 50 percent. In many cases,

BOX 4.2.

FIGHTING MOLD AND DECAY IN
THE TWENTY-FIRST CENTURY AT
THE WINTERTHUR MUSEUM, GARDEN,
AND LIBRARY IN DELAWARE

By Michael Dixon

The building that houses the Winterthur Library is a four-story structure totaling over 68,000 square feet. The top two floors house the conservation labs and offices. The second floor is primarily an administrative area, but also houses some collections. The first floor is primarily a public space that houses collection objects.

The crucial measure of a research library, however, is its ability to store, in an accessible manner, its voluminous reference materials. In the Winterthur Library, this is achieved through a five-level stack that occupies a 3,200 square foot footprint at the end of the building, stretching from the basement level through the second floor. While this may have seemed like a vast volume of space in 1969, in 1999 it was bulging with printed material and suffering from wide swings in environmental conditions.

Before embarking on an ambitious project to upgrade the library HVAC systems, extensive effort was undertaken to verify that such an investment was prudent, given the age and design of the building. A primary consideration was whether the building had the space capacity to accommodate the growing collection for a period of time that would allow the desired return on investment. This effort was led by Dr. Gary Kulik, Deputy Director of Library and Academic Programs. His prospectus, written in April 1999, established that if steps were taken to maximize the use of available storage space, the Library could exist within the current building for another twenty years, thus justifying the expenditures of over $3,000,000 to replace the 30-year-old mechanical equipment, while improving compliance with environmental standards.

The effect of this conclusion was to expand the project to consolidate administrative operations, in order to create more space for collections storage. With this expanded scope of the project, local authorities having jurisdiction over fire systems and elevators mandated other system upgrades. The construction period was also chosen to complete a long-needed upgrade of the security system.

The argument against investing in upgrades for a 30-year-old library building is the widely held belief that, in the not-too-distant future, library materials would be fully accessible via electronic media. Library professionals, however, make a strong case for the fact that research libraries will never be a fully digital resource. Their research relies as much on the construction and materials of literary works as they do on the contents.

While the quality of the results of imaging efforts has improved greatly in recent years, the cost of converting collections to other media has not fallen. It is still a labor-intensive effort, whether microfilming or digitizing—especially given the fragile condition of some of these materials. Most cultural institutions are not in a position to assume additional operating costs, and the Winterthur is no exception.

For more than ten years, the Winterthur has attempted to maintain an environment of 72 degrees Fahrenheit (F) and 50 percent relative humidity. But the original system design has allowed conditions to vary to 60 percent relative humidity and higher during the humid summers in Delaware. At those humidity levels, the Winterthur's conservators estimate that a major portion of the at-risk collections would severely deteriorate within 50 years.

The most aggressive institutions are currently designing for 35 or 40 percent relative humidity in modern buildings, and are reducing temperature set points to 65 degrees F. Library conservation staff at the Winterthur estimated that the useful life of the at-risk collections would increase to over 100 years under these conditions. They believe that, by then, other preservation technologies would be cost-effective.

Complicating the establishment of new standards is the variety of collection materials within the Library. In addition to published materials, there are photographic and slide collections, maps and prints, archived paper-based materials, film, and tape. Add people to the mix and it is obvious that one standard cannot be applied to every space.

Thus, the environmental control specification [for the Winterthur's new standards were] broken into four separate applications.

Average conditions: Suitable for most occupied spaces
- Temperature of 68–72 degrees F
- Relative humidity of less than 55 percent

Archive storage: Paper-based materials, including rare books
- Temperature of 55–65 degrees F (68 degrees for reading rooms)
- Relative humidity of 40 percent

Archive storage: Artworks
- Temperature of 60–72 degrees
- Relative humidity of 40 percent

Archive storage: Film and tape
- Temperature of 65 degrees F
- Relative humidity of 40 percent

The major impact of the new standards is the cooling required in order to achieve the 40 percent relative humidity specification in the archive storage spaces. In order to deliver 40 percent relative humidity air to these spaces, chilled water at 40 degrees F is required. However, the current chilled water system delivers only 44 degrees F chilled water. In order to deliver 40 degree F chilled water, an additional chiller and cooling tower would be required at a considerable capital investment and ongoing operating cost.

[The] project manager . . . worked with [the] engineers . . . to develop a plan to reallocate collection spaces and reconfigure the air-handling systems so that all archive materials would be stored within the stacks and the 40 percent relative humidity condition would be maintained only within that space. In order to do that, a variety of air-cooled glycol chillers were investigated, that have the capability of delivering the 40 degree F water to the air-handler for that space.

A system was eventually selected that utilizes the existing 44 degree F chilled water supply as the condenser cooling media, instead of air. The package fits into the existing mechanical room, and will operate at a lower cost than a centrifugal chiller. The major benefit of the water-cooled chiller is that it can be placed indoors, avoiding the noise and appearance issues that accompany any equipment installed adjacent to a public garden.

The original system design utilized a single chiller to provide all the cooling to this building, with a very cumbersome backup procedure in case of a major equipment failure. As part of the project aimed at increasing cooling capacity of the building, that chiller was integrated into a loop with two other chillers within the same central cooling plant. All three chillers were retrofitted with new control systems . . . with variable-speed drives and their Adaptive Capacity Control that learns and remembers optimum motor speed and the position of the pre-rotation vanes for a given set of load and water temperature combinations. The addition of variable-speed drives to the three cells of the cooling tower also contributes to a more efficient system.

Tying together the whole package is a . . . chiller plant automation (CPA) computer system that manages the total cooling load in conjunction with the existing . . . direct digital control (DDC) system. The CPA system controls the speed and sequence of all three chillers, plus the variable-speed drives for the primary chilled water pumps, the condenser water pumps and the secondary chilled water pumps, as well as the cooling tower fans and the isolation valves. In addition to these control functions, the system also provides history, trending, alarm and emergency call-out capabilities.

The calculated payback period for the additional control features is 3.3 years. The savings will more than offset the increased cost associated with the more stringent environmental specifications for the archive storage area.

Until the costs for digital storage of fragile materials, and access to those images, is further reduced, collection materials must be preserved while also remaining accessible. Facility managers must be able to provide environmental conditions that ensure the long-term survival of even the most susceptible materials, maintaining their availability to scholars well into the foreseeable future.

Source: Dixon (Summer 2003). "Old Buildings, Old Systems and Older Books: Fighting Mold and Decay in the Twenty-First Century." *Papyrus: A Publication of the International Association of Museum Facility Administrators* 4(3): 29–31. Available at www.iamfa.org.

collections objects are not allowed to go on loan to an outside museum, unless it can be proven that temperature and RH conditions consistently fall within these parameters.

Temperature and relative humidity are inextricably linked, and it is important to have a holistic plan in place for managing these environmental factors together. As mentioned earlier, if the temperature in a space rises, the relative humidity will drop, and vice versa. If dangerously low or high RH levels are identified during monitoring of facility's relative humidity, it is important to look for the cause immediately. Relative humidity can be affected by the presence of moisture in a number of areas on the cultural institution's site and within the cultural institution's building itself. For example, inadequate surface or soil drainage near the building can cause relative humidity to increase inside museum spaces, exposing collections to damp conditions. Dampness is an especially prominent problem for collections kept in basements, on the ground floor in buildings without basements, and under roofs or terraces. During cold weather, it is also possible for areas near exterior walls to experience an increase in relative humidity unsafe for collections. For this reason, shelving or cabinets that will hold RH-sensitive pieces of the collection should not be placed near exterior walls. Additionally, attics lacking proper ventilation can become too hot, and, thus, the relative humidity may be too low to safely house collections. Areas immediate to bright windows or heaters may also be prone to unsafe, low relative-humidity levels.

Basic strategies to reduce indoor relative humidity include making certain that effective vapor barriers are installed on the "warm side" of exterior walls, roof surfaces, and crawl spaces. Joints around windows, doors, electrical outlets, and seams should be sealed. It is also important to ensure proper drainage away from the building's foundation, including drainage of rainwater from the roof. In addition, dehumidifiers can be employed to reduce humidity; however, it is important to try to prevent high RH in the first place, rather than removing excess moisture after the fact (Michalski 2011a).

In historic buildings that hold art and artifacts, controlling temperature and relative humidity can be even more challenging, as these structures were often not built to meet the necessary, exacting environmental constraints. In addition, historic buildings themselves are sensitive to temperature and humidity fluctuations, and conditions that are desirable for artifacts may not necessarily be healthy for these buildings. Richard Kerschner, director of preservation and conservation at the Shelburne Museum in Ferrisburgh, Vermont, suggests several "practical climate control actions" that can be employed to manage temperature and humidity in historic buildings (1992, p. 69). The first practical action that Kerschner suggests is to monitor temperature and relative humidity conditions in different areas of the building during each season. In turn, the actions that follow should center on remediating any issues discovered during initial monitoring. One common issue stems from moisture seeping into the basement. This added moisture ultimately intensifies RH levels throughout the entire building. For this reason, it is essential that rainwater is rerouted away from the foundation of the building.

Though exterior shrubbery may not come to mind as a potential hazard to the moisture conditions inside buildings, it is actually an important element to consider when regulating RH levels. When trees and shrubs are planted close to a building, moisture can become confined in the space between the walls and the trees and shrubs. Ultimately, this prevents air from circulating, and the walls may become moist. To prevent this, shrubs should be trimmed or moved away from the building to allow ample circulation. Attic areas should also be well insulated and have proper ventilation. This two-pronged approach—insulating and ventilating—ultimately helps lessen heat accumulation during the summer.

Heating during the winter can cause relative humidity levels to drop to dangerously low levels (as low as 5–10 percent RH). These very low RH conditions can be avoided, in part, by permitting the indoor temperature in collections areas to drift lower during the cold periods of the year. Because of the inverse relationship between temperature and relative humidity, allowing the temperature to drift lower will help keep RH levels from falling to dangerously low temperatures. The indoor temperature may become uncomfortably cool when allowing the temperature to drift lower, and care must be taken that water is kept circulating in the pipes so that it does not freeze. For the sake of human comfort, if the temperatures become very cool, visitors may be encouraged to wear warm clothing for their tours and the staff work area can be heated separately.

If the temperature in a space is allowed to drift lower during the cooler months, but requires heating for a particular program or workshop to be held in the space, it should be heated slowly leading up to the program, and then cooled back down at a similarly slow rate after the program is over. Because of the preferably slow rate of heating and cooling a space, careful scheduling is important. Kerschner advises that "it is better to hold five workshops in one week during the winter than one workshop a week for five weeks because the building can be gradually heated and then cooled over a two-week period instead of being suddenly heated and cooled five times over a five-week period" (1992, p. 71).

Changes in humidity commonly affect sensitive collections items at a much greater extent than do changes in temperature. For this reason, some argue that it may be more important to prioritize RH control over temperature control in environments that house sensitive artifacts. One way to achieve particular relative humidity constraints within a set range is to install a humidistat, rather than a thermostat. A humidistat works much like a thermostat. However, rather than turning the heating or cooling on or off when the temperature falls below or rises above a certain temperature, it turns off or on when the relative humidity falls below or rises above a predetermined range. For example, when the relative humidity increases above an ideal set point, like 45 percent, the heat will turn on and run until the RH returns to the set point, then it will turn off. In this way, the RH is held steady through the use of strategic temperature fluctuation (Kerschner 1992).

One example of a humidistat in practice is at the Prince Edward Island Heritage Foundation, where they employ humidistatically controlled heating in their collections storage facility. The facility's humidistat turns the heaters on when the humidity climbs above 50 percent RH. To supplement this climate control, when the RH is particularly high during the summer season, additional portable dehumidifiers are utilized to reduce RH levels (Michalski 2011a). In any case—whether using a humidistat, allowing seasonal drift, or adding insulation—it is important for conservators to collaborate with facility managers and engineers in order to come to a solution that will keep collections safe, keep occupants comfortable, and be financially feasible for the cultural institution.

Ongoing Debate about Temperature and Humidity Control

> I think that what is most important in this discussion is that we realize that there has been no "standard" that has been written down for temperature and relative humidity. We have all assumed that 70 degrees Fahrenheit (20 degrees Celsius) and 50 percent [RH] is a standard that we must abide by. But the reality is that there is no doctrine, no written law that says that. It is just our perception.
>
> —Cecily M. Grzywacz, Facilities Scientist (AIC/IIC 2010)

As Grzywacz points out, the current temperature and humidity standards are "assumed," but where and how did they originate? Actually, current environmental standards within museums are said to have originated in the United Kingdom during World Wars I and II. Beginning with the First World War, the British Museum temporarily stored its collections in underground rail tunnels. Following this temporary storage effort, formal research into the consequences of exposing artwork to humidity began in the 1930s. During World War II, a number of galleries and museums stored their collections in environmentally steady slate quarries in Wales. Following the war, the environmental conditions of these quarries—particularly temperature and humidity levels—were cited as being ideal for museum collections. These conditions have, in turn, influenced the common standards of 70 degrees Fahrenheit and 50 percent relative humidity that we see today.

Another major development in temperature and RH guidelines came in 1994, when the Smithsonian Institution's Conservation Analytical Laboratory (SICAL) released groundbreaking guidelines that permitted up to 15 percent variation in relative humidity—from 35 percent to 65 percent—and, for temperature, a range between 52 degrees and 88 degrees Fahrenheit, no matter the type of collections held within the space. Since that time, debate over these guidelines has continued, but several institutions have chosen to relax their guidelines and have defended their decisions from the standpoint of economics and sustainability. These institutions have used the SICAL research to back up their conservation strategy when expanding their acceptable ranges for temperature and RH (Anderson 2010).

The Indianapolis Museum of Art (IMA) is among the institutions that have relaxed their standards in the face of SICAL's 1994 guidelines. Speaking of their relaxed standards, IMA director Maxwell Anderson suggests that "flexibility in the working environment among each other's communities: the conservators, scientists, engineers and administrators" is necessary. A part of this flexibility involves accepting that collection environments cannot necessarily achieve the desired conditions at all times (AIC/IIC 2010). On the IMA website, their strategy is further explained:

> The Indianapolis Museum of Art has recently expanded the temperature and relative humidity ranges in its permanent collection galleries and storage areas based on studies conducted by the Smithsonian Institution Conservation Analytical Laboratory in 1994. New ranges have been implemented of 50% RH +/− 8 (with a variation percentage of +/− 6% in a 24 hour period) and 70°F +/− 4 (with a variation percentage of +/− 2° in a 24 hour period) with small monthly seasonal adjustments within these ranges to achieve efficiencies in energy consumption without adversely affecting the condition of collection objects and loans. (IMA 2012)

As a part of relaxing their standards, the IMA also gave its lenders the option of taking pieces back from the museum if they disagreed with its new environmental policy. And, notably, none of the IMA's lenders opted to remove their pieces following initial implementation of the policy (Humphrey and Bickersteth 2011).

To help reduce museums' carbon footprints, the United Kingdom's National Museums Directors Conference assembled a set of guidelines in 2009. These guidelines provide valuable food for thought when determining strategies for temperature and humidity regulation:

1. Environmental standards should become more intelligent and better tailored to clearly identified needs. Blanket conditions should no longer apply.

2. Care of collections should be achieved in a way that does not rely solely upon air-conditioning or other forms of active maintenance. Passive methods and simple technologies that are easy to maintain, as well as lower-energy solutions, should be considered.

3. Natural and sustainable environmental controls should be explored.

4. When designing and constructing new buildings, or renovating old ones, architects and engineers should be guided to reduce significantly the building's carbon footprint as a primary objective. (Quoted from Humphrey and Bickersteth 2011, p. 38)

These guidelines, which highlight the importance of appreciating the context surrounding a particular museum facility and its collections, similarly highlight the opportunities for conservators and facility managers to work together to achieve solutions that are sustainable for collections, facilities, and the museum's bottom line. No matter the situation, there is value in museum staff members at all levels working together to achieve mutually agreeable environmental conditions.

Summary

An understanding of the primary agents of deterioration that affect cultural institution collections—air pollution, unnecessary light, and dangerous temperature and humidity levels—is essential for museum facility managers who want to provide the optimal environmental conditions for their facilities. This understanding makes it possible for cultural institution facility managers to work closely with other museum staff, like conservators and exhibition designers, for the purpose of keeping collections safe, while ensuring that the museum spaces are dynamic and supportive of the museum's mission. As the conversation surrounding whether environmental guidelines can be relaxed in museum environments continues to evolve, an integrated team of staff members from throughout the museum, which includes the facility manager, can continue to evaluate these guidelines with an eye toward balancing sustainability, staff and visitor comfort, and conservation.

CHAPTER FIVE
MANAGING CULTURAL FACILITY MAINTENANCE AND OPERATIONS

Space is a resource as important to the proper functioning of the organization as are people and money. Poor management of facility space results in staff inefficiency, poor staff morale, and increased operating costs. . . . [P]oor management can also result in the failure of the museum to fulfill one of its primary responsibilities, to provide for the long-term preservation of its collections. Good space management begins at the top, for these decisions affect all occupants of the museum facility—people and collections alike.

—Vincent Wilcox (1995, p. 41), director emeritus,
Smithsonian Institution Museum Support Center

A museum facility manager helps the museum achieve its mission through ongoing maintenance of facility components and thoughtful execution of operations. How do we distinguish between maintenance and operations? Maintenance is ongoing work that keeps an asset in good working order for its anticipated service life, like inspecting and repairing HVAC equipment. By contrast, we can think of operations as activities that do not extend the life of the asset but instead support its performance, like paying utility bills or collecting recycling (Eppley Institute for Parks and Public Lands 2013). Both maintenance and operations activities are crucial to the success of a museum and must be carefully planned, documented, evaluated, and adjusted over time.

This chapter provides an overview of different maintenance strategies, including reactive, preventive, predictive, and reliability-centered maintenance. In addition, planning for several aspects of museum facility operations is discussed, including cleaning, pest management, moving management, and storage management. Strategies for documenting practices in an operations and maintenance (O&M) manual, for benchmarking facility performance against that of similar facilities, and for choosing an in-house or outsourced staff are also covered in this chapter.

Implementing a Long-Term Maintenance Program

Most cultural institutions probably have a maintenance program in place in some form or another. Perhaps the maintenance program has been codified and is enthusiastically supported by the institution's director. Or, maybe, the program is based on a "first-to-fail, first-served" mantra. In any case, becoming familiar with different ways a maintenance program can be organized—each with its own opportunities and pitfalls—can help make the museum's maintenance program more successful moving forward. Becoming familiar with various approaches to maintenance programs will also help make a clear case to the museum's management or board when it comes time to budget for next year's maintenance costs.

The four common types of maintenance programs are reactive, preventive, predictive, and reliability-centered maintenance. Studies of maintenance standards over the past ten years show that most facilities' equipment is not kept in suitable working order. Instead of investing in the resources to properly maintain equipment, organizations commonly delay maintenance until a piece of equipment breaks down. By ignoring the regular maintenance called for in the equipment's operating manuals, these facility managers do little to ensure their equipment meets or surpasses its life expectancy. That said, it is not fair to place blame entirely on these facility managers. They are often hired into organizations that have allowed maintenance to fall by the wayside, organizations with insufficient funding set aside for facility management, or buildings in which ongoing maintenance was not considered during planning, design, construction, or expansion. If a cultural institution is facing these challenges, the road to a healthy facility is not an easy one. However, through careful planning and a great deal of advocacy on behalf of the facility when speaking to staff, management, donors, and governing boards, it is possible to implement a predictive or reliability-centered maintenance plan that will standardize maintenance and keep operations running smoothly, rather than tending to assets only when they are not working.

The practice of tending to equipment only when it is *not* working, or "running equipment to failure," is termed *reactive maintenance*. At first glance, reactive maintenance may seem like a reasonable strategy—an institution can save money by not hiring additional staff to continually maintain equipment that seems to be operating just fine. However, when the equipment breaks down—especially if it is something essential to the museum's operation, like a chiller—the museum is on the hook for labor costs to repair the equipment. It must quickly come up with the parts necessary for the repair or keep a large inventory of parts on hand for these situations. In addition, the failure of one essential piece of equipment may ultimately cause another mechanism to fail, resulting in further costs to the organization. Ultimately, running equipment to failure time and again results in added capital costs. This equipment will not last as long and must be replaced more often, likely at great expense to the institution.

In contrast to reactive maintenance, a preventive maintenance program adheres to the maintenance schedule recommended by the designer. Investing in regularly scheduled maintenance means the museum is more likely to see equipment meet or surpass its life expectancy, while also being more reliable during its lifetime. In addition, equipment that is serviced regularly will tend to run more efficiently, resulting in possible energy savings.

With fewer replacement costs and increased reliability, organizations that implement preventive maintenance normally see savings of 12–18 percent over those organizations that implement purely reactive maintenance programs. It is even possible that moving from a reactive maintenance program to a program based on prevention could save more than 18 percent. Of course, preventive maintenance cannot prevent all equipment failures; however, it should reduce the overall failures over the lifetime of the museum's equipment. Among the drawbacks of a preventive maintenance program are that it is labor intensive, it is possible that unnecessary maintenance is performed, and there is the added possibility that damage might occur to equipment as the result of unnecessary maintenance.

While preventive maintenance demonstrates major benefits over reactive maintenance, there are still more sophisticated means of maintaining a museum facility, one being predictive maintenance. The foundation of predictive maintenance (PM) is pinpointing exactly the right time to carry out a maintenance procedure. While most equipment manuals will recommend maintenance based on a particular interval of time, a predictive maintenance plan makes use of diagnostic equipment to identify which maintenance is needed and the time it is most appropriately performed.

The U.S. Department of Energy's Federal Energy Management Program (FEMP) provides a great analogy for understanding the difference between preventive and predictive maintenance:

> [M]ost people change the oil in their vehicles every 3,000 to 5,000 miles traveled. This is effectively basing the oil change needs on equipment run time. No concern is given to the actual condition and performance capability of the oil. It is changed because it is time. This methodology would be analogous to a preventive maintenance task. If, on the other hand, the operator of the car discounted the vehicle run time and had the oil analyzed at some periodicity to determine its actual condition and lubrication properties [a strategy analogous to predictive maintenance], he/she may be able to extend the oil change until the vehicle had traveled 10,000 miles. (U.S. Department of Energy [DOE] 2010, p. 5.4)

Setting up a predictive maintenance program can be costly, as it requires an investment in diagnostic equipment and extensive staff training. Facility management operations that do establish predictive maintenance programs see an average savings of between 8 and 12 percent over programs that pursue only preventive maintenance. By contrast, a program that utilizes reactive maintenance could see savings of between 30 and 40 percent by transitioning to a predictive maintenance program.

Despite these huge savings, it can often be difficult to convince museum management of the overall benefit of implementing the predictive maintenance program. The intensive training and setup costs required to commit to a predictive maintenance program may overwhelm cultural institution administrators at first, so it is important that a clear plan be laid out that demonstrates the anticipated reduction in maintenance costs and the expected payback period. Among the advantages that can be highlighted when making the case for predictive maintenance are improved safety and security of collections, improved worker safety and morale, a decrease in equipment downtime, a decrease in expenses for parts and labor, the ability to make corrective actions *before* equipment fails, and energy savings.

What types of diagnostic equipment and tests are commonly used in a predictive maintenance program? Table 5.1 lists many of the technologies, tests, and equipment used in PM programs, as well as their applications for common pieces of facility equipment. While in-depth descriptions of

Table 5.1. Common Predictive Maintenance Technologies and Their Application to Facilities Equipment

Technologies, Tests, and Inspections	Applications										
	Pumps	Electrical Motors	Diesel Generators	Condensers	Heavy-Equipment/Cranes	Circuit Breakers	Valves	Heat Exchangers	Electrical Systems	Transformers	Tank Piping
Bearing and temperature analysis	X	X	X		X						
Electrical monitoring									X	X	
Infrared thermography	X	X	X	X	X	X	X	X	X	X	
Insulation resistance		X	X			X			X	X	
Lubricant and fuel analysis	X	X	X		X					X	
Motor circuit analysis		X				X			X		
Motor current signature analysis		X									
Nondestructive testing (thickness)				X				X			X
Performance monitoring	X	X	X	X				X		X	
Polarization index		X	X						X		
Ultrasonic flow	X			X			X	X			
Ultrasonic noise detection	X	X	X	X			X	X		X	
Vibration monitoring and analysis	X	X	X		X						
Visual inspection	X	X	X	X	X	X	X	X	X	X	X
Wear particle analysis	X	X	X		X						

Source: NASA (2000, pp. 4–58).

specialized equipment are beyond the scope of this book, it is worth briefly introducing several common preventive maintenance tools: infrared thermography, ultrasonic analysis, vibration analysis, and oil analysis. For additional resources related to PM diagnostic equipment and processes, please see the "Resources" section of this book.

Infrared (IR) thermography has, potentially, hundreds of applications for detecting hidden problems within facilities and their equipment. It works by creating images on a liquid crystal display (LCD) screen that represent temperature differences on surfaces of objects or buildings. These temperature differences can be detected because any object that has a temperature above absolute zero will emit infrared energy at a level proportionate to its temperature. IR detection devices are able to capture IR data and convert it into a graphic that displays relative temperatures of the equipment and/or spaces seen in a particular snapshot.

These snapshots become very helpful when diagnosing otherwise "invisible" problems happening inside of equipment or buried within walls. IR imaging cameras can show temperature differences as a result of frictional change in rotating equipment, corroded electrical connections, leaking roofs, and many other issues. The cost of IR equipment can vary from $500 to $2,500 for a spot radiometer (which gives a temperature reading but no image) to $7,000 to $20,000 for an IR imager that does not have radiometric capabilities, to $18,000 to $65,000 for a fully functional IR camera. Because of the great expense associated with purchasing the most sophisticated IR technology, small cultural institutions would likely benefit from contracting out IR survey work. These contracted services can range between $600 and $1,200 for a day of readings (DOE 2010).

At the Smithsonian Institution, IR thermography is viewed as a valuable tool for diagnosing many issues, including moisture intrusion. In one circumstance at the Smithsonian's Hirshhorn Museum, moisture became visible on the building's exterior concrete surface. However, the origin of the moisture was unclear. By taking IR thermography images of the exterior of the building, it became clear that the moisture was actually coming from within the building. This was evident from the fact that the areas of moisture intrusion were measured as being warmer than the outdoor ambient temperature. This temperature difference indicated that the water penetration had come from the building's warmer interior. Using this IR technology allowed Smithsonian facility management staff to quickly determine the source of the water and remedy the intrusion (Mecklenburg and Pride 2005).

While infrared thermography makes it possible to see otherwise invisible temperature data, ultrasound analysis makes it possible to hear sounds that are normally out of the range of human hearing. Ultrasonic wave detectors are able to render these normally unheard sounds in frequencies that people can hear or read on the face of a meter. In addition, some detectors are able to save their readings for later reference as a baseline, if equipment is healthy at the time of the reading, or to notice any trends in its condition over time. Rotating equipment or equipment that has the potential to leak are two equipment types that can benefit from ultrasonic analysis, as ultrasonic wave detectors can pick up telltale sounds if a problem exists. Ultrasonic analysis equipment is much less costly than IR thermography equipment, coming in between $750 and $10,000 for a set that includes a scanner, software, and probes, and, often, this equipment has a payback period of six months or fewer.

As they move, rotating machine parts produce patterns of vibration, and, over time, these patterns of vibration may change as the condition of parts degrade or come out of alignment. To pick up on these changes, vibration analysis uses vibration transducers to measure vibration. These measurements are then converted to an electronic signal that allows the magnitude of the vibration to be read directly from a sensing meter at the site of the reading. There are also more sophisticated equipment and software that can analyze this vibration data to help diagnose issues with assets. As with other types of predictive maintenance equipment, vibration analysis equipment can be purchased at a range of price points and capabilities. Simple vibration metering devices without capacity for analysis start at around $1,000, while an equipment and software package capable of providing analysis may surpass the $30,000 mark. Because of the great expense associated with a sophisticated vibration analysis package, a small cultural institution may not benefit from investing in such a system. Instead, purchasing a simple metering device for regular monitoring and performing analysis manually, or hiring a contractor, may be more cost effective.

Oil analysis, in which oil is sampled from a piece of equipment and tested for a variety of factors—for example, whether oil additives are present in the right quantities, whether the oil has been contaminated, and whether wear particles from the machine are present—can be a cost-effective way to help plan oil changes and schedule the maintenance necessary to keep a piece of machinery in good working order. Normally, oil analysis is performed by a laboratory specializing in this service. These laboratories ease the process by providing collection containers, labels, and return-mailing supplies. Facilities personnel must collect the sample properly (a process that requires training) and be sure that it is sampled from the same place each time. Compared to other types of predictive maintenance discussed here, oil analysis is fairly inexpensive—coming in between $15 and $100 per sample analyzed, depending on the sophistication of the analysis.

While predictive maintenance is largely seen as a best practice, reliability-centered maintenance (RCM) is gaining currency among cultural institution facility managers, including those at the Smithsonian Institution (see box. 5.1). RCM combines predictive maintenance strategies with the understanding that not every piece of equipment bears equal importance, value, or susceptibility to failure. Taking this into consideration, an RCM program requires that a facility's equipment and resources are evaluated. After evaluating the museum's equipment and available resources, an RCM plan is formulated and put in place. This plan employs predictive maintenance testing—like vibration analysis, IR thermography, or ultrasonic analysis—on the most crucial or valuable equipment; reactive maintenance for less important or less expensive equipment; and preventive maintenance on other equipment, as identified in the plan (see table 5.2 for suggested maintenance applications for these different maintenance strategies). RCM shares many advantages with predictive maintenance with the added advantage of being able to pick and choose maintenance strategies (i.e., reactive, preventive, or predictive) for each piece of equipment, depending on the resources the institution has available (DOE 2010).

If a museum is ready to begin implementing an RCM program, there are free resources available online that provide very detailed information that can help to tailor a program to suit the museum facility's needs. One such resource is the *Reliability Centered Maintenance Guide for Facilities and Collateral Equipment* (2000), published by the National Aeronautics and Space Administration (NASA) and available on their website. As one may suspect, coming from NASA, this guide is incredibly detailed and very technical; however, readers will come away from this guide with a solid foundation for implementing an RCM plan. The NASA guide points out several key principles that distinguish RCM from other maintenance strategies. For example, RCM is function oriented and system focused—this means that an RCM plan prioritizes the overall function of the system over the functioning of a particular component. Also among these key principles is the importance of using a logic tree to assign maintenance tasks.

Before the facility manager gets to the point of using a logic tree to assign tasks, it is necessary to have a clear sense of the equipment used in the facility. A master equipment list that includes all of the equipment in the

BOX 5.1.

RELIABILITY-CENTERED MAINTENANCE AT THE SMITHSONIAN INSTITUTION

At the Smithsonian Institution, where the Office of Facility Management and Reliability (OFMR) oversees facility management in nineteen museums and various other research facilities, the maintenance plan is centered around performing "the right maintenance on the right equipment at the right time." In this case, "right" means finding an appropriate balance between two key areas: available resources and maintenance best practices.

To develop the Smithsonian's RCM program, OFMR hired a consultant to help analyze equipment failures in Smithsonian facilities. This analysis paid particular attention to the following:

- The functions and performance standards of the equipment that will be maintained,
- The failure modes of that equipment,
- The causes of each failure,
- The effects of failure,
- The tasks that could predict or prevent failure, and
- Workarounds if there are no proactive tasks to mitigate failure. (List quoted from NRC 2012, p. 63)

Data from the analysis helped determine what types of maintenance different types of equipment would require.

In turn, nondestructive predictive testing and inspection (PT&I) tools were acquired. These tools reduce the amount of downtime, because equipment can be tested while it is running. Based on test results, maintenance and repair are scheduled. All data obtained from PT&I testing are logged in OFMR's computerized maintenance management system (CMMS). Saving these data is important, because they help reveal potential issues prior to their becoming severe.

Source: NRC (2012).

Table 5.2. Reliability-Centered Maintenance (RCM): Suggested Applications

Before implementing an RCM program, your equipment should be evaluated, for example, on the basis of its cost, how crucial it is to supporting your cultural institution's activities, and the potential cost of downtime should it fail. After evaluating each piece of equipment, it can be organized according to whether it would benefit from a reactive, preventive, or predictive maintenance approach. This table provides suggested maintenance applications, depending on the characteristics of a given piece of equipment.

Possible Reactive Maintenance Applications	Possible Preventive Maintenance Applications	Possible Predictive Maintenance Applications
Small parts and equipment	Equipment subject to wear	Equipment with random failure patterns
Noncritical equipment	Consumable equipment	Critical equipment
Equipment likely to fail	Equipment with known failure patterns	Equipment not subject to wear
Redundant systems	Manufacturer recommendations	Systems for which failure may be induced by incorrect preventive maintenance

Source: DOE (2010).

cultural institution facility must be developed. Additionally, each piece of equipment, or asset, should be prioritized on the basis of how critical it is to the facility's operation and/or mission. Sample prioritization categories include the following (DOE 2010, p. 5.6):

Level 1   Emergency (e.g., the equipment is critical to life, health, and safety)

Level 2   Urgent (e.g., continuous operation of the facility may not be possible without this equipment)

Level 3   Priority (e.g., this equipment provides support to the mission and project deadlines)

Level 4   Routine (e.g., this equipment is prioritized and will be serviced on a first-come, first-served basis)

Level 5   Discretionary (e.g., this equipment is desirable but not absolutely necessary)

Level 6   Deferred (e.g., this equipment will be serviced only when resources permit)

After equipment has been inventoried and prioritized, it is time to begin looking at what will be required to maintain each piece of equipment in order for it to properly support the facility over time. Things to consider include the history of the equipment, such as why it has failed in the past; manufacturers' manuals; and the size of the maintenance staff. Also consider how much time staff members are able to devote to preventive, predictive, and reactive maintenance tasks each day (DOE 2010). At this time, it is appropriate to begin using an RCM decision logic tree (table 5.3) to help assign a preventive, predictive, or reactive maintenance approach for each piece of equipment, using the information that has been gathered up to this point for guidance.

The process for implementing a maintenance program, as described here, may sound simple—but in reality, it will take time and a lot of fine-tuning to settle on a plan that works with the museum's level of staffing, budget, and unique facility. What matters is that the cultural facility is not treated as an entity that can be "updated" once every couple of decades, then forgotten until funds are raised for the next restoration. Instead of planning major maintenance efforts every so often, it is much more effective to implement an ongoing program that expends resources little by little over time. This proactive approach to planned maintenance, one that takes a holistic view of the facility as a living system, not only saves the cultural institution money but also keeps the building in better condition overall (New South Wales Heritage Office 2012).

Tracking the Maintenance Program

Whether done manually or using specialized computer software, it is important that maintenance is planned and tracked using a dedicated system. A good rule of thumb is that buildings larger than 100,000 square feet should use a computerized maintenance management system (CMMS). In either case—whether manually documenting maintenance schedules or using specialized software—it is important that maintenance goals are set and tracked accordingly. The Society for Maintenance and Reliability Professionals (SMRP) is one organization that helps facility managers implement CMMS in their facilities. For help from SMRP, visit www.smrp.org (Cotts et al. 2010).

When the Canadian Museum of Civilization (CMC), located in Gatineau, Quebec, decided it was time to implement a computerized maintenance management system, it worked with a contractor to develop a specialized solution. For this system to be effective, the museum and its contractor determined that five criteria had to be met. First, no work could occur "outside"

Table 5.3. Reliability-Centered Maintenance (RCM) Decision Logic Tree

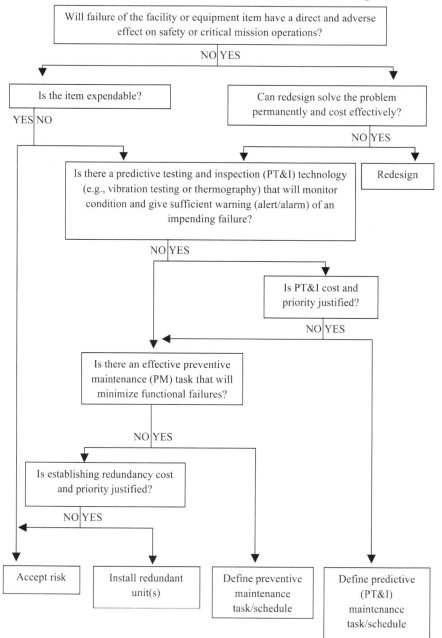

Source: NASA (2000, pp. 2–12).

of the tracking system. That is to say, all facility management activities had to be recorded using the CMMS software in order for historical trending to be represented accurately. Second, all information had to be recorded in the CMMS system in a timely manner. Third, any changes made to existing facility systems had to be updated right away, so the records wouldn't become obsolete. Fourth, the information produced by the CMMS had to be put to use in order to improve operational efficiency. And, fifth, the system had to be viewed as an important tool by both the museum management and its facility managers. By cohering to these five guidelines, the CMC ensured that it would get the most out of its investment in the CMMS.

At the CMC, this software was used for a variety of purposes, including tracking the museum's maintenance and operations budget and aiding in the museum's preventive maintenance program. The CMMS held an equipment database of more than 4,000 pieces of the museum's equipment and documented manufacturer names, parts numbers, and equipment specifications that maintenance staff could use as a reference for preventive maintenance work. After being implemented, the CMMS was able to generate around 2,800 preventive maintenance work orders and approximately 3,400 unscheduled work orders per year (Harding and Richard 2002).

In addition to CMMS, there are several other systems available to help with maintaining healthy cultural institution facilities. Among these systems are computer-aided facilities management (CAFM) systems, integrated workplace management systems (IWMS), environmental management systems (EMS), and building management systems (BMS). Computer aided facilities management programs are similar to CMMS; however, they have expanded functionality that includes several facilities activities that may not be covered by a CMMS. Among the added functionalities of CAFM systems are room booking, resource scheduling, stock control, purchase ordering, and health, safety, and fleet management. For very small cultural institutions, CAFM systems may be beyond the scope of what is necessary to manage the facility.

Integrated workplace management systems are comparable to CAFM systems—they assist with resource and maintenance management. An IWMS typically has the added functionality of estate portfolio and space management, and they may be helpful for cultural institutions that have amassed a portfolio of leased storage spaces that must be tracked and maintained. Environmental management systems, which are not necessarily software driven, help organizations monitor how their activities affect the environment (Whalley 2010). In the United States, the Environmental Protection Agency provides free guidance for implementing an EMS online at www.epa.gov/ems/.

A building management system is a computerized control system that can monitor and control indoor environmental conditions, as well as control plant and energy management and lighting, heating, ventilation, and air-conditioning systems (Victoria and Albert Museum 2003). Because of the specialized environmental control requirements in museums and cultural institutions, a BMS is a valuable tool for both small and large institutions. In their *Manual of Museum Management* (1997), Lord and Lord predicted that electronic BMS technology would replace traditional, mechanical means of recording temperature and relative humidity in the twenty-first century. They went so far as to say that "no new museum and no major renovation should be undertaken without including a BMS room" (p. 148). Now, more than 15 years after their prediction, the convenience of automated data collection and the peace of mind afforded by a BMS make it an important tool for many cultural institutions.

The Facility Condition Index (FCI) can be an important tool for understanding maintenance deficiencies in the museum and explaining them to senior leadership. Often compiled using CMMS data, a facility's FCI is the "ratio of the cost of remedying maintenance deficiencies to the current replacement value" of the facility (APPA 2013). For example, if the FCI ratio is between 0 and 5 percent, the facility is considered to be in "Good" condition. If the FCI is between 5 and 10 percent, the facility is in "Fair" condition; and an FCI between 10 and 30 percent indicates "Poor" condition. Facilities with an FCI greater than 30 percent are in "Critical" condition. By translating the facility's condition into simple terminology (e.g. good, fair, poor, or critical), the FCI makes it easier for those who do not specialize in facility management, like museum directors and board members, to understand the impact of deferred maintenance on facilities and, in turn, allocate the funds necessary to keep the facility operational (IFMA 2013).

Implementing a Building Service, or Housekeeping, Plan

While it is commonly known as a *housekeeping plan*, in this chapter we will use more contemporary terminology and, instead, refer to this important resource as a *building service plan*. Those who perform this critical work are referred to as *building service workers*, rather than *housekeeping staff*. In cultural facilities, implementing a clear building service plan is a crucial step toward maintaining the integrity of collections and the facility. This plan serves as a guiding document, outlining for building service workers the procedures and frequencies for cleaning different areas of the facility. Many common cleaning chemicals and processes can be harmful to both collections objects and human occupants who experience sustained exposure to them. It is important that a conservator verify that cleaning procedures and substances are appropriate for the spaces in which they will be used. To ensure the safety of artifacts, training for building service workers is particularly vital in a cultural institution setting (Genoways and Ireland 2003).

Of course, before building service workers can be properly trained, a building service plan must be carefully assembled and reviewed. This is a process that should involve museum conservators, as well as staff members who will carry out the work. When assembling this plan, keep in mind that a good building service plan:

- considers the nature and condition of museum collections;
- identifies the location of museum collections;
- identifies both routine housekeeping tasks and special housekeeping projects;
- identifies equipment, materials, and techniques for carrying out housekeeping tasks;
- identifies staff persons responsible for carrying out housekeeping tasks;
- establishes a schedule for completing the tasks; and
- records completed tasks. (Quoted from NPS 1998, p. 13:2)

By ensuring that the building service plan embodies each of these elements, the plan becomes a guiding document capable of supporting preventive conservation of the artifacts as well as the cultural institution.

While appearing clean is important in a museum environment, cleaning for the sake of appearance should not be the end goal of cleaning in a museum. What constitutes "clean" in the museum environment is not necessarily a pristine clean. The primary goal is to keep objects in the collection in good condition by reducing their exposure to agents of deterioration. Some professional organizations offer guidelines for cleaning standards that museums can use to help set cleaning goals in their facilities. For example, APPA (formerly the Association of Physical Plant Administrators, now known as "APPA, Leadership in Educational Facilities") describes five levels of cleanliness:

- Level 1: Exceptional

- Level 2: Exceeds Standards

- Level 3: Meets Standards

- Level 4: Marginal

- Level 5: Unacceptable (Missouri University of Science and Technology 2013)

For more information on APPA cleaning standards, see "Determining APPA Levels of Cleanliness in Buildings" (Glazner 2011).

It is important to know the *ways* in which pests, dirt, and contaminants can enter the space. This will allow efforts to be concentrated on preventing their entry, like placing mats at entryways that collect dirt from visitors' feet or putting gravel around the perimeter of the building that will deter insects from sneaking into the building. It is also important to understand the level of foot traffic that the space experiences each day. When deciding how frequently a space should be cleaned, there are a number of factors to take into consideration. It is necessary to inspect the space, noting exactly where dust and dirt accumulate and how frequently it builds up to an unacceptable level. Of course, after a building service plan has been implemented, it is important to continually adjust the frequency of cleaning in a particular space, as necessary.

The U.S. National Park Service (NPS) suggests that a museum's cleaning plan should include five basic elements—a title page, a narrative section, reference file sheets, task sheets, and schedules. The title page includes an appropriate title for the plan, the name of the cultural institution, and signature lines for applicable administrative staff to sign, affirming that the plan is to be implemented within the institution. The narrative section provides an opportunity to describe the significance of the plan within the museum environment and an overview of what the plan will cover; for example, the narrative might mention when and where cleaning tasks will be carried out and by whom, as well as the techniques, supplies, and equipment necessary for cleaning. Among the information included in the reference file section might be the museum's collection management plan, the collection condition survey, environmental-monitoring records, and equipment handbooks.

Consider including information about particular environmental concerns in each space, how environmental monitoring is carried out for the space, as well as other collection-specific information. For example, at the National Portrait Gallery (NPG) in Washington, DC, curators feel that waxing or polishing the floor would produce a sheen that detracts from a prominent portrait of George Washington. As a result, the building service workers at the NPG do not wax or polish the floor directly in front of this portrait. In addition, the building service workers at the National Portrait Gallery use cleaning practices that require less water so as not to increase the humidity levels around collections, and this is exactly the type of information that would be included in the reference file sheets.

The information included in the reference file sheets can be used to organize the task sheets for the plan. The task sheets list the detailed procedures, equipment and supplies, and frequencies for each building service task. In support of a holistic approach, task sheets should be prepared in cooperation with the personnel who will be responsible for overseeing and/or completing the tasks, including building service workers, conservators, and facility supervisors. Task sheets can also include time and cost estimates for each task. These sheets should be reviewed and updated annually and whenever other organization-wide documents are updated. Because of their detailed nature, task sheets are useful when requesting additional resources from management. The final component of the plan is the schedule, which outlines when tasks must be completed, helps to track when tasks have been carried out, and acts as a mechanism to keep tasks from being overlooked or from piling up. For a detailed description of the sections of the plan, including tips for assembling the reference file and task sheets, see chapter 13, "Museum Housekeeping," of the NPS' *Museum Handbook* (1998).

Assignment sheets are valuable tools that remind building service workers of key safety and duty requirements while helping to keep the cleaning schedule on track. For example, the National Museum of the American Indian (NMAI) has developed an assignment sheet for its building service workers that lists safety reminders and the equipment necessary for the day, as well as a schedule of primary duties. Because NMAI utilizes a color-coded cloth and mop system, where a specific color of cloth or mop is used for a given application (e.g., a blue cloth is used for general cleaning, while a red cloth is used for toilets or urinals), this system is also outlined on the assignment sheet. See boxes 5.2 and 5.3 for an example of the NMAI assignment sheet.

Though this section is dedicated specifically to developing a building service plan, it is worth briefly discussing two important cleaning concerns: dust reduction and cleaning supply selection. Keeping dust away from collections objects is particularly important, because dust can contain substances that affect collection objects and attract harmful pests (Edson and Dean 1994). Walk-off mats and entry grates are valuable tools for reducing the amount of dirt and moisture that gets tracked into a cultural facility. It is much easier to clean a moveable mat than it is to clean permanent carpeting. Making sure that debris that enters the building or debris that accumulates just outside an entrance is removed right away is another strategy for preventing buildup of unwanted matter inside, thus reducing the need for indoor cleaning (Brophy and Wylie 2008).

When dust does begin to accumulate indoors, it is crucial that it is captured and removed rather than simply redistributed around the space (Edson and Dean 1994). Another important strategy for reducing dust accumulation is to use vacuums with high-efficiency particulate air (HEPA) filters. HEPA filters can capture very small particles, including lead dust, arsenic, asbestos, and other contaminants, at a rate of 99.97 percent for particles measuring 0.3 microns and larger (Alten 1997).

In addition to dust reduction, another area worth mentioning is cleaning supply selection. Not only are these supplies potentially hazardous to people and collections, but also they are very expensive. To use cleaners wisely, Westerkamp suggests a few strategies:

- Use mild cleaners for daily cleaning.
- Reserve heavy-duty cleaners for weekly, or less frequent, cleaning.
- Avoid toxic or environmentally harmful ingredients.
- Prioritize using no chemicals where possible, and then using green chemicals before turning to using harsher chemicals. Always use as few chemicals as possible.
- Measuring concentrates carefully, not estimating, saves [money]. (2009, p. 19)

For example, it is possible to clean restroom mirrors without using any chemicals—only water and a squeegee. For information about specific cleaning methods in cultural institution facilities, please see the "Resources" section of this book.

BOX 5.2.

SAMPLE FACILITY SERVICE WORKER ASSIGNMENT SHEET: PRIMARY DUTIES

OFFICE OF FACILITIES MANAGEMENT AND RELIABILITY

JOB ASSIGNMENT: FACILITY SERVICE WORKER		**Job #0000**
ASSIGNMENT SITE LOCATION:		
TOUR OF DUTY: 11 am – 7 pm		
DAILY ACTIVITIES:	Total Wash-up time:	30 minutes
	Safety talk	15 minutes
Name:	Computer time	15 minutes

FACILITY SERVICE WORKER SAFETY REMINDERS

BE AWARE OF YOUR SURROUNDINGS AND WEAR THE PROPER PERSONAL PROTECTIVE EQUIPMENT

- ◆ Inspect PPE
- ◆ Know the JHA associated with the task
- ◆ Know where to find the MSDS
- ◆ Lift safely & use appropriate equipment
- ◆ Connect/disconnect/store equipment properly
- ◆ Store/dispose of PPE properly
- ◆ Read all chemical labels
- ◆ Inspect the work area
- ◆ Offer and/or ask for assistance
- ◆ Operate equipment two feet from wall
- ◆ Be prepared with Bloodborne Pathogen requirements: Red bags, rubber gloves & absorbent powder

CART EQUIPMENT & SUPPLIES	CLEANING CLOTHS	CLEANING MOPS
- Absorbent powder - Red bags - Furniture polish - Glass cleaner - Dust pan & broom - Putty knife - Rubber gloves - Trash can liners - Shovel	● Red – toilets, urinals ○ Yellow w/ red liners – all other restroom surfaces ● Blue – general cleaning, (offices, lobbies, classrooms, mirrors, Plexiglas, glass) ● Green – kitchens, breakrooms ○ White – metal surfaces and specialty areas	● Red – restrooms ● Orange – Sani-glaze restrooms ● Blue – multi-use, non-restrooms ● Green – tile, marble, granite

PRIMARY DUTIES: MAINTAIN BUILDING INTERIOR AND EXTERIOR

Activity	Building Interior	Building Exterior
Special Events -	☐ set-up/breakdown	☐ set-up/breakdown
Trash Cans -	☐ emptying/cleaning	☐ emptying/cleaning
Stairwells/Escalators/ Elevators -	☐ clean	☐ clean
Hard Floors -	☐ mopping	
	☐ stripping	
	☐ waxing	
	☐ buffing	
Carpeted Floors -	☐ vacuum	
	☐ shampoo	
Restrooms -	☐ clean	
	☐ dust	
	☐ vacuum	
	☐ service	
Office areas/Galleries/Break Rooms	☐ maintain?	
Terraces/Parking Lots -		☐ clean
Sidewalks/Entryways		☐ clean
Entrance Glass & Frames -		☐ clean
Signage -	☐ clean	☐ clean
Snow/Ice -		☐ remove
		☐ slip protection

This is the front side of an assignment sheet that was developed for building service workers at the Smithsonian Institution's National Museum of the American Indian by the Office of Facilities Management and Reliability (OFMR) Cleaning Standards Taskforce. For the back side of the sheet, "Work Schedule," see box 5.3.

Source: Reproduced with permission of the Smithsonian Institution Office of Facilities Management and Reliability.

BOX 5.3.

SAMPLE FACILITY SERVICE WORKER ASSIGNMENT SHEET: WORK SCHEDULE

OFFICE OF FACILITIES MANAGEMENT AND RELIABILITY

WORK SCHEDULE

11 AM – 12 PM	12:15 – 1:45 PM	2:45 – 5:30 PM	5:30 – 6:00 PM	6:00 – 7:00 PM
Safety talk	Clean security restroom	Clean 1st floor ladies restroom (Room 1007)	Clean and dust staff entrance doors	Clean and service 1st floor restroom
Service 1st floor ladies room	Clean all basement gear rooms	Clean 2nd floor ladies restroom	Sweep and damp mop stone floor around mat	Clean and service unisex restroom at Visitor's Desk
Clean entrance glass/staff entry doors	Spot clean basement walls	Police 1st floor	Vacuum entrance mat	
Police first floor	Spot clean elevator #4	Spot clean staff entrance doors		
	Spot clean first floor vestibule	Police entrances		
	Check trash and recycle containers; empty and clean surfaces as needed	Police 1st floor from staff entrance to visitor's elevator		
	Act as swing person for absent staff			
	Perform other assigned tasks			
Thoroughly clean Room 1007 the first and third Wednesdays of every month				

TOOLS REQUIRED FOR TOUR COMPLETION

TOUR	TASKS	TOOLS/CHEMICALS REQUIRED
Walls	Remove streaks, dust, dirt, urine stains, smudges	Cleaning cloth & recommended cleaner
Mirror/glass	Remove streaks, dust, smudges	Cleaning cloth & recommended cleaner
Commodes/urinals	Remove streaks, dust, dirt, urine stains, smudges, encrustations	Cleaning cloths, scrubbing pad, cleaner, soft brush , commode brush
Chrome	Remove streaks, urine stains, dirt, encrustation, shine	Cleaning cloths, cleaner, white scrubbing pad
Trash cans	Remove dust, stains, dirt from all surfaces	Cleaning cloth & recommended cleaner
Lockers	Remove dust, stains, dirt from all surfaces	Cleaning cloth & recommended cleaner
Baby Changing Stations	Remove dust, stains, dirt from all surfaces	Cleaning cloth & recommended cleaner
Vents (ceiling, walls, doors)	Remove dust, stains, dirt from all surfaces	Cleaning cloth & recommended cleaner
Floors (tile, marble, cement, granite, stairwells)	Remove gum, stains, dirt	Gum remover, window cleaner, putty knife, recommended cleaner, mop, bucket, dust pan & broom, strip-seal-wax mop, dust mop

This is the back side of an assignment sheet that was developed for building service workers at the Smithsonian Institution's National Museum of the American Indian by the Office of Facilities Management and Reliability (OFMR) Cleaning Standards Taskforce. For the front side of the sheet, "Primary Duties," see box 5.2.

Source: Reproduced with permission of the Smithsonian Institution Office of Facilities Management and Reliability.

As mentioned earlier, conservators must approve any cleaning substances that will be used around objects in the museum's collection. At zoos and aquariums, where cleaning chemicals have the potential to affect the health of animals, it is particularly important that zookeepers approve all substances used in close proximity to their living collections. Similarly, children's museums should carefully select their cleaning substances, keeping in mind that children often put their mouths and hands in unexpected places.

Material Safety Data Sheets (MSDS) are required by the U.S. Occupational Safety and Health Administration (OSHA), and these sheets describe safe handling procedures and hazards associated with potentially hazardous substances. To ensure proper use and safety, each worker who uses a potentially harmful substance as a part of his or her job needs to be familiar with the MSDS for each product he or she uses and be able to access this information easily (Westerkamp 2009).

Implementing an Integrated Pest Management (IPM) Plan

No matter the climate or geographic region, every locale is susceptible to pests, which can be very damaging to cultural institution buildings and their collections. Unfortunately, a 2004 survey of over 1,200 museums conducted by the American Association of Museums (AAM, now known as the American Alliance of Museums) revealed that only 54 percent of respondents actually practiced IPM, while only 39 percent had an IPM plan in place. The cultural institution facility manager is often responsible for the design and implementation of an IPM plan that protects the facilities, as well as the collections, from pest infestation. Carrying out this plan requires buy-in from the institution's entire staff—everyone from building service workers to security guards can be on the lookout for potential pest entry points and help identify early signs of an infestation (Merritt 2005).

Pests affecting cultural institutions generally fall into three categories: microorganisms, insects, and vertebrates. In museum environments, woodborer beetles, dermestid beetles, cockroaches, rodents, and birds—like pigeons and starlings—are among the most common pests. Because of the wide variety of potential pests and the broad range of entry points through which they gain access to collection areas, it is important to monitor them through both direct observation and periodic sampling, including setting insect traps in the facility. When a pest has been identified, it is important to document each occurrence. A trend in this data can indicate an infestation that can then be addressed early on, rather than after it has become a larger problem. Recording the kinds of pests present in the facility also helps tailor the museum's IPM plan to manage the specific pests that affect the facility (Genoways and Ireland 2003).

IPM, which originated as a commercial agricultural practice, is seen as a preventative, less toxic way to prevent pests in a facility (Smithsonian Institution 2006). As illustrated in box 5.4, IPM in the museum environment can be conceptualized as a sequence of nested layers, with collections placed at the center of this layered protection system. The layers that must be protected, in turn, are the institution's grounds, the building envelope, the exhibition and storage rooms, the exhibition and storage cases, and the actual collections objects themselves.

For the outer layer, the institution's grounds, facility managers and horticulturalists should take care to select plants that do not attract insects that have the potential to become indoor pests. For the next layer, the museum building envelope, special care needs to be paid to cracks, crevasses, and openings that may allow pests to enter. These entry points include everything from visitor entrances to air intakes and windows to loading docks. Any cracks should be sealed to prevent entry of pests.

The next layer to consider is the room in which collections are actually stored or displayed. Though it can be difficult to keep this space airtight, especially if visitors are allowed into the space, it is important to strive for airtight, dust-free conditions. Keeping food out of these areas, as well as being sure to empty any trash bins daily, will also help reduce pest infestations. Dust makes enticing food for insects, so it is important that building service workers pay special attention to areas in which dust may accumulate, including under storage cases and on fixtures. In addition, prior to entering collection areas, all shipping boxes must be treated for pests through fumigation or freezing. The final layer, the storage cases that house pieces of the collection, should be airtight and acid free in order to keep harmful insects, dust, and other irritants from coming in contact with the collections (Genoways and Ireland 2003). See box 5.5 for a checklist for pest management specifically related to collection storage areas.

IPM means finding a balance between keeping pests out of the building and away from collections, while also being sensitive to human health concerns that arise when using pesticides and other poisons. As a part of finding this balance, the British Museum in London employs a specially trained

BOX 5.4.

INTEGRATED PEST MANAGEMENT (IPM): A NESTED APPROACH

Originally developed for commercial agricultural application, IPM is helpful for museum environments as well. This system ensures that pest intrusion is reduced at a variety of scales, including at the levels of the grounds, building, room, storage case, and actual collection item. IPM allows for an ecosystem approach that reduces the cost of chemical applications, as well as staff and collections' exposure to such chemicals.

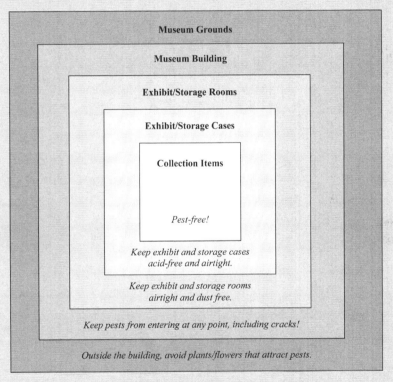

Source: Genoways and Ireland (2003, p. 209). *Figure source:* © Angela Person-Harm 2013.

BOX 5.5.

CHECKLIST FOR PEST MANAGEMENT IN COLLECTIONS STORAGE FACILITIES

Physical Space:

- ❑ Collections storage should be a dedicated space, and should be separate from collections exhibition and processing areas, food preparation and consumption areas, staff offices, laboratories, and other work areas.
- ❑ Collections storage should be located in an interior room of the museum building.
- ❑ All access to the storage area should be through an interior door.
- ❑ All doors to the space should be gasketed on four sides to fit snugly in the door frame.
- ❑ Joints between walls and floor, and walls and ceiling should be caulked.
- ❑ All interior surfaces of the room should be smooth and free of cracks and gaps.
- ❑ All gaps around pipe and conduit penetrations in the walls, floor, and ceiling should be sealed.
- ❑ Drop ceilings should be eliminated.
- ❑ Flooring materials should be made of materials that are easily cleaned, such as vinyl tile or sealed concrete.
- ❑ All materials that are vulnerable to pest infestation should be stored inside of tightly sealed storage equipment or containers.
- ❑ For some oversize specimens, the room should be constructed as a tightly sealed storage cabinet.
- ❑ Specimens should not be overcrowded.

Storage Equipment and Supplies:

- ❑ Storage equipment should be elevated at least 15 cm (6 in.) to permit cleaning.
- ❑ Cabinets should be properly placed and designed so that all areas are accessible for inspection and cleaning.
- ❑ Storage cabinets should have gaskets and be tightly sealed.
- ❑ Storage cabinets should be easy to clean with no interior ridges or hollow drawer runners.
- ❑ All cabinets should have floors.
- ❑ Cabinets should be white in color. Exterior surfaces should have no ridges or indentations to trap debris.

- ❑ All drawers in cabinets should be completely removable.
- ❑ All storage and packing supplies should be stored outside of collection storage areas.

Building Maintenance:
- ❑ The building should be routinely inspected for problems such as roof leaks, condensation, and leaking pipes and faucets. Repairs should be made immediately.
- ❑ All door gaskets should be inspected on a regular basis and repaired immediately.
- ❑ Cracks in walls, floors and ceilings should be filled immediately.
- ❑ Collection storage areas should be kept clean and free of dust and clutter: collection storage areas should be vacuumed weekly.
- ❑ Cleaning schedules should be established and cleaning efforts should be documented.
- ❑ All trash receptacles should be emptied at the end of each day.
- ❑ All cleaning supplies and equipment should be stored outside of collections storage.

Collection Storage Maintenance:
- ❑ Specimens should be inspected thoroughly and determined to be pest-free before placement in storage.
- ❑ No specimens should remain outside of sealed cabinets or other sealed containers overnight.

Pest Awareness and Monitoring:
- ❑ All staff should receive training in pest awareness.
- ❑ A pest monitoring program should be established. A variety of monitoring techniques should be employed depending upon the target organisms. All monitoring data should be documented and evaluated regularly.
- ❑ One person should be in charge to receive, report, and interpret pest monitoring data, and to determine response.
- ❑ All materials susceptible to pests should be inspected at least once a year.
- ❑ Pest inspections should be documented.
- ❑ All observations of biological activity should be documented.
- ❑ All pests should be identified to determine if the collections are threatened.

Infestations:
- ❏ Infested materials should be bagged and removed from storage areas. Pests should be eradicated by appropriate methods. All treatments should be documented.
- ❏ The extent and cause of infestation should be identified and documented.
- ❏ Appropriate actions should be taken to deter reinfestation.

Source: Jessup (1995). "Checklist for Pest Management in Collections Storage Facilities," in Carolyn L. Rose, Catharine A. Hawks, and Hugh H. Genoways, eds. *Storage of Natural History Collections: A Preventive Conservation Approach* (Volume 1). Washington, DC: Society for the Preservation of Natural History Collections, pp. 219–220. © 1995, used with permission from the Society for the Preservation of Natural History Collections.

canine that identifies active rodent infestations, and then traps can be placed in the most effective locations. This is especially helpful in the catering and student lunch areas of the museum and has allowed the British Museum to use fewer traps and less rodenticide (Carroll 2011).

Not all cultural institutions are lucky enough to have an entomologist on staff to aid in identifying pests in and around their facilities. To address this, several applications, or apps, have recently been developed for mobile devices to help laypersons identify pests on the spot. While we do not endorse any particular application, we offer descriptions of several available apps. For example, the app "Museum Pests Ref" is designed to help identify pests common to museums and libraries using mobile devices. This guide is based on the information from the Integrated Pest Management Working Group's (IPM-WG) website, www.museumpests.net. The IPM-WG is a group of professionals including collection managers, conservators, entomologists, and others interested in IPM in institutions with pest-sensitive collections. Both the IPM-WG's website and "Museum Pests Ref" app provide reference photos for use during identification. The IPM-WG website also supplies information about prevention, monitoring, and potential solutions.

The University of Florida–Gainesville has developed three mobile apps: iPest1, iPest2, and iPest3. Each app is geared toward identifying distinct types of pests and supplies information about individual pests, including their geographic distribution, habitat, biology, and behavior. The iPest and Museum Pests Ref apps are two that have been recognized by the Northern States Conservation Center (NSCC) as viable identification aids; however, because of the quick pace at which mobile apps are developed, it is important to check frequently for updates and new applications as they become available (NSCC 2012).

Moving Management in Cultural Facilities

The involvement of cultural facility personnel during moves can take all different forms—from typical jobs like helping to relocate office furniture to exhilarating jobs like helping to move a live tiger at a zoo—and each type of move presents different challenges. In any case, managing the movement of collections objects into, out of, and around cultural facilities requires coordination of staff from throughout the institution. For example, curators and conservators must communicate with facility managers to ensure that the space is ready to accept new objects and that there is a procedure in place for the object to make a safe move. Some considerations that should be discussed include whether the new space meets all of the necessary temperature and relative humidity requirements, whether all supplies necessary for the move are available, and whether facility personnel require special training in order to properly assist with the move.

Collection objects are more likely to be damaged when they are being handled or moved, which makes careful and effective moving management particularly crucial. In order to reduce the possibility of damage, there are several guidelines to take into account before and during the move process. First and foremost, it is important that all staff members involved in handling and moving objects, including facility staff, are properly trained in order to reduce the risks associated with incorrect practices. When it is time for an object to be moved, the staff involved should meet to determine the route and each person's responsibility during the move. As part of this planning process, the object being moved should be inspected, and this inspection should take into account the stability, construction, weight, dimensions, and shape of the object. These characteristics will help with selecting the equipment needed and the route for the move.

The route should be inspected to ensure that corridors, doorways, and stairs can safely accommodate the object, its movers, and any necessary move equipment. Any obstacles should be removed from the path that will be taken during the move, and the object's new location should be inspected and prepared for its safe storage or display. The moving equipment must also be identified and assembled before the move, as this will help determine the route and roles of movers throughout the process. If a cart is necessary for the move, it should have shock-absorbent tires and padded trays that will hold the object and keep it from shifting or falling.

Before moving an object, it is important to make sure that staff is appropriately dressed. Those involved in the move should dress in comfortable clothing and wear nonslip footwear. Rings, bracelets, and other jewelry should not be worn during the move to avoid damage to the object. Gloves—made from plain cotton or nitrile rubber—should be worn by those handling the object; if gloves are not worn, all hands should be washed very well.

Before the object is picked up, the move team needs to decide which parts can be handled, if any. Parts of the object that may protrude should be accounted for during the move, as they are particularly vulnerable to damage. When carrying a small object alone, both hands should be used and as little pressure as possible should be applied. One hand should be put under the heaviest part of the object, while the other hand supports the object. When carrying an object on a cart, it is important that the object be fully supported and that it be protected from vibration and impact during the move. The cart should be moved slowly and steadily, at a regular speed without any quick movements or sudden stops (United Nations Educational, Scientific and Cultural Organization [UNESCO] 2010). These guidelines provide only basic direction for moving collections items.

No matter how far the object is being moved or how long it is being handled, it is at much greater risk of being damaged during the moving process than when it is lying at rest. It is important that a member of the collections staff provides guidance when moving each piece of a museum's collection. In addition to guidance from collections staff, specialized training in the use of moving equipment, such as rigging equipment, may be necessary prior to moving fragile collection pieces.

One facility management team recently faced a large-scale move challenge when they helped coordinate the move of NASA's space shuttle *Discovery* to its final resting place at the National Air and Space Museum (NASM) Steven F. Udvar-Hazy Center in Chantilly, Virginia. The shuttle required extensive planning and preparation for its move, due in large part to its size—it measures 122 feet long, 57 feet high, and 78 feet wide, and weighs in at around 150,000 pounds. All told, more than 30 meetings were held to make moving arrangements for this gargantuan space artifact. Involved in the planning were more than 100 NASA and NASM staff; and all 17 members of the NASM facility management group were included in the move process.

The facility management staff provided support throughout the move in a number of ways. Prior to moving *Discovery* into the museum, its look-alike, the prototype shuttle *Enterprise*, had to be removed from the hangar–exhibition space to make room. *Enterprise* then made its own journey to its new home in New York. Before *Enterprise* could be moved out of the hangar, the facility team coordinated the removal and later repair of a section of the hangar wall to accommodate the height of *Enterprise*'s tailfin as it exited the space. After *Enterprise* made it safely out of the building, the facility team began supporting the move of *Discovery* into the hangar. The team inspected the area for the potential of foreign object damage that could be caused by objects on the ground as the shuttle rolled by. The FM staff also provided generators and other supplies, including a 125-foot boom, for the move.

In addition, the facility team was tasked with ensuring that environmental conditions met the requirements set for *Discovery*, as well as the museum's other collection items: 70 degrees Fahrenheit (+/–4 degrees) and 45 percent relative humidity (+/–8 percent). During the move, maintaining these conditions presented a particular challenge, as the very large hangar doors that opened to let *Enterprise* in and *Discovery* out remained open all throughout the moving day's welcoming ceremony. In order to reduce temperature and humidity fluctuation during this time, the building had to be pressurized (Lewis 2012).

The move of space shuttle *Discovery* is worth mentioning, because it illustrates the importance of integrating the talents of cultural institution staff from throughout the organization, including facility management staff, to get a sensitive job done. Without careful planning and the involvement of a variety of staff members early on, this moving job may have resulted in damage to one of the iconic shuttles. Instead, clear communication and ample time for preparation led to a well-orchestrated day that everyone could enjoy. Ultimately, any cultural institution move project could benefit from a process that mirrors these key strategies.

Storage Management for Cultural Facilities

A 2011 survey of nearly 1,500 cultural institutions from more than 130 countries revealed that "all over the world, museum collections in storage suffer from poor management and lack of maintenance, adequate space and equipment" (Lambert 2011–2012, p. 23). This international survey, conducted by the International Centre for the Study of the Preservation and Restoration of Cultural Property (ICCROM) and UNESCO, showed that museums in both developing and developed countries face problems related to insufficient storage.

To understand the nature of these problems, it is helpful to review some key statistics from the ICCROM–UNESCO survey that demonstrate reasons for, and symptoms of, inadequate collections storage. The following issues were identified as being either major problems (i.e., requiring several months' work) or drastic problems (i.e., indicating an extreme case):

- 67 percent of museums face a lack of space.

- 50 percent of museums face a lack of storage units and/or overcrowded storage units.

- 40 percent of museums face a lack of management support for activities related to storage, have too few trained staff, face a large backlog of objects that require accessioning, and have storage spaces that are not properly tailored to the types of objects stored within.

- 33 percent of museums have unclear methods for managing storage and it is unclear who is responsible for storage; do not have regular cleaning of storage; and have buildings in poor repair.

- 25 percent of museums have no object movement register; lack an accession register, or, if they have a register, it is out of date; do not have location codes for storage units or aisles; place objects directly on top of the floor; and have difficulty moving in storage areas.

- 20 percent of museums have unsecured doors and windows; have damage from flooding, earthquakes, hurricanes, or fires; keep items other than collections items in storage; and store items in nonstorage spaces, such as hallways or offices.

- 10 percent of museums have faced object theft. (ICCROM-UNESCO 2011)

Glancing down this list, we can see that correcting many of these problems falls under the purview of cultural facility managers. That is not to say that these problems can be blamed on lack of facility management. There are likely a variety of factors at work, and forming a partnership between facility management and members of staff responsible for collections is an important step toward improving cultural facility storage conditions.

Functionally speaking, collections storage space is expected to meet three requirements: (1) to consistently supply environmental conditions that facilitate preservation of collections, (2) to provide access so objects can be stored and retrieved in a safe manner, and (3) to organize collections in a way that effectively makes use of the space, while complying with the first two requirements. Because of their intimate knowledge of the spaces within their facilities, cultural facility managers are uniquely equipped to support updates to and reconfiguration of storage spaces so these three requirements can be met.

As evidenced by the ICCROM-UNESCO list above, successful integration of facility management practices is currently lagging in cultural facilities the world over. A part of the problem may be that facility managers are simply not tapped for their expertise in terms of space planning, environmental conditioning, and moving management. By working with collections staff, facility managers can play a key role in identifying storage solutions and space requirements. For example, the facility manager can recommend equipment for moving collections items in and out of the storage area, such as forklifts, pallet jacks, hand trucks, carts, and ladders. In addition, because doorways and hallways have an effect on how the space is accessed, the facility manager can help select moving equipment particular to the space or, in turn, work to alter entry points to facilitate movement of collections (Wilcox 1995).

There are a number of ways that cultural facility managers can contribute to building a healthy storage management program. Facility managers must ensure that doors and windows are secure from pests and deter access of unqualified persons who may try to enter the space. In addition, when damage occurs to storage space—whether from a natural disaster or other event—the facility manager is often responsible for organizing cleanup and recovery of the storage area. The facility manager can oversee a use policy that governs what can and cannot enter the storage space. When collection objects are stored outside the storage area, the facility manager may also take responsibility for finding additional space, as necessary, to accommodate these objects—whether through leasing more space or reorganizing existing space. Ensuring that the space is kept clean and in good repair is, of course, another way in which the facility manager supports safe storage of collections.

As mentioned earlier, the facility manager should always work with collections staff when making decisions that affect spaces in which collections will be stored or displayed. To help get started, there are some general guidelines for creating a safe storage space that facility managers can share with their museum director and collections staff to ensure they are keeping the collection as safe as possible. For example, if a museum has the opportunity to build a new storage area or if it is relocating stored items within its facility, there are several important elements to consider. The storage area should be easily accessed from the outside, as well as from exhibition areas and conservation areas. This means, for example, that hallways that lead from the loading dock to the storage area should be of a width sufficient to accommodate safe transportation of collection objects. It is better for the storage area to be centrally located within the building, rather than on the perimeter, as a central location helps guard collections against temperature fluctuations. Basements or attics are almost never appropriate locations for collection storage due to extremes in temperature and/or humidity inherent to these locations.

A cleaning policy, or building service plan, for the storage area should be implemented, and dust, in particular, should be kept out of the space. To aid in dust reduction, any concrete surfaces in the storage area should be sealed with epoxy or water-based polyurethane, and walls should be smooth and painted with latex paint. In a perfect setting, potentially harmful wiring, pipes, and ducts will not come in contact with the storage area. Any wiring that is in the storage area should be insulated and maintained in good condition to reduce the risk of fire. It is important that the storage area's walls and ceiling are clad in a fire-resistant material, like stone or gypsum. Any fire extinguishers that are located in the space must not spray powder, because it can harm collections. Either carbon dioxide or pressurized-water fire extinguishers are better options. In addition to an easy-to-reach fire extinguisher, the storage space should have smoke detectors, and these detectors should be tested on a regular basis.

So that facility personnel can easily access control panels, these panels should be located outside of the storage areas. To keep the space secure, storage area doors should either be metal plated or built of solid wood, and dependable locks should be installed. To keep the space safe from outside pests, the storage area should have good ventilation and be kept dry. This will help keep mold from developing. Doors and windows should be closed at all times, and the building should be inspected for small openings that need to be sealed. Any openings that are necessary for ventilation should be covered with fine mesh screens; these screens will help keep potentially harmful insects out of the building (UNESCO 2010).

Free online resources exist to help cultural institutions plan and maintain safe storage for their collections. For example, ICCROM and UNESCO have come together to develop RE-ORG, a free online tool designed to help museum personnel improve documentation and storage of their collections (www.re-org.info). By registering on the RE-ORG website, members of museum staff are able to break their storage reorganization plan into a series of discrete tasks that can then be tracked using RE-ORG's online tracking tool. For additional information about creating optimal storage conditions in the cultural facility, please consult the "Resources" section of this book.

Many cultural institutions lease storage space, and, in these cases, the lease should address facility management, including how all of the specialized storage conditions mentioned earlier will be met and by whom—the owner of the leased space or staff from the cultural institution. In many cases, the cultural institution's facility manager is in the best position to negotiate a lease that is sure to address, up front, how the space will be maintained rather than as an afterthought.

Developing an Operations and Maintenance (O&M) Manual

Any well-managed facility—particularly a specialized facility, like a museum or cultural institution—must develop and make use of an O&M manual that specifically documents how the facility will be cared for over time. To accomplish this, an O&M manual should document and describe the facility, its purpose, and unique challenges posed by the facility and its mission, as well as the processes necessary for ongoing maintenance of its components and the strategies necessary to sustain effective operations. Other important elements that an O&M manual may include are information about on-the-job safety precautions, space assignment, and descriptions of sustainability strategies employed in the facility. The O&M manual also presents an excellent opportunity to describe the role that facility personnel play in the museum's emergency preparedness and emergency management plans.

An O&M manual cannot be assembled without also developing a comprehensive maintenance plan, like the plans discussed earlier in this chapter. In many ways, a museum's maintenance plan becomes the roadmap that guides the development of its O&M manual. If the maintenance plan is the roadmap, then the manual serves as the turn-by-turn directions for members of the museum facility management team. The manual also educates members of the museum staff in terms of the services offered and how the facility management team can support them, as well as defining the protocol museum staff should follow when requesting facility management services.

When beginning to develop an O&M manual, there are several guiding principles to keep in mind. First, it is important that the manual is created in a manner that will be easy to update, add to, and reconfigure as the organization changes and processes evolve. Several years ago, a large museum facility management organization created its O&M manual using complex design software that not many people in the organization had access to or were comfortable using. Recently, when it became necessary to update that manual, the organization found it necessary to painstakingly convert the manual to a more user-friendly format using software that facility management staff was comfortable using and could easily access.

In addition to ensuring that the manual can be easily updated, it is also important that it be assembled with input from a diverse team capable of thoroughly outlining all of the important O&M methods in a user-friendly manner. For a museum facility, the team creating the O&M manual may include the facility manager, engineering technicians, building service workers, a member of staff who handles training, and a capable editor. Staff members who are familiar with maintaining and troubleshooting the facility's specialized systems, like building automation systems, should also be included. In addition, much like during the strategic planning process, involving museum staff from outside of the facility management team, including the museum director and conservators, ensures that the manual addresses all of the needs of the facility and its occupants.

This team can gather information about the facility and its equipment through site inspections and by talking to staff, equipment manufacturers, and other knowledgeable parties. Next, the team can "review, analyze, and evaluate" the facility using the information they have collected. After performing this data collection and analysis, the team is ready to begin building a straightforward O&M manual that includes a thorough introduction to the facility, pertinent requirements of the facility, instructions for requesting and logging maintenance activities, and descriptions of facility systems and safety requirements.

The National Institute of Building Sciences' *Whole Building Design Guide* (WBDG) recommends incorporating a number of particular elements into an O&M manual (Hunt 2011), and we will discuss several of these elements here, including ways that museums can approach them in their own manuals. However, it is important to keep the unique circumstances of each and every facility in mind when developing an O&M manual—there is no one-size-fits-all approach, and the WBDG suggestions are merely offered here as a starting point.

First, the WBDG recommends including an introduction that familiarizes users with the facility, while also describing how the manual can be used and giving an overview of the information covered. For museums and cultural institutions, this is a good place to point out the specialized needs of the facility, depending on the nature of the collections. For example, if very particular temperature and humidity requirements must be met, these standards can be introduced here. The introduction can also include a list of emergency contacts and point out where additional information not available in the manual can be found—like as-built drawings, test data, and construction specifications.

Next, it is essential to provide a description of safety hazards associated with the systems and equipment in the facility and ways to prevent injuries on the job. After safety has been addressed, a description of utility systems, including water supply systems, electrical systems, and natural gas, sanitary waste, communications, security, and other systems important to the facility's operation, can also be included. A description of the cultural facility's interior and exterior maintenance plans, including housekeeping (building services) and general maintenance requirements, is also vital to the O&M manual. This section is a good place to describe cleaning guidelines particular to the cultural institution—for example, certain substances that cannot be used in the presence of collections objects, whether conservators or building service staff will clean in collection cases, and other guidelines specific to cleaning in the cultural institution. In addition, this section can cover why it is crucial to conduct regular inspections and how they can be documented.

It is also important to include a description of the facility's plumbing operation and maintenance standards for both the domestic and sanitary waste systems, as well as the standards for maintaining its HVAC systems. The HVAC section can reiterate specialized environmental requirements that must be met in order to properly preserve collections and why these requirements are so important. This section may also address policies regarding space heaters, centralized air systems, and automated controls in the museum.

Defining the operation and maintenance standards for the facility's fire protection system can be essential to ensuring that the system works properly in a fire emergency, and these standards can be included in the manual. In addition, an explanation of the facility's alarm systems, including fire detection and intrusion alarms, and how they should be inspected and cared for is key to keeping visitors, staff, and artifacts safe. An overview of the facility's electrical systems, including the operation and maintenance of power distribution equipment and any emergency backup equipment, like generators, is important to document. Additional systems that are not covered by earlier sections should also be described in terms of their key characteristics and recommended maintenance. For example, in the museum environment, this may include lighting systems and which lamps are allowable in exhibition and storage spaces so as to prevent light damage to collections. If applicable, a description of the facility's conveying systems, including preventive maintenance requirements for the museum's conveyors, wheelchair lifts, elevators, and escalators, can be included.

After all systems have been described, it is important to outline why and how maintenance logs are used to track maintenance activities in the cultural facility. This section should also include a list of the specific tasks that must be completed as part of the maintenance routine, as well as how often each task must be completed. In addition to maintenance logs, it is also important to include a section that lists key service contacts for the facility's equipment and a sample work order form. The O&M manual can also include a list of manufacturers' literature, like manuals and cut sheets, and where these resources can be found. This literature supplements information in the O&M manual, giving more specific advice about operating, maintaining, and repairing the facility's equipment. The manuals and cut sheets need to be well organized and clearly labeled so they can be found quickly when they are needed. To make this literature accessible to all staff members, it is a good idea to scan as much of it as possible and place clearly labeled digital versions in an "O&M Manufacturer's Literature" folder on the museum's intranet.

Hunt (2011) also recommends including general operating procedures for major equipment within the facility, like how the controls work, how to power the equipment down, how to initiate an emergency override, and the steps necessary for seasonal changeover. Including "fault tree analysis" tables that direct maintenance personnel through a step-by-step process to determine a potential problem with a piece of equipment and how it can be remedied help facilitate troubleshooting. Floor plans, system and equipment tag locations, and labeled photographs of particular pieces of equipment can also be helpful to include in the manual. In addition, schematics for electrical systems, airflow, and plumbing serve as important resources. The manual might also include the number, location, size, type, and standard position of valves within the facility (Hunt 2011).

While we have considered the O&M manual components suggested by the *Whole Building Design Guide*, let us now consider how one particular cultural institution has organized its own O&M manual. The Smithsonian Institution's *Operations and Maintenance Manual* (OFMR 2010) is organized into six sections, each of which is further broken down into more specific subsections. These six sections include

- an introductory section;

- a structure and strategy section;

- a policies, procedures, and safety section;

- a maintenance section;

- an operations section; and

- appendices.

The Smithsonian's *Operations and Maintenance Manual* begins with an introduction and executive summary, and provides an overview of the Office of Facilities Management and Reliability's (OFMR) structure and strategy. This overview spans topics such as the Smithsonian and OFMR mission, sustainability strategies, and expected levels of service. In addition, it also covers lifecycle modeling and commissioning for Smithsonian facilities, key performance indicators (KPIs), and several other topics related to the OFMR structure and strategy.

The next section of the Smithsonian O&M manual describes important policies, procedures, and safety precautions. Among the topics in this section is a description of administrative operations, accountable property and bar-coding procedures, and where construction documents can be found. In addition, this section describes accident and medical emergency protocol, emergency and disaster response guidelines, and hazardous materials and lock-out and tag-out procedures. This section also outlines the integrated workplace management software used to manage maintenance tasks each day, purchasing guidelines, and how work orders are processed once received, among other topics.

The maintenance section of the Smithsonian O&M manual provides an overview of its key maintenance strategies—including RCM—as well as specific information about lighting, the high-pressure steam system, and performing electrical work. Among other topics in this section are shop inventory and equipment maintenance records, maintenance emergency protocol, and project execution. The operations section addresses appearance inspections, audiovisual support, and loading dock use. In addition, the operations section outlines emergency preparedness guidelines, snow and ice removal, and alarm monitoring procedures. Building automation systems and building service procedures are also addressed in this section, along with several additional operations-related topics.

The manual closes with appendices that define acronyms, list resources and references, and provide relevant maintenance and operations forms. The appendices include a description of the cutting-edge technologies used in RCM, applicable Smithsonian directives, a sample statement of work, and a list of topics that are planned for incorporation into the next draft of the O&M manual.

As we see when comparing the WBDG O&M manual recommendations (Hunt 2011) to the content of the Smithsonian's O&M manual, there are different means of structuring this important guiding document. Of course, the way that a museum decides to structure its O&M manual will depend largely on the type and size of its facility and its systems, the mission of the cultural institution, and the role that the facility management organization plays in supporting this mission. What matters most is that this document is available and is viewed as useful for and relevant to the day-to-day operations. Ultimately, the manual should aid in maintaining the safety and integrity of a cultural facility by helping the facility management team to perform to the highest standards possible.

Benchmarking for Cultural Facilities

Benchmarking has been defined as "The search for industry best practices that lead to superior performance" (Camp 1989). Within facility management organizations, benchmarking is a helpful tool that identifies, for example, strategies that help save on utility bills, innovative maintenance techniques, and how a particular facility is performing in relation to other, similar facilities. Traditionally, benchmarking efforts are organized by an outside organization, such as the International Facility Management Association (IFMA) or a consulting firm. These organizations or firms generate benchmarking reports by compiling data provided by facilities on topics such as square footage, utility rates and expenditures, building service costs, and maintenance and operations practices. An individual facility organization can, in turn, pay for a benchmarking report that pits its own data and practices against those of comparable facility management organizations. This comparison helps facility managers understand how their facilities are performing in relation to those of their peers in terms of a predetermined set of KPIs, and where savings might be found. Benchmarking can also help identify practices that may benefit the overall condition of their facilities.

For museum facilities, there are several prominent efforts geared toward capturing data specific to these specialized institutions. One text, *Covering Your Assets: Facilities and Risk Management in Museums*, provides results from a survey of over 1,200 museums (Merritt 2005). This text presents data on size, types of policies in place, facility use, number of maintenance staff members, attendance, insurance costs, and income and expenses, among other items. Though this information is now more than a few years old, much of it, including essays on crucial topics like insurance and pest management, can still be of help to today's institutions.

For organizations that want to participate in an annual benchmarking effort tailored specifically to cultural facilities, the International Association of Museum Facility Administrators' (IAMFA) annual benchmarking survey may be a good fit. IAMFA benchmarking reports capture a broad range of museum facility data. For example, its 2011 benchmarking survey documented, among other topics, averages of electrical consumption per square foot, custodial costs per square foot cleaned, and maintenance cost per square foot, as well as the average facility management budget as a percentage of the total budget for each of its survey participants. In addition, the IAMFA benchmarking report captures and documents trends among participating museum facilities. Among the trends cited in the 2011 report include increased use of photovoltaic and solar hot-water technologies, increased use of daylight and motion sensors, and more efficient use of space (Facility Issues 2011).

Institutions that contribute their data to the IAMFA benchmarking effort are invited to attend a benchmarking seminar held at IAMFA's annual meeting. This seminar provides an opportunity to discuss issues with other cultural institution facility managers, to ask questions about why their facility's data may differ from others' data, and to collectively brainstorm for solutions to tricky museum facility issues. Registration and data entry for the IAMFA benchmarking exercise are generally completed each spring (from March to June), while the follow-up seminar is held in the fall. More information, including registration costs and timelines, can be found on the IAMFA website (www.iamfa.org).

The IFMA provides an online benchmarking survey that captures information about a broad array of facility types. This survey is free and open to facility managers of all facility types from around the world. Once the IFMA survey has accumulated enough data to be considered statistically significant, a benchmarking report that compiles all of the data is generated and made available for purchase. Though this benchmarking effort is not held specifically for cultural institutions, it generates information about facility management costs and practices that may be helpful to museums. Any facility that contributes its data to the IFMA benchmarking study can receive access to the final report for free. For more information about this benchmarking effort, visit https://ifma.enetrix.com.

Energy Star, a program of the U.S. Environmental Protection Agency, advocates the use of energy-efficient practices and products and offers free benchmarking through its online Portfolio Manager. The Portfolio Manager allows facility managers to input their facilities' data into its online database, which, in turn, helps them compare their facilities' performance to the performance of other, similar buildings found throughout the United States. The Portfolio Manager also assigns a *benchmark score* to each facility on a scale from 1 to 100. If a building is assigned a benchmark score of 75 or higher, it qualifies for an Energy Star Label. Earning the Energy Star designation is a significant feat; buildings with this label use about 40 percent less energy than the average building while maintaining comfortable environments and providing expected services (Energy Star 2012). For more information about the Energy Star Portfolio Manager program, visit www.energystar.gov.

Within the Energy Star benchmarking program, museums are classified as and benchmarked against "entertainment facilities," a category that includes stadiums, convention centers, theaters, and museums. In this category, the Mark Twain House and Museum in Hartford, Connecticut, was one of the first museums in the country to become an Energy Star partner. Being an Energy Star partner differs from receiving the Energy Star Label. While earning the label requires a particular benchmarking score, Energy Star partners must make the commitment to (1) measure, track, and benchmark their energy performance; (2) develop and put in place a plan to improve their energy performance; and (3) teach the public, as well as staff, about this partnership and what is being achieved as an Energy Star partner.

Because the Mark Twain House and Museum was invested in sustainability and resource conservation, developing an energy management program was a logical next step for the museum. The Mark Twain property consists of several facilities with a range of sizes and ages. The 12,298 square foot Main House and the 4,935 square foot Carriage House were both built in 1874. Its 33,000 square foot Museum Center was built in 2003.

Among the strategies that the Mark Twain House and Museum employed were shutting off and unplugging equipment that was not being used, installing occupancy sensors in the Museum Center, adjusting the boiler and HVAC systems through recommissioning, and installing more efficient LED lamps in place of incandescent and halogen lamps. In 2009, just nine months after beginning to make adjustments based on benchmarking, the museum saw a reduction of 38 percent in their electricity and natural gas costs. In terms of power, this reduction was significant: the museum used 138 kBtu per square foot less than it used during the baseline period the year before. The Mark Twain House and Museum did not stop there. They continued to make plans for the next year, including installing LEDs in the historic house and exploring solar energy for the museum (Energy Star 2010). The Mark Twain House and Museum demonstrates how benchmarking—even when using a free program, like Energy Star—can help realize savings as well as environmental benefits.

With options ranging from the free, federal Energy Star program to the more specialized, fee-based IAMFA program, cultural facility managers have no shortage of ways to track and compare their facilities' data and practices to those of other facilities. It is important that each cultural institution takes time to truly evaluate their practices, ensuring that they are not doing things one way simply because that is how "things have always been done." By benchmarking along with other organizations with a similar mission or of a similar size, a museum can keep its FM practices current, while also sharing its knowledge and experiences with other cultural facilities organizations.

While the benefits of benchmarking are many, it is important to note one frequent downside of benchmarking: facility managers are often overwhelmed by the amount of data they receive. As a result, benchmarking reports may be left on a shelf, where they do not get put to use. For the benchmarking effort to be worth the work that is put into it, a clear plan for the resulting data to be studied, and, in turn, a timeline for changes to be implemented must be put in place. One helpful way to keep from forgetting about the benchmarking report is to implement an end-of-cycle reporting mechanism.

With end-of-cycle reporting, the facility manager repackages the facility's benchmarking information into mini-reports that make sense to different audiences in the institution. For example, he or she might put together a presentation for museum management that informs them of the key benchmarking findings and next actions, write a short summary for museum visitors and general staff that describes how the facility is performing in relation to other facilities and where improvements can be made, and post important benchmarking information for facility management staff to review in a highly visible location (Facility Issues 2011). By sharing benchmarking information and next steps with each of these audiences, facility managers ensure that everyone understands why their facilities are participating in benchmarking and what is being accomplished as a result of these efforts, while making themselves accountable for following through on their word. It is much harder to ignore the benchmarking report and delay implementation of next steps when so many other people have been informed and are now expecting specific goals to be met.

Staffing Cultural Facility Management Functions

The decision to develop an in-house staff, to outsource, or to combine both staffing strategies must ultimately support the facility's maintenance program and strategic plan. In addition to ensuring that the staffing plan supports the strategic plan, staffing decisions should take into account a number of other factors, including how staff is trained, staffing turnover rates, and institutional memory retention. These three factors are especially important in cultural institutions where resources are scarce and where providing the correct environmental conditions and levels of cleanliness is vital to the conservation of collections.

The Smithsonian's OFMR relies upon a primarily in-house facilities staff in order to care for the Smithsonian's specialized facilities and its collections.

As the former director of OFMR, Nancy Bechtol, put it, "After all, there is only one Hope Diamond and one pair of Ruby Slippers." She continued,

> As a result, I prefer to have in-house staff. When you hire people directly, they become dedicated to their buildings and know them like the back of their hands. Someone who has been part of our team for many years can sense something is wrong before it happens. They are sensitive to any changes in the building environment before they occur—and take corrective action quickly to minimize any potential damage. (*Facilities Engineering Journal* 2010)

Here, Bechtol, who is now director of the Smithsonian's Office of Facilities Engineering and Operations, illustrates one of the primary benefits of developing in-house maintenance staff: these employees have the ability to become intimately acquainted with their buildings over time. The Smithsonian invests in its in-house staff by providing intensive training and certification opportunities geared to developing the knowledge, skills, and abilities required to perform their jobs.

In-house facilities personnel offer a number of benefits to their organizations, including stability, flexibility, and added security and institutional knowledge. For example, in-house building service workers often accumulate more years of experience working in a particular facility than do their contracted peers. Over time, this constancy helps customers recognize who should be contacted in a given facilities situation. In-house employees also encourage a "sense of continuity and order," and this stability can help prevent mistakes and disorder that can result from a high turnover rate. In-house staff also amasses knowledge about their facility that is indispensable in terms of identifying, remedying, and preventing problems.

Among other benefits of in-house personnel is the sense of ownership and pride that these staff members can develop over time. In-house staff also have the opportunity to become invested in the institution's mission and identity over time. This allows these staff members to better reflect the organizational culture to the staff and visitors who come in contact with them as they clean and maintain the facilities. This appearance is particularly important in cultural institutions, as curious museum visitors often approach facility staff members to seek information or ask for assistance. Daily exposure to the facility also gives in-house staff the ability to notice when things are not quite right, and this adds to the safety and security of the facility. In the event of a facility emergency—like a flood or a last-minute special event—

BOX 5.6.

FACILITY MANAGER PROFILE: DAVID SAMEC, PE, CFM, CHIEF OF FACILITIES MANAGEMENT, NATIONAL GALLERY OF ART, WASHINGTON, DC

"All facilities need to be cleaned, and monumental museums, such as the National Gallery of Art in Washington, DC [above], take a significant facilities work effort."

Number of years in facility management (FM) for a cultural facility:
   16 years as a facility manager in Washington, DC.

Facilities managed and their ages:
   East Building, 35 years old; West Building, 72 years old.

Favorite aspect of being a facility manager in a cultural facility:
   "My favorite aspect is the daily closeness to historically significant art and artifacts. Additionally, most cultural institutions rotate collections and exhibits, thereby making this 'perk' even more dynamic. I enjoy the satisfaction that I am helping to conserve American treasures to the best possible standards available so they will be preserved for generations to come."

Most challenging experience as a facility manager in a cultural facility:

"In January 2012 I was involved with providing the exact environmental conditions needed to preserve precious international art that came to the United States and the National Gallery of Art for public display. Through that experience, I learned: Never assume anything. Build in contingencies and se-quels to your plans. Rehearse with your staff."

Most important advice for facility managers making the transition into working for a museum or cultural institution:

"At some point, even the best FMs have to be hands on in order to get the job done: the sooner in their careers, the better. This may mean starting off in a 'trades' job. Even home project 'do-it-yourselfers' gain a better understanding of what it takes to get facility work done. It takes time and practice to develop people skills as well, so starting out in small teams is a good way to learn. FMs who think they can jump right out of college and into 6-figure salary jobs will have an extremely difficult time in this business. They will eventually be foiled by their own staff if they try to take over all FM operations at their facility. Com-petition is tough for FM jobs today, especially in cultural institutions, where you are protecting priceless art. You have to know all of the FM core competencies [see box 2.1] very well. There is no room for failure."

Source: Samec (2012). Photo by David Samec, 2012.

in-house staff can provide support that contracted personnel who also serve other facilities may not have the insights or flexibility to provide. (See box 5.6 for a profile of David Samec, the in-house chief of facilities management at the National Gallery of Art in Washington, DC.)

While the benefits of cultivating an in-house facilities staff are many, outsourcing can be beneficial as well. For example, contracting for facility services, such as cleaning, is often less expensive than providing these ser-vices in-house. In addition, contractors often can adjust staffing numbers more easily than can in-house staff. Outsourcing is also seen as a way to leave more time for on-site staff to focus on the core mission of the orga-nization (Bigger and Bigger 2007).

The decision to outsource is sometimes driven by the desire to improve quality. According to a 2006 IFMA survey, one-third of organizations that outsourced facility work saw an improvement in quality. Outsourcing also means that personnel issues, like payroll processing, labor relations, time keeping, and disciplinary actions, can be taken care of by the contractor. Likewise, often-expensive employee benefits that may have to be paid on behalf of in-house staff do not have to be accounted for when outsourcing the duties. Contractors may also be able to provide specialty services and technologies that in-house operations are unable to provide. In addition, contractors are often able to provide training for their staff that in-house operations simply cannot afford.

Many organizations do not have exclusively in-house or exclusively outsourced facility operations; instead, these organizations out-task certain specialized needs while retaining others in-house. As an example, in-house staff could complete day-to-day cleaning operations, while tasks like window cleaning and carpet cleaning are contracted out to specialists (Bigger and Bigger 2007). That said, before deciding what to provide in-house and what to outsource, it is important to determine the types of expertise that are needed.

To evaluate how the different staffing strategies—in-house, outsourced, and out-tasked—meet the needs of the facility, Guy Larocque, former president of the IAMFA, suggests using a weighted evaluation table like the one found in box 5.7 (Larocque 2006–2007). This evaluation table helps compare how different staffing strategies might perform with respect to the factors that are identified as important for the facility. This table can be used as a decision-making tool, as well as a way to justify staffing decisions to museum management.

Ultimately, if the facility manager is leaning toward outsourcing any of the facility's functions, it is crucial to keep a number of managerial, human resource, and business issues in mind when navigating the outsourcing process. For example, it is important to retain adequate in-house staff to manage facility-related contracts. These in-house staff members should understand the intricacies of the museum's mission, environmental needs, and preferences and, in turn, help get the most out of each contract. By extension, the facility's strategic plan, policies, standards, and procedures should also remain under the control of in-house staff. This will ensure that the cultural institution's facility is maintained in a way that is truly reflective of its strategic plan and specialized mission.

When negotiating each contract for facility work that will be outsourced, there are a number of rights that should be reserved on behalf of the cultural

BOX 5.7.

SAMPLE EVALUATION OF FACILITY MANAGEMENT STAFFING OPTIONS USING WEIGHTING FACTORS

One way to weigh staffing options is by using an evaluation table. To do this, former International Association of Museum Facility Administrators (IAMFA) President Guy Larocque suggests that cultural facilities identify a list of factors that will be affected by whether the facility has an outsourced, in-house, or hybrid (both in-house and outsourced) facilities staff. Larocque cautions that the factors chosen will be different for each cultural facility, depending on its budget, strategic plan, and other unique circumstances.

The below table is an example of Larocque's weighting system, and the factors used are not necessarily applicable to all institutions. Note that each factor is rated on a scale from 1 to 10, in terms of how favorably it will be affected by an outsourced, in-house, or hybrid staffing plan, with 1 being least favorable and 10 being most favorable. Each factor's score is then weighted in terms of its relative importance, or weighting factor. This system helps when comparing different staffing strategies, because it reveals strong and weak points of each staffing method in terms of the factors that are important to a particular facility. After tallying the weighted scores for each staffing plan, these total scores can be compared side by side in terms of their overall expected benefit.

Sample Factor	Weighting Factor	Totally Outsourced	Totally In-House	Hybrid Out/In
Value for money	25%			
Corporate memory retention	10%			
Core business	10%			
Complementary to organizational structure	20%			
Human resources management	10%			
Turnover rates	10%			
Eliminate duplication	15%			
Total scores	100%			

Source: Larocque (Fall/Winter 2006–2007). "Is Outsourcing Right for Your Organization?" *Papyrus: A publication of the International Association of Museum Facility Administrators* (8)1: 16. Available at www.iamfa.org.

institution. For example, the cultural institution should reserve the right to overrule the contractor's choice of staff. The institution should consider reserving the right to solicit bids for any additional facility-related work that arises in the facility. It is also important that the cultural institution develops a contingency plan, should the contract need to be terminated.

While the contract is in place, the contractor's performance should be benchmarked against the performance of similar operations at other facilities, just like when performance is benchmarked for operations and maintenance tasks performed by an in-house staff. The contractor should be expected to improve its performance over time, and an in-house facility manager can track performance and encourage this improvement. During regularly scheduled meetings, performance should be reviewed with the contractor. During these meetings is also a good time to ask if the contractor can suggest any adjustments for the facility's operations and maintenance plan that may reduce costs and/or lessen the environmental impact of the facility. Facility managers can and should build collaborative relationships with their service providers. This relationship helps the service providers become truly invested in finding the best solutions for the unique facilities they serve.

It is also important that a relationship be cultivated between the service provider and cultural institution staff and visitors. Even though the cultural institution does not formally employ them, contracted workers are still seen by visitors as representatives of the institution. These workers should be kind, courteous, and professional in their interactions with staff and guests and be able to direct visitors toward finding answers to their questions about the museum. Visitors do not know—or necessarily care—whether a museum worker is an in-house staff member or if they are contracted. What guests will remember, however, is whether representatives of the museum treat them helpfully and respectfully during their visit, and contractors count among these representatives.

A recent visit to a prominent Washington, DC, cultural institution illustrates the importance of proper contractor–guest interaction. During the visit, an elevator was shared with a security contractor who had been detailed to the museum. Rather than engaging the guests in the elevator and asking about their visit, the contractor told crude jokes. In doing so, the image he projected was not in line with the professionalism of the museum's own mission. This scenario reinforces the importance of contractors receiving the same guest relations training and education about the museum's mission that in-house staff receives.

Summary

Operations and maintenance are essential elements to consider when planning for the future of each cultural institution facility. By taking into consideration, for example, how maintenance will be carried out for each valuable asset in the facility, how the facility will be cleaned, and how these processes will be documented and evaluated, the facility manager contributes not only to maintaining and operating the facility but also to the safety of the museum's collections, the well-being of staff, and the exceptional experience of visitors.

CHAPTER SIX

CAPITAL IMPROVEMENT PLANNING
AND IMPLEMENTATION

The design of buildings requires the integration of many kinds of information into an elegant, useful, and durable whole. . . . The best buildings result from continual, organized collaboration among all players.

—*Whole Building Design Guide* (2012)

Careful capital improvement planning and implementation are important in cultural institutions, where the facilities must be operated efficiently while also meeting the needs of staff, visitors, and collections. To ensure that these needs are met, capital costs, the onetime costs related to purchasing a site and constructing a facility or updating a preexisting facility, must be carefully estimated and planned for (Crimm et al. 2009). Whether the capital improvements under consideration entail the construction of an entirely new facility or investing in a new heating, ventilation, and air-conditioning (HVAC) system, integrating the facility manager's perspective into the capital project planning, implementation, and evaluation processes helps to ensure that the museum's new or updated facility can be operated efficiently and reliably—and within the organization's budget. On the other hand, if facility management–related considerations are not taken into account, the resulting facility may be prohibitively expensive to operate and maintain, causing problems that reverberate throughout the institution for years to come.

This chapter describes the cultural facility manager's role during the capital program planning and implementation stages. Further, this chapter discusses why it is essential to include a facility management perspective during the planning process, as not doing so can result in negative consequences and added costs once the program is complete. In addition to covering the facility manager's role in the process, this chapter includes several examples that demonstrate lessons learned in past capital projects at cultural institutions.

Cultural Facility Capital Improvement Planning Basics

As missions evolve, collections grow, and facilities age, capital projects are unavoidable for many cultural institutions. When the need for capital improvements is identified, it is important that a planning team be carefully assembled and that programming requirements be clearly outlined. In addition, a competent contractor must be identified who can complete the work on time and within the museum's budget. The quality of any work performed must also be verified throughout the capital improvement process.

That said, capital projects are not always the most worthwhile investments, especially when energy savings is the primary goal of the project. For example, capital projects can take a year or more to implement, whereas simply adjusting operations and maintenance practices can yield instant payback in terms of energy savings (Sullivan et al. 2010). Prior to investing in a capital improvement, especially those focused in increasing energy efficiency, a cultural institution should make attempts to evaluate and adjust its practices.

Forming a Capital Improvement Planning Team

Large and complex capital improvement projects must be planned and implemented with an eye toward ensuring that the museum is able to carry out its mission, taking into account such factors as keeping collections in good condition, enabling staff to effectively perform their work, and enhancing visitors' experiences. Because of the diverse array of stakeholders—collections, staff, and visitors—in the museum environment, it is important that capital improvements are planned by a team that includes members of in-house personnel, as well as the outside experts necessary to complete the project to the highest standards possible within the given time and budgetary constraints.

Though planning teams should always include a variety of unique perspectives, their composition and size will vary, depending on the scale of each capital improvement project. For example, some teams may include the museum director, project manager, owner's representative (construction manager), and leaders of subteams related to the building and museum, as well as a cost consultant (Lord et al. 2012) and commissioning agent. If the capital improvement project is very large—for example, if it involves constructing a new facility for the cultural institution—the planning team may consider forming a number of working groups dedicated to addressing collections, operations, exhibitions and programming, development and public relations, sustainability, and community outreach concerns related to the new facility (Crimm et al. 2009).

No matter the scale of a capital improvement project, the cultural institution's facility manager should be involved in the planning process to some degree. The facility manager's perspective is invaluable in terms of informing the design team about the practical considerations that will arise once the facility is occupied. For example, at one prominent cultural institution in Washington, DC, a recent multimillion-dollar renovation specified glass and stainless steel, which has since caused countless headaches for the building service workers who struggle to keep up with the fingerprints left by the thousands of school children—and adults—on these easily fingerprinted surfaces. Involving the facility manager and building service workers in the planning process could have helped to avoid the additional work caused by using these particular surfaces in such high-traffic areas. As Cotts et al. say, "[T]he facility manager must live with and operate the building long after the design firm has moved on" (2010, pp. 226–227), so he or she will make crucial contributions to the planning team.

In addition to identified steering-team members, capital improvement projects frequently require a dedicated project manager who is responsible for shepherding the project through each phase of completion. Because the museum's facility manager is familiar with the museum's unique mission-related requirements and how these requirements are supported by the facility, he or she is likely a good project manager. However, if the facility manager does not have sufficient time to dedicate to a particularly large capital improvement project, it may be necessary to identify another member of the museum's staff or, alternatively, hire someone from outside the museum to manage the project. In any case, it is necessary for the project manager to have a thorough comprehension of the museum's operations, and some experience with design and construction is also desirable (Crimm et al. 2009).

Planning for Future Facility Requirements

As discussed in chapter 3, cultural institution strategic plans should be supported by a facility management strategic plan. The facility management strategic plan outlines specific goals and objectives of the cultural institution's facility management organization, and it can be supplemented by a facility strategy or functional program. The facility strategy or functional program is a more specific document than the strategic plan and presents the spatial, technical, and budgetary requirements for facilities that support the cultural institution's mission. For example, if capital improvements are planned, the facility strategy document might describe the specific facility planning goals, principles, and assumptions.

The plan's goals, which are likely developed by the planning team, describe what the museum expects the facility to achieve in relation to the institution's mission, vision, long-term expectations, and other desirable outcomes. As the capital improvement planning process progresses, the planning team identifies its preferred planning principles, such as accrediting organizations' standards like those of the American Alliance of Museums; the preferred level of sustainable performance; and programmatic expectations. In turn, the planning assumptions can be researched and refined until they realistically represent the concrete requirements of the facility. Planning assumptions identify the facility's size, the types and sizes of events it must accommodate, the number of years the facility is reasonably expected to meet the needs of the institution, the daily occupancy of the institution, and the dimensions of the biggest collection objects that are expected to be moved within the facility, among other critical requirements of the facility (Lord et al. 2012).

Opportunities in Cultural Institution Capital Planning

As discussed earlier, one of the primary challenges of managing cultural institution facilities is meeting the rigorous temperature and humidity requirements necessary to create the ideal environment for collections. Museums often have the opportunity to address concerns related to temperature and humidity through capital projects—via either new construction or updates to their existing facilities. In either case, it is crucial that the planning team look for ways to achieve these exacting environmental conditions while ensuring that the museum facility can be operated and maintained within a reasonable budget.

While a great deal of emphasis is often placed on specifying the correct mechanical system, the building itself is often the determining factor when it comes to maintaining the desired environmental conditions and achieving energy efficiency. For example, how the building is oriented on its site and the quality of its envelope are both features that affect performance. Completed in 2012, the Barnes Foundation's Philadelphia, Pennsylvania, campus was designed and engineered to be efficient and to create the conditions necessary to preserve Impressionist and Early Modern paintings. By employing several strategies required to create an airtight envelope, such as precisely detailing the connections between windows and walls and using air and vapor barriers, the design team significantly reduced the likelihood that outside air and moisture would seep into the facility and vice versa (Gonchar 2012).

In addition to taking into account how careful design and construction can help achieve a museum's exacting environmental conditions, capital planning needs to consider how decisions made during design and construction will affect the operation of the facility during its useful life. As an example, the Taubman Museum of Art (TMA) in Richmond, Virginia, was completed in 2008 at a cost of $66 million. In November 2010, just two years after opening the doors of its new facility, the TMA was in the news because it was facing a financial crisis. While the museum brought in $119,000 in admission fees each year, it cost *over* $871,000 to maintain its new facility annually. At the time, its executive director, David Mickenburg, felt that, in hindsight, the facility should be smaller and some of the funds used during construction should have been saved.

In addition to addressing collections, museum programming, and staff requirements, many cultural institutions must also tackle other important issues, such as sustainability, mandated Americans with Disabilities Act (ADA) upgrades, and historic preservation strategies through capital improvement projects. Each of these issues is of concern to the institution's facility manager, and he or she should be engaged as they are considered.

Sustainable Capital Improvement Practices

The Taubman Museum of Art example illustrates the significant expense that maintenance costs can represent if care is not taken to minimize the impact of these costs during the design stages. While the design and construction phases of a museum capture a great deal of attention with the excitement that comes along with a new facility, in actuality, over a 30-year period, construction costs account for only 2 percent of the facility's total costs. By contrast, operations and maintenance costs account for 6 percent, and the remaining 92 percent of costs are attributable to personnel costs.

To help reduce the expense of operations and maintenance over the life of the facility and its equipment, capital improvement decision making can be aided by performing lifecycle cost analyses (LCCAs). An LCCA takes into account the cost of a project or piece of equipment from cradle to grave—the cost of its purchase, the costs of ownership, and the cost of disposal. More specifically, costs that may be considered in a LCCA include purchase costs; fuel costs; operation, maintenance, and repair costs; replacement costs; finance charges; residual values, such as resale or salvage values; and any nonmonetary benefits or costs (Fuller 2010).

Members of a capital improvement planning team, especially the facility manager, should familiarize themselves with the steps required to perform LCCAs. Several introductions to LCCAs are available for free online. For example, the National Institute of Building Sciences provides detailed information about performing LCCAs in its *Whole Building Design Guide* (Fuller 2010). The U.S. Federal Energy Management Program has made information about conducting LCCAs available for free online at www.energy.gov/femp.

While LCCAs can influence design and purchasing decisions, a cultural institution should also use a holistic lifecycle management approach throughout the life of the facility. For example, the Smithsonian Institution's facilities are managed using a lifecycle management approach. Each of the Smithsonian's buildings is considered in terms of three phases: "Phase 1," Design and Construction; "Phase 2," Operation and Maintenance; and "Phase 3," Capital Asset Management. The final two phases can be thought of as the "stewardship phases," in which the building is kept in good condition through preventive and corrective maintenance (Smithsonian Institution 2010). See chapter 5 for more information about implementing an operations and maintenance plan that ensures the stewardship of the cultural institution facility.

The LCCA is one very important component of sustainable capital improvement planning, and other sustainable planning practices are discussed in chapter 7. Capital improvement planning provides a valuable opportunity for cultural institutions to integrate energy-saving and water-saving elements into their facilities, pursue strategies that improve the health and satisfaction of occupants, and reduce waste production in the facility for years to come. For example, the William J. Clinton Presidential Library in Little Rock, Arkansas, engaged a number of sustainable strategies when completing its facility. The Clinton Library includes a green roof that lessens storm water runoff, reduces the heat island effect, and contributes to energy efficiency and clean air, among other benefits. It also has over 300 solar panels that help power the building, and has glass and screens that lessen solar heat gain by 50 percent. Cultural institution facilities that invest in LCCA and pursue sustainable practices during the capital planning process can benefit people, the planet, and their organizations' bottom lines for years to come.

The Americans with Disabilities Act (ADA) and Universal Design Considerations

Disabilities are physical or mental impairments that affect "one or more major life activities," like seeing, hearing, or mobility (Cornell University 2013, p. 7). In 1990, the U.S. Congress enacted the ADA prohibiting discrimination on the basis of a person's disability. The passage of the ADA means that cultural institutions in the United States have a legal mandate to invest in upgrades that make their facilities more accessible to those with disabilities. Because each cultural institution has a unique mission, each facility will require very specific adjustments in order for its special events, exhibits, and programming to be made equally accessible to those with disabilities.

The American Alliance of Museums (AAM) suggests several steps that can be taken to cultivate an accessible museum environment. Crucial to capital improvement planning, the AAM recommends that a museum's facilities and programs are reviewed in order to identify existing obstacles to accessibility, and, in turn, short- and long-term plans should be made to address issues that are identified. In addition, by making an explicit commitment to accessibility in the museum's mission statement, appointing an accessibility coordinator, and getting feedback from persons with disabilities, the museum demonstrates its commitment to accessibility while making possible meaningful changes to its environment. Staff should be trained with respect to accessibility issues, ADA requirements, and reasonable accommodations. The museum should also advertise its accessibility and provide contact information for its accessibility coordinator to ensure that persons with disabilities feel welcome in the facility. A grievance process should be identified so that staff knows how to address any conflicts with the promotion of accessibility. Finally, all efforts to make the museum more accessible should be continually reviewed and adjusted (Salmen 1998).

When capital improvement projects have the potential to affect facility occupants, it is important for the planning team to take ADA requirements into account throughout the planning process. To help institutions understand how the law applies to their facilities, the U.S. Department of Justice (DOJ) and Department of Transportation (DOT) established ADA Standards, which are periodically updated. The specific DOJ and DOT regulations and design standards that apply to nonprofits are published online at www.ada.gov. In addition to federal laws, cultural institutions must also take into account state and local laws and codes pertaining to making accommodations for those with disabilities.

In addition to taking ADA requirements into account, many cultural institutions now utilize a universal design philosophy when planning their facilities. Whereas the emphasis of ADA is on making facilities accessible to those with disabilities, universal design strives to place "the entire range of human capability . . . at the heart of the design process" (Zimmerman 2006). In essence, universal design works to make spaces that account for each stage of people's lives and a range of human abilities, without making anyone feel like they are being treated differently from everyone else simply because their abilities differ. In other words, environments in which universal design is applied do not require special adaptations in order to be made accessible—they are accessible to all.

Applying universal design principles to cultural institutions makes good sense, because they are often visited by a diverse range of guests throughout each year. In their *Manual of Museum Planning* (2012), Lord et al. make a passionate call for the application of universal design in museum planning:

> The extent and scope of universal design ranges across the museum planning process from spatial layout and physical configuration of spaces to issues such as ensuring adequate access to learning in the museum environment and the perceptibility and legibility of museum graphics. As well as ensuring access and capacity for the universal spectrum of potential patrons, it is also universal in its scope and range of application—virtually no portion of the museum planning process can afford to ignore universal design, and its integration from the initiation of the planning process is of vital concern. (p. 154)

What types of issues might be considered when taking a universal design approach? To help answer this question, the Center for Universal Design (CUD) at North Carolina State University developed a list of seven universal design principles that should be sought: (1) equitable use, (2) flexibility in use, (3) simple and intuitive, (4) perceptible information, (5) tolerance for error, (6) low physical effort, and (7) size and space for approach and use (Center for Universal Design 1997).

Providing family restrooms is an example of how these universal design strategies can be applied. Clearly marked family restrooms make it possible for adults and children who require assistance in the restroom to have the space necessary for them to be safe and comfortable, while also achieving a degree of privacy. Elements as small as hand dryers can also be considered from a universal design perspective to ensure that they are located in places that serve a variety of people (Zimmerman 2006).

Professional associations, such as the American Alliance of Museums, the Association of Zoos and Aquariums, the International Association of Museum Facility Administrators, and the Museums/Cultural Institutions Council of IFMA, also provide networking opportunities for museum professionals to learn how other cultural institutions integrate universal design principles and address ADA requirements in their facilities. In addition to networking and referencing the CUD principles and ADA requirements, see Lord et al.'s (2010) detailed suggestions for accessibility; these suggestions relate to physical design, control and operations, lighting, way finding, and other essential aspects of museum environments, including restrooms, ramps, and elevators, and they are a valuable resource for cultural institution planning teams (pp. 163–186).

Capital Improvements to Historic Properties

Frequently, cultural institutions are housed in existing buildings, and, sometimes, these buildings have unique historic preservation requirements. If the building has been identified as historic, facility managers and capital improvement planning teams have the opportunity to preserve the building's history and authenticity while also updating the building to enhance its systems, life safety and security capabilities, and accessibility. How carefully these updates are pursued will ultimately determine the success of a historic preservation project (Historic Preservation Subcommittee [HPS] 2012).

The U.S. Secretary of the Interior (SOI) outlines four ways that historic buildings can be treated—*preservation*, *rehabilitation*, *restoration*, and *reconstruction*—in its "Standards for the Treatment of Historic Properties" (National Park Service [NPS] 1995). *Preservation* entails repairing and maintaining the historic property, whereas *rehabilitation* entails making changes or additions to a historic property while keeping its original character. *Restoration* means returning the historic property to a condition that reflects a particular time period, and *reconstruction* entails recreating parts of a historic building that no longer exist. These treatments are not necessarily carried out one at a time—it is certainly possible for them to be combined and completed during one capital project (HPS 2012). For an example of a rehabilitation project at the Library of Parliament in Ottawa, see box 6.1.

When addressing capital improvement projects in historic facilities, the planning team should include at least one historic preservation professional. To help with selecting a historic preservation professional, the SOI's "Professional Qualification Standards," available online, identify baseline criteria for qualified candidates (NPS 2013). Just as capital improvement projects for nonhistoric buildings involve a facility strategy, treatment of historic properties requires a treatment plan. The treatment plan will identify the type of treatment appropriate for the property, as well as how the property will need to be adjusted in order to meet the mission of the cultural institution. The facility and its site should be assessed in order to identify the building's historic "character-defining features and qualities." Normally, the planning team should work to keep the architecture in its original form, and a list of preservation priorities should be developed before work begins on the historic facility project (HPS 2012).

The Role of Cultural Institution Facility Management in Capital Planning

As discussed earlier, cultural institution facility managers should be involved in the capital planning and implementation process. Sometimes, they are involved as members of planning teams, and, other times, they are solely responsible for identifying and managing multiyear capital programs. In either case, the facility manager will be responsible for pulling together critical information that informs decision making related to the project. Among the information the facility manager can bring to the table is the midrange facility plan, the annual work plan, sustainability policies,

BOX 6.1.

THE LIBRARY OF PARLIAMENT— READY FOR A NEW GENERATION

The Library of Parliament building in Ottawa is the only remaining part of Canada's original Parliament building—the only part of the Centre Block to have survived the devastating fire of 1916. Although joined to the Centre Block, the Library was saved by a quick-thinking librarian who closed the iron doors separating the two buildings.

A considerable measure of the Library building's heritage value resides in its continued operation as the Library of the Parliament of Canada. Public Works and Government Services Canada (PWGSC) is leading a major rehabilitation project to ensure that the significance and importance of the Library building is protected for future generations.

From the outset of planning in 1995, to the day in 2006 when the last books [were] expected to be returned to the Library's shelves, the challenge has been finding solutions which respect and enhance this historic asset, while meeting the requirements of those who use it. This effort takes in not only the Library's vast and valuable collections and its commitment to service, but also its desire to improve the visitor experience for the more than 400,000 people who take guided tours of the Centre Block each year.

Building for the Future

Due to the building's large, open configuration, undertaking any extensive interior work requires that the Library's assets and staff be relocated while the work is carried out. Temporarily moving the Library to an alternative location is an expensive and disruptive proposition. Likewise, major work on a historical building can be both hard on the structure and intrusive. However the Library building has not actually undergone any major work since it suffered its own fire and water damage in 1952—when it required the most extensive repairs undertaken since its completion in 1876.

Our approach to the conservation, rehabilitation and upgrade of the Library of Parliament is a long-term investment, expected to last at least 50 years or more. This means a focus on the basics, and on quality craftsmanship. It also means taking advantage of a rare opportunity to restore a national architectural treasure, and entails taking the time to put comprehensive yet flexible planning in place. Above all, it means having the determination to ensure that the job is completed before the deterioration becomes irreversible.

Starting with a Solid Foundation

Our first priority was to look after the structure and the building envelope: masonry stabilization, seismic reinforcement of the historic iron dome, window repair and upgrading, roof rebuilding, waterproofing of the foundation, improving energy efficiency and weather-tightness, and addressing code compliance. An equally important but parallel priority was to look after the Library's requirements, its valuable collections, and its vision for the future. A high standard of technical expertise was required from the designers, and a high quality of workmanship was required of all contractors. Pre-qualification of sub-trades was used for a number of the specialties; for example, wood, masonry and ironwork conservation, and plaster repairs. For many aspects of the job, mock-ups were required before work was allowed to proceed.

As work progressed, we remained in awe of the craftsmanship that had gone before us, and were reassured that our careful approach was justified. The Gothic detail, and the beauty and variety of the stonework, woodwork, ironwork and plaster carvings were inspiring. Contemplating the sheer act of building such a complex structure with its 16 bays, thick stone walls, flying buttresses and huge pre-fabricated iron dome—particularly without the benefit of modern technology—is humbling. It is easy to understand why it took 17 years to build the original Library. We also set, and are exceeding, high standards for responsible construction. Over 80 percent of construction waste was being diverted from landfill. New materials are low in off-gassing, low in maintenance, and are durable.

Adopting a Practical Conservation Approach

The conservation strategy which guides the work was developed by the project architects—a joint venture of four architectural firms: Ogilvie and Hogg (Ottawa), Desnoyers Mercure et associés (Montreal), Spencer Higgins (Toronto) and Lundholm Associates (Toronto). The approach, which they named "Layers of History," was endorsed by the project team because it respects the work that has gone before, but adds our own generation's new layer.

This is not a period restoration, but a minimal intervention within the confines of the other project objectives, including the not-insignificant demands of asset longevity and of the Library's essential operations.

Source: This is an excerpt from an article that originally appeared in Soper, Mary F. (Spring 2005). "The Library of Parliament—Ready for a New Generation." *Papyrus: A publication of the International Association of Museum Facility Administrators* (6)1: 1–4. Available at www.iamfa.org.

and data pertaining to recently completed projects (Cotts et al. 2010). In order for this information to be available to support capital planning, it is important that it be kept current.

Identifying, Prioritizing, and Budgeting for Capital Improvements to Facility Assets

When the cultural institution facility manager is solely responsible for tracking the condition of key facility assets, including the building's roof, HVAC systems, and envelope, he or she must have a clear process for identifying capital improvements, calculating the projected costs of these improvements, and prioritizing the improvements by using the cultural institution's objectives. The facility manager should also explore the effects of various spending levels for required improvements. Then, taking into account the projected costs and timeline for these improvements, the facility manager can develop a capital plan and accompanying budget that illustrates to the institution's director, board, and other key stakeholders the value and criticality of these improvements.

Facility managers can employ a seven-step process for planning and managing upgrades to capital assets. Defined by VFA, a facilities capital planning consulting firm, seven steps to consider are as follows:

- Define the process.

- Gather data.

- Analyze benchmarks.

- Prioritize capital projects.

- Demonstrate impact of funding.

- Create defensible budgets.

- Develop process for continuous update. (VFA 2011)

In the first step, "define the process," the facility manager and his or her team identify strategic organizational goals relevant to the future of the organization and its facilities, as well as applicable metrics that can be used to track progress toward achieving these goals. The second step, "gather data," involves conducting a facility condition assessment (FCA) through a series of walk-through inspections conducted by qualified engineers or in-house staff in order to gather baseline data. The data gathered during this step include information about the age, size, location, and type of construction of the facility; the condition of the facility's assets, including its HVAC, roof, and exterior; code violations and critical systems; and other assorted data that are not related to the facility's condition but that may affect the institution, such as risk and programmatic concerns.

The third step, "analyze benchmarks," takes the data gathered during the facility condition assessment and translates them into a Facility Condition Index (FCI) so they can be benchmarked alongside the data of other, comparable facilities. As discussed in chapter 5, the FCI is the ratio of the cost of repairing deficient assets to the cost of replacing them (VFA 2011). Facilities with an overall FCI between 0 and 5 percent are normally considered to be in "Good" condition, while an FCI between 5 and 10 percent indicates "Fair" condition, and an FCI between 10 and 30 percent indicates "Poor" condition. Facilities with an FCI greater than 30 percent are in "Critical" condition (International Facility Management Association [IFMA] 2013). By comparing the cultural institution facility's FCI to those of other facilities, a minimum condition standard can be set for the facility, and the planning team can begin prioritizing capital projects to achieve this standard.

The fourth step, "prioritize capital projects," normally involves placing capital projects into categories, such as projects mandated in order to comply with regulations, significant operations and maintenance projects, and projects that fulfill strategic initiatives, such as new buildings. Each project should then be weighted in terms of its relationship to the institution's goals, and, after all projects are weighted, they should be prioritized in terms of their overall ranking. The fifth step, "demonstrate impact of funding," requires that the facility management team shows how different levels of funding for capital projects will affect the condition of a facility over time. For example, the funding analysis could depict how three different funding scenarios might affect the facility's FCI over a hypothetical 30-year period. The sixth step, "create defensible budgets," combines the project rankings compiled in the fourth step and the funding impacts from the fifth step in order to budget for capital expenditures over the following years.

The seventh and final step, "develop process for continuous update," codifies the process for maintaining, updating, and storing facility-related data, as well as a timeline for completing subsequent facility condition assessments. It is considered a best practice to gather data and assess an organization's facility portfolio in its entirety every four years, with 25 percent of the total assessment performed each year. In addition, the goals identified in step 1 may change over time, so it is important to continually update the way that capital projects are weighted and prioritized in accordance with evolving organizational goals (VFA 2011).

The VFA method represents just one approach to strategic facilities planning. Prior to beginning the planning process, it is valuable for cultural institution facility managers and capital improvement planning teams to explore the range of planning strategies available before settling on just one. For an example of another approach to the strategic facility planning process, see "Strategic Facility Planning: A White Paper" (Roper et al. 2009), published by the International Facility Management Association.

Capital Planning That Supports Facility Management

How capital improvements affect the functionality of the facility management team should be considered during the planning process of new museum facilities. For example, maintenance staff must be given the space necessary for them to access and perform work within mechanical rooms, and sufficient space needs to be allocated for the collection and easy pickup of recycling and garbage. Existing automated building management systems need to be integrated into any new additions to the facility.

Dedicated staff and storage spaces that support facility management must be provided. Facility renovations or plans for new facilities need to include a facility management office for the facility manager and space for his or her administrative staff. This office should have a conference room and enough storage for all of the hard-copy documents related to the facility, including as-built drawings, emergency plans, and other important documents. Cultural institutions that have in-house engineers will also require an engineers' office. Additionally, if the institution's facility management team is large enough, they may need their own locker room and break room.

In terms of storage and work areas, the facility management team may require a machine shop with enough space to organize supplies and safety equipment, as well as in-house paint and carpentry shops. A lamp room that provides sufficient storage for the facility's stock of replacement lamps, as well as the tools necessary to replace them, is also helpful, as is storage for air-handling unit filters. Building service workers and staff who care for the institution's landscaping will require their own storage spaces, and these spaces may need to be rather large to accommodate *all* of the supplies and equipment necessary to perform tasks like buffing or waxing floors, removing snow, and cleaning restrooms (Lord et al. 2012).

Careful planning of capital projects can also contribute to higher levels of cleanliness and ease of maintenance. For example, at a cultural institution facility in Washington, DC, an inaccessible, large flat surface has continually collected dust since the facility's opening. Because this surface is not easily accessible, it is unable to be cleaned with regularity, yet it is visible to the public and very noticeable as people descend the museum's grand staircase. Other institutions' facility management teams experience difficulties like changing light bulbs that are positioned in very hard-to-reach places, cleaning surfaces that show fingerprints very easily yet are prone to being touched, and cleaning textured fixtures that collect dust and grime deep within their grooves. Integrating cultural facility management team members into the design process will help to ensure that the cultural institution facility can be kept at the level of cleanliness preferred by the institution.

Design-Build-Operate-Maintain (DBOM)

When it is time for a cultural institution to select an architect and construction firm, the institution may want to consider a firm that specializes in the DBOM delivery system. When design and construction teams work collaboratively on a project, it is referred to as a design-build delivery system. Projects delivered using design-build are able to incorporate feedback from the construction team into the design in a way that often enhances the project's outcome. By extension, a DBOM system introduces an operations and maintenance perspective to a project's design process. Within DBOM, members of the design, construction, and facility management teams have the opportunity to develop a collaborative relationship that informs and respects the interests of each party. The result of an integrated DBOM delivery system is often a facility that is maintained in a way that reflects the designer's original intent and that operates more efficiently and effectively over its useful lifetime.

DBOM teams are normally a joint venture between a design-build firm and a firm that handles building operations. This DBOM partnership, in turn, enters into a contract with the building owner that guarantees the performance of the building, generally for a period ranging between 10 and 15 years. The costs to operate and maintain the facility during this period are determined at the outset of the project and outlined in the contract, and the design team must specify systems that are able to perform without exceeding this preset budget. If the building's maintenance and operations costs exceed the costs identified in the contract, the DBOM partnership is responsible for these excess costs. Contractual obligation motivates the DBOM team to make careful decisions during the design process in order to reduce maintenance and operations costs.

While DBOM has many advantages, including increased sustainability, lower long-term operating costs, and enhanced quality, several disadvantages are worth considering. For example, the cultural institution may not be able to provide as much input as it desires during both the design and operation of the facility (Dahl et al. 2005). In addition, because it is packaged into the DBOM contract, the operations and maintenance of the facility are outsourced. As discussed in chapter 5, outsourcing operations and maintenance staffing may not be desirable for cultural institutions that prefer the stability, flexibility, and institutional knowledge of in-house staff. Additionally, the cultural institution may want to keep a facility manager in-house to manage the operations and maintenance aspects of the DBOM contract, oversee facility-related issues not covered by the contract, and implement museum sustainability initiatives. For a brief discussion of the importance of considering O&M costs within the framework of capital planning, see box 6.2.

Evaluation and Certification of Capital Improvement Projects

Capital improvement projects can be evaluated in stages through commissioning evaluations, which evaluate a project throughout its planning and early completion phases, and postoccupancy evaluations (POEs), which are conducted after the facility is occupied. For example, the U.S. General Services Administration (GSA) performs commissioning of its facilities during planning and until tenants occupy the facilities. The GSA's POEs then take place between six months and two years after the tenants have begun their occupancy (GSA 2013). In addition to commissioning and postoccupancy evaluations, cultural institutions can also pursue certifications that verify that their facilities are performing to the rigorous standards established by the certifying party.

BOX 6.2.

O&M COST CONSIDERATIONS FOR CAPITAL PROJECTS

Above: The Barnes Foundation's Philadelphia, Pennsylvania, campus. This building was designed with an airtight envelope in mind through strategies such as precisely detailing the connections between windows and walls and using air and vapor barriers. The design team significantly reduced the likelihood that outside air and moisture would seep into the facility and vice versa.

Capital projects are physical improvements to systematically acquire, construct, replace, upgrade, and/or rehabilitate the built environment and associated assets, including systems. While these improvements include the planning, design, and construction of specific projects, it is also very important to include the critical aspect of operations and maintenance (O&M) costs when considering a capital project. These costs are sometimes not included in the planning of capital projects, and this can result in inadequate O&M funding, and, subsequently, asset performance degrades due to lack of maintenance.

Given the variety of sources of capital funding and the variety of cultural facilities that utilize capital funds for new construction and extensive renovations, it is impossible to provide any one-size-fits-all process for managing these projects and tracking their funds. Since capital projects for cultural facilities are funded through a variety of financial mechanisms (which may include federal, state, or local government funding; trust funds; retail revenue; grants; and donations or bequests), it is important that institutional leadership understand the complexities and ramifications of managing a capital budget.

The operations, maintenance, and environmental conditioning of space in cultural facilities should be one of the primary considerations when making plans for capital improvements. Assets should be evaluated in terms of their effects on climate conditioning, code compliance, security, operational efficiency, system performance, and their abilities to adapt to changing programmatic requirements. Equipment and design features have a significant impact on preservation of collections and the visitor experience, as well as overall O&M costs. For this reason, responsible management of the built environment includes effective facility management and careful monitoring of operations and maintenance performance.

Bundling maintenance projects together is one way to control the capital budget, the facilities footprint, and, ultimately, the operations and maintenance costs. Bundling can be done either systemically or geographically. Systemic bundling is the replacement of a major piece of equipment or system and then expanding the scope to assess the condition of related systems or minor components of the system. An example of systemic bundling would be the replacement of a heating system that did not include the replacement of any deteriorated steam lines that feed into the system. In this scenario, the cost of not capitalizing the whole project could result in higher operations and maintenance costs and compromised performance. Geographic bundling is based on the geographic area and adjacency of equipment and systems. For example, capitalizing the replacement of three chillers located in approximately the same area may be more advantageous than replacing them on a rotating basis, which could result in the entire process beginning again immediately after completion.

One very common approach to capital planning is to identify and define requirements in accordance with a master plan, and then prioritize, rank, and refine the requirements to develop a five-year funding plan. Planning the renewal of the built environment within this process is one of the most important aspects of capital project management, particularly when taking into account the remaining useful life of equipment. Being aware of organizational growth is critically important to controlling capital costs. Many cultural facilities are committed to expanding exhibition, research, and collections storage space, yet do not take the associated O&M costs into account when considering capital improvements or requirements. More space used differently always translates into more operations and maintenance costs, and efficient and effective organizations realize and plan for that eventuality.

Managing a capital program requires expertise, communication, planning, understanding operations and maintenance, and knowledge. When the right team is involved throughout the process, it can create the circumstances for successful completion of projects. When carefully planned, these projects can reduce the amount of funding that must be allocated to O&M year after year. Over the life of a building, these savings can be significant.

Photo source: Digital Image © The Barnes Foundation.

Commissioning

Commissioning is sometimes thought of as the testing that occurs when construction of a facility is complete. In actuality, commissioning is a collaborative process that begins when a commissioning agent (CxA) is brought onto a planning team; this happens well before completion of the facility. Introducing the CxA to the project early on helps ensure that the agent is able to participate in the development of project requirements, that the operations and maintenance manual is developed, and that all important records can be documented during the planning process.

Throughout the planning and early occupancy stages, the commissioning agent works variously with the planning, design, construction, and facility management teams to achieve the following:

1. Define and document requirements clearly at the outset of each [design] phase and update through the process

2. Verify and document compliance at each completion level

3. Establish and document commissioning process tasks for subsequent phase delivery team members

4. Deliver buildings and construction projects that meet the owner's needs, at the time of completion

5. Verify that operation and maintenance personnel and occupants are properly trained

6. Maintain facility performance across its life cycle. (Quoted from Project Management Committee [PMC] 2012)

The benefits of commissioning are many—commissioning results in detailed preventive and predictive maintenance plans, operating plans, and training standards; improves energy efficiency, environmental health, and safety; and offers savings over the life of the facility. For example, when commissioning is thoroughly integrated throughout each phase of the planning, construction, and early occupation stages of a new facility, the facility can expect its energy performance to be between 8 and 30 percent better than if it had not been commissioned (PMC 2012). After the building is initially commissioned, it should be periodically recommissioned to ensure that it is operating effectively—approximately every five years (Robertson 2011).

For information about the most commonly referenced commissioning standards, see the American Society of Heating, Refrigeration and Air-Conditioning Engineers' guidebook, *ASHRAE Guideline 0-2005, The Commissioning Process* (ASHRAE 2005).

Postoccupancy Evaluation

The POE is the process of evaluating a building's performance after it has been occupied for a short time, generally a period of 6–18 months (Cotts et al. 2010). POEs may be conducted by in-house staff or by a consultant, and they can range from a cursory evaluation to a comprehensive analysis. Examples of topics explored during a POE include the satisfaction of occupants throughout the facility, its sustainability performance, its operational effectiveness, and whether the facility is serving the organization's mission (GSA 2013).

Data gathered during the POE can be used to identify and address problem areas and to recommend changes to the planning of future capital improvement projects. For the POE data to be truly effective, the facility management organization must develop and implement a process for documenting its POE data, for archiving lessons learned, and for sharing this valuable information with members of the organization (Federal Facilities Council [FFC] 2002). If key performance indicators (KPIs) were established by the planning team, these can be assessed after the facility is occupied. Examples of key performance indicators include maintenance expenditures per square foot, energy use per square foot, and the suitability of the facility in light of the institution's mission-based requirements. For more information regarding key performance indicators, see Cable and Davis (2005).

Cultural institutions have a variety of resources to turn to when shaping their processes for post-occupancy evaluation. For example, the Higher Education Funding Council for England (HEFCE) details a seven-step process for POE in its *Guide to Post Occupancy Evaluation* (2006). These steps are to identify the POE strategy, choose an approach, define the process in a *POE brief*, plan the POE, carry out the POE, prepare a report on the findings, and act in response to the findings. The FFC also offers a 138-page guidebook, *Learning from Our Buildings: A State-of-the-Practice Summary of Post-Occupancy Evaluation* (2002), which is available online from the National Academies Press (www.nap.edu). *Learning from Our Buildings* offers sample POE surveys and information about evaluating universal design performance, integrating technology into the POE process, and maximizing learning from POE-generated data. In addition, this guide describes a balanced scorecard approach to the POE that takes into account four categories—financial, business, stakeholder, and human resource–related outcomes.

Third-Party Certification of Cultural Institution Facility Performance

Cultural institutions may be interested in pursuing third-party certification of their capital improvement projects. Leadership in Energy and Environmental Design (LEED) certification, developed by the U.S. Green Building Council (USGBC), and Energy Star Label certification, overseen by the U.S. Environmental Protection Agency, are two examples of certification programs that verify that facilities are performing to rigorous, preset performance standards.

Facilities pursuing LEED certification must register their projects with the USGBC and pay a registration fee (Zimmerman 2008). Several LEED certification options are available, including the "LEED for Existing Buildings: Operations and Maintenance" (LEED-EBOM) credential and the "LEED for New Construction and Major Renovation" (LEED-NC) credential. Facilities that pursue LEED-EBOM must demonstrate a commitment to sustainable operations and maintenance practices by earning credits toward certification in a range of areas, including indoor environmental air quality, water efficiency, and sustainable sites. Facilities that pursue LEED-

NC must also earn credits toward certification in similar preset categories. Once a facility has compiled and submitted the documentation necessary to earn LEED certification, the information is submitted to the USGBC for review, and, if it is approved, the facility is certified. Note that there are varying levels of LEED certification; these levels, in order from most to least credits required, are "Platinum," "Gold," "Silver," and "Certified." In order to maintain any level of LEED certification, a facility must periodically re-certify (USGBC 2013).

Facilities that pursue the Energy Star Label show a commitment to effective energy management practices and often achieve savings for their organizations. Please note that the Energy Star Label is not currently available to museum facilities specifically, but it can be applied to facilities that are sometimes part of a museum or cultural institution's campus, such as data centers and dormitories. To earn the Energy Star Label, facilities must enter data related to their energy management and performance into the Environmental Protection Agency's online *Portfolio Manager* tool. The online tool will then calculate a score between 1 and 100 for the facility. This score represents how the facility is performing in relation to other, similar facilities; for example, a score of 75 means that the facility performs better than 75 percent of similar facilities in the United States. Facilities that earn a score of 75 or above may be eligible for the Energy Star Label, but they must first apply for certification through the *Portfolio Manager*. If the application is approved, the facility's Energy Star Label will be valid for one year. After one year, energy performance data and an accompanying application must again be submitted for review (Energy Star 2013).

Cultural institution resources must be allocated very carefully, and it is important that the pursuit of certification is linked to a cultural institution's mission. Before entering into the certification process, cultural institutions should also be aware that certification can require a significant investment of time and money that may not be offset by the benefits of certification. Regardless of whether or not an institution chooses to pursue certification, certification performance standards are valuable benchmarking tools that can be used to evaluate a facility's operation.

Summary

The capital program planning and implementation process affords a valuable opportunity to bring together staff from across a cultural institution who can work together to create a facility that will serve the institution's mission for years to come. By including the institution's facility manager on the capital improvement planning team, the project will be planned with an eye toward accommodating maintenance of the facility, reducing the cost of operations, and fostering higher levels of cleanliness. Once capital improvement projects are complete, it is often the facility manager's job to spearhead evaluation and third-party certification efforts related to the finished facility. Continually evaluating capital improvement projects and seeking third-party certification help to ensure that the cultural institution facility is serving its intended purpose, while meeting rigorous standards for sustainability and energy management.

SUSTAINABLE CULTURAL FACILITY MANAGEMENT

As a well-known proverb says, "We do not inherit the earth from our ancestors; we borrow it from our children." The Smithsonian is doing its part to make sure that we return our fragile planet in better shape than we received it. Economically, environmentally and ethically, sustainability is the right thing to do.

—Dr. G. Wayne Clough (2012), 12th secretary of the
Smithsonian Institution and president emeritus
of the Georgia Institute of Technology

Sustainability can be defined as "living on the earth's income rather than eroding its capital" (Museums Australia [MA] 2003, p. 3). In turn, sustainable actions can be thought of as actions that do not compromise the well-being of natural and cultural conditions in the future. In 2011, over 40 percent of U.S. energy use was linked to consumption in our buildings (U.S. Energy Information Administration 2013). With so much of our energy use, as well as much of our consumption of other natural resources—like water—attributable to the built environment, attempts to operate more sustainably require that we look closely at practices in and around the facilities we use each day.

Museum and cultural institution facilities, whose delicate collections often require additional resources in order to maintain ideal conservation conditions, need special attention when considering sustainable initiatives. Despite the challenges inherent to preserving sensitive collections, sustainable initiatives are not out of reach. Each cultural institution must decide how best to approach sustainable facility management, given such factors as its mission, strategic plan, and budget, as well as the talents of its personnel and volunteers.

For institutions that aspire to become accredited by professional associations, like the American Alliance of Museums (AAM, formerly the American Association of Museums) or the Association of Zoos & Aquariums (AZA), it is important to note that these associations have begun encouraging sustainability among their members as well. For example, in 2012, the AAM launched its "Sustainability Standards in Museums" initiative. As part of this initiative, the AAM is continuously gathering data on sustainability practices from museums (Sustainability Standards in Museums 2013). Many of these practices are shared on the AAM's sustainability website, pic-green.net.

The AZA recently published "The Zoo & Aquarium Green Guide: Suggestions for Beginning or Expanding a Sustainability Program" (2011). This guide clearly and concisely outlines seven, largely facility management–related areas in which zoos and aquariums can become more sustainable: energy, water, chemicals, waste, purchasing, awareness, and innovation. Though it is tailored to zoos and aquariums, any cultural institution can cull helpful strategies from this guide, which range from practical tips like when a facility's boiler should be replaced to ways to educate guests about sustainability efforts. The AZA "Green Guide" represents just one resource in an ever-growing collection of references for museums and cultural institutions interested in pursuing sustainable practices in their facilities.

In addition to identifying helpful resources for museums and cultural institutions interested in "going green," this chapter addresses the importance of linking sustainable practices to the achievement of the institution's mission. This chapter also provides an overview of the triple bottom line approach to sharing sustainability metrics and the process for developing a sustainability policy for the facility. Benchmarking, auditing, and waste stream analyses of a cultural institution facility are discussed, as well as emerging best practices for sustainable museum facility management. The information shared in this chapter helps build a foundation for cultural institution facility managers interested in strengthening sustainability initiatives for their facilities.

Measuring Sustainability: The Triple Bottom Line

Over the past decade, cultural institutions have begun to realize savings, to increase community outreach, and to reduce environmental impact through their sustainability efforts. This three-pronged approach that integrates concerns for the "three Ps" of sustainability—profit, people, and the planet—can be defined and measured using the triple bottom line (TBL) framework. The TBL framework is helpful when making the case for continued sustainability efforts, because it accounts not only for sustainability-related economic benefits but for social and environmental benefits as well (Slaper and Hall 2011). Put another way, the TBL "captures the essence of sustainability by measuring the impact of an organization's activities on the world" (Savitz and Weber 2006, p. xiii). Clearly communicating the impact of sustainable practices to key stakeholders helps to earn the support necessary to advance sustainable practices in an institution.

While the triple bottom line provides a structure for assessing the value of sustainability initiatives, deciding how to measure each TBL component can be challenging. Profit can be quantified in dollars, but the impact of sustainability on people and the planet can be measured in any number of ways. A museum might quantify the positive impact of its sustainability measures on the planet by describing how many gallons of water were saved, improvements made in air quality, reductions in energy use, and increases in waste diversion over a set period of time. It might quantify the positive impact of its sustainable measures on people by describing the number of community outreach events hosted in its facility, the sustainability training hours provided to employees, or any increase in employee retention or satisfaction in the museum that can be attributed to sustainability efforts. The key is in taking the museum's stakeholders into account when choosing how to represent the impact of sustainability efforts on people and the planet.

Publishing a report like the Smithsonian's "Strategic Sustainability Performance Plan" is one way to share triple bottom line metrics with stakeholders. (This report can be viewed online at www.si.edu/About/Policies.) Other ways to share information about sustainability initiatives include posting this information online or through strategically placed signage in a facility. Cultural institutions have documented and shared sustainability initiatives in other ways, including:

- The Victoria and Albert (V&A) Museum in London, which shares a comparison of its carbon footprints over a four-year period on its website (V&A 2013);

- The Reid Park Zoo in Tucson, Arizona, which describes its green building, recycling, composting, and reclaimed water practices on the "conservation" page of its website (Reid Park Zoo 2013);

- The Golisano Children's Museum of Naples, Florida, which integrates information about people's influence on the environment into its exhibitions and programming (Golisano Children's Museum 2013); and

- The Happy Hollow Park and Zoo in San Jose, California, which provides guests with a "green tour" walking map tailored specifically to touring the Zoo's sustainable facilities and grounds (Happy Hollow Park and Zoo 2012).

In each instance, the cultural institution shares sustainability-related outcomes in a way that is meaningful to its key stakeholders.

Consider how key stakeholders can be educated with regard to a triple bottom line. Will docent-led tours that highlight how the museum has been greening its facilities be offered? Will a semiannual e-newsletter to donors be distributed that describes the sustainability initiatives made possible by their recent contributions? Will information be included in exhibition catalogs or on signage about the sustainable measures taken in the exhibition spaces, like the use of low-VOC (volatile organic compound) paints or installation of light-emitting diode (LED) lighting? Will green cleaning techniques be demonstrated during semiannual community workshops?

By working together with staff from throughout a museum, the triple bottom line, or "three P," data can be tailored to speak to different audiences, like donors, visitors, and board members, as well as other museum employees, in ways that help build support for further sustainability efforts.

Pursuing Mission-Based Sustainability

In their book *The Green Museum: A Primer on Environmental Practice* (2008), Sarah Brophy and Elizabeth Wylie describe the relationship between a museum's mission and sustainability implementation in this way: "The environmental sustainability of your institution is a mission-based decision; implementation should come from mission-driven decisions made on a daily basis using your institutional policy for green" (p. 4). That is to say, to successfully implement sustainable initiatives, these initiatives must be linked to achieving the museum's mission. Linking the pursuit of sustainable initiatives to the achievement of the institution's mission clarifies for the governing board, administrators, donors, and other stakeholders why sustainability is worth the investment of the museum's valuable time and resources.

Take a moment to look over an institution's mission. Does it include words evocative of sustainability principles, like *preserve, sustain, educate, future, community,* or *responsibility*? If so, the institution can try to use these words as a jumping-off point when building its case for pursuing organization-wide sustainable practices in the management of its facility. It is possible—but not probable—to review a cultural institution's mission and feel there is no clear way to connect sustainability to the institution's mandate. In this case, it is worth looking at the organization's strategic plan and its interactions with the community and other existing practices for clues that might help build an argument for implementation of sustainable practices. For example, it may be that although an institution's mission does not explicitly support sustainability, long-term cost savings are written into its strategic plan. Is it possible that these savings can be achieved, in part, by investing in more efficient HVAC systems that will save money over time? Connecting sustainable initiatives, like installing more efficient HVAC systems, to an institution's existing plans, such as plans to pursue savings, helps introduce sustainability into the management of a facility in a way that is hard to argue against.

For an example of linking sustainable facility management practices to the achievement of museum-wide goals, we can look at how the Smithsonian Institution's sustainability initiatives are connected to the Smithsonian's strategic plan. One of the grand challenges identified in the Smithsonian's 2010–2015 strategic plan is "Understanding and Sustaining a Biodiverse Planet." By pledging to sustain a biodiverse planet, the Smithsonian promises to look closely at how its day-to-day operations affect the world at large. By pursuing sustainable initiatives, the Smithsonian comes closer to meeting this challenge. To this end, it is actively pursuing environmentally sound practices, like composting, sustainable purchasing, and alternative fuel use, to name a few. For the sake of transparency between itself and its key stakeholders, the Smithsonian shares its eight sustainability goals, along with performance metrics for each goal, in its "Strategic Sustainability Performance Plan," mentioned earlier (Office of Facilities Engineering and Operations 2012). All told, the museum complex is making good on Smithsonian Secretary Wayne Clough's avowal that "economically, environmentally and ethically, sustainability is the right thing to do" (Clough 2012).

Defining a Sustainability Policy

A sustainability policy is the guiding document that helps a museum bridge the gap between its current practices and a more sustainable future. Developing a sustainability policy can be approached in several ways. If a museum is not ready to pursue sustainability organization-wide, the policy can be written to relate only to facility management practices. Alternatively, the policy can be drafted to cover all of the museum's practices. How broadly—or narrowly—the policy is written is a decision that should be made in concert with a museum's director and, if applicable, key stakeholders.

If a museum does not already have a "green team," a committee dedicated to finding ways that the organization can become more sustainable, it is a good idea to form one to help with writing and implementing its sustainability policy. A green team should include staff members from all areas of the museum and can also include board members and members of the museum (Brophy and Wylie 2008). Gathering a group of people who have diverse backgrounds but share a passion for sustainability will make the final sustainability policy more relevant to all parts of a museum and, ultimately, more achievable.

The areas for improvement identified during benchmarking and energy and waste audits can form the basis for a sustainability policy as it relates to facility management. As the green team decides how these areas for improvement will be addressed in the policy, it can consider how any elements of the policy may affect the museum's mission in terms of environmental, social, and economic outcomes. In other words, the sustainability policy should be written with quantifiable targets (e.g., to divert waste, reduce energy consumption, and increase public outreach) that will positively affect the museum's triple bottom line.

According to the Canadian Museums Association (CMA), a museum's sustainable development policy must do the following:

- Be adapted to the museum's values and mission
- Be developed in conjunction with stakeholders (including personnel)
- Have senior management support
- Be communicated to personnel
- Be made available to the general public
- Incorporate a commitment to continuous improvement
- Incorporate a commitment to pollution prevention, health and safety promotion, both on the job and during visits

- Incorporate clear, realistic and measurable objectives with respect to each dimension of sustainable development. (Quoted from CMA 2010)

These tips provide a good starting point as a museum develops its sustainability policy. It is also important to "take a long-term perspective" and consider how the policy will affect both current and future museum operations (MA 2003).

Before drafting a new policy, it is a good idea to review existing sustainability policies from similar organizations. A handful of museums have made their sustainability policies available online, including the National Museum of Science and Industry in London (2010) and the Royal British Columbia museum in Victoria, British Columbia (2008). Universities have established themselves as leaders in sustainability policy development, and there is no shortage of university policies for a green team to consider. Concise examples include the sustainability policies of the Freud Museum (see box 7.1), the University of North Carolina (2009), and Rice University (2013). Please see the bibliography for links to the university sustainability policies.

Once the policy has been drafted and approved, a green team should identify a clear plan for "rolling out" the policy that states how it will be communicated, promoted, and, most importantly, integrated into daily activities. For example, to communicate the new policy, members of the green team might visit different units within the museum to discuss how the policy relates to each unit's daily work and answer any questions. To promote the policy, the green team might publish a sustainability newsletter with tips for how staff can contribute to more sustainable operations, as well as progress reports for particular initiatives, like recycling or energy saving. To help integrate the policy into daily activities, members of the museum's staff should be trained with respect to how the policy affects their individual practices. This training is an extension of communicating the policy and can help staff identify sustainable strategies and tactics specific to their roles in the museum.

As the green team maps out the implementation process, remember that the sustainability policy does not have to be implemented all at once. As the CMA reminds us, "[I]t is preferable to focus on a few realistic objectives than to become discouraged by an insurmountable task" (2010). By targeting several achievable objectives early on, implementation of the policy as a whole will seem more manageable.

BOX 7.1.

FREUD MUSEUM ENVIRONMENTAL SUSTAINABILITY POLICY

FREUD MUSEUM LONDON

Freud Museum Environmental Sustainability Policy

In this policy the term 'sustainability' includes the natural, built, economic and social environments of the Freud Museum London. The Museum recognises its sustainability obligations to its staff, visitors, communities and stakeholders – both locally and globally – and to present and succeeding generations.

The Freud Museum London commits itself to:

1. Communicate its environmental policy to staff volunteers and other stakeholders and to raise awareness amongst these groups of their own environmental responsibilities and requirement to commit to environmental improvements;

2 Implement the requirements of all relevant sustainability legislation and regulations and, where possible, exceeding any relevant minimum requirements.

3 Reduce its carbon footprint through prudent use of fossil fuels (through energy conservation, management and efficiency within buildings) and to switch to low-carbon fuel alternatives where possible;

4 Manage and reduce water consumption;

5 Encourage walking, cycling and the use of public transport as principal means of commuting to work and for travel by staff on museum business;

6 Reduce waste created and where possible to reuse and recycle before responsible disposal of surplus materials; to use recycled and recyclable materials wherever possible;

7 Integrate principles of environmental sustainability within all museum policies and practices, specifically to those relating to procurement of goods and services;

8 The Museum will encourage staff and volunteers to attend appropriate sustainability training and development.

Carol Seigel
Director

Review date: May 2011

Source: Reproduced with permission from the Freud Museum, www.freud.org.uk.

Sustainable Purchasing Practices in Cultural Facilities

How cultural institutions choose to approach procurement has the potential to make or break their sustainability efforts. The goods and services that are purchased by and used within a cultural facility tangibly represent the types of environmental practices supported by the organization. While facility management–related purchases count toward only a portion of a cultural institution's overall purchasing, these purchases are nonetheless significant. For example, if a museum renovation project is using unsustainably harvested flooring that was transported from overseas, the museum is neither practicing nor exemplifying sustainable principles.

Selecting local and renewable construction materials represents just one area in which an institution's procurement process can become more sustainable. When developing a sustainable procurement policy, some institutions may decide to write a policy that pertains to the *entire* range of the goods and services that they purchase. Alternatively, institutions may implement a procurement policy that governs only one area of procurement, such as facilities-related purchases.

Before continuing our discussion of sustainable procurement, it is first important to define this concept as a whole. The term *environmentally preferable* is one phrase used to describe products that cohere to sustainable procurement standards. Environmentally preferable products can be defined as "products or services that have a lesser or reduced effect on human health and the environment when compared with competing products or services that serve the same purpose" (Executive Order 13423, 2007).

The United Nations provides us with yet another way to look at sustainable procurement. The United Nations, which has developed very clear requirements related to its own sustainable procurement, defines the concept in a way that mimics the triple bottom line approach discussed earlier. As per the United Nations Global Marketplace (2010),

> Procurement is called sustainable when it integrates requirements, specifications and criteria that are compatible and in favour of the protection of the environment, of social progress and in support of economic development, namely by seeking resource efficiency, improving the quality of products and services and ultimately optimizing costs.

In practice, accounting for these economic, environmental, and social concerns within an organization's procurement practices means keeping track of a broad range of factors.

For example, the United Nations suggests that sustainable procurement practices should be predicated upon

- economic considerations: best value for money, price, quality, availability, functionality;
- environmental aspects, that is, green procurement: the impacts on the environment that the product and/or service has over its whole life-cycle, from cradle to grave; and
- social aspects: effects of purchasing decisions on issues such as poverty eradication, international equity in the distribution of resources, labour conditions, human rights. (Quoted from UNGM 2010)

By keeping tabs on these economic, environmental, and social factors, a cultural institution not only demonstrates to suppliers that there is, indeed, a market for sustainable goods and services, but also shows suppliers that sustainability does not just mean being "green": sustainable products and services can also embody notions of value and quality, as well as respect for human rights. As more and more organizations continue to implement sustainable procurement policies, suppliers will strive to make more and more sustainable goods and services available—at prices that are increasingly comparable to those of their less sustainable counterparts.

As discussed earlier, successfully implementing sustainable initiatives in a facility requires buy-in from others throughout the institution. When it comes to developing and implementing a sustainable procurement policy, the need for buy-in is no different. Though sustainable goods and services do not always cost more than their less sustainable alternatives, it is possible for additional costs to be incurred when pursuing some sustainable goods. For example, high-efficiency light bulbs often cost more per bulb than traditional light bulbs; however, they use less energy and are often replaced less frequently. So, while sustainable purchases have the potential to affect an organization's overall budget at the point of purchase, they can often have financial benefits in the long run.

The museum's director and financial officer must be among the strongest advocates of sustainable purchasing if the policy is to truly carry any weight. As the policy is being developed, these leaders should be engaged in the process. They can help to establish to what degree the museum can reasonably accommodate sustainable purchasing within its budget. For example, they might specify that, if a similarly priced sustainable alternative is available, it should be purchased in lieu of other available products; however, if the sustainable alternative costs significantly more than other products, a senior leader should be consulted prior to making the purchase. Note that what qualifies as "significantly more" would need to be defined clearly within the policy.

In addition to asking members of the leadership team for input, it is also very important to include staff members from throughout the cultural institution who participate in purchasing activities in the development of the sustainable procurement policy. By bringing their unique experiences of working with suppliers and contractors to the table, these individuals can help articulate a sustainable procurement policy that truly works when put into practice. Members of the museum's green team can also be invited to help draft the policy. The staff members who actually use the products should also be involved. For example, building service workers should be asked for their opinions regarding cleaning products they have had experience with, whether these products are effective, and any recommendations they have for the policy.

When beginning these discussions about what a sustainable procurement policy will look like in a facility, one of the first questions should be "What do our institution's *existing* procurement policies look like?" There may already be guidelines in place that encourage sustainable procurement practices, like purchasing products made of recycled materials or domestically produced goods. Carrying over these guidelines into the new sustainable procurement policy may help stimulate buy-in, because the new policy is grounded in preexisting sustainable practices.

Another question to ask early on when developing a sustainable procurement policy is "What, exactly, is being purchased by our institution?" This may sound like an obvious question, but, if purchasing is done by multiple parties throughout an institution, there may not be a single document that records *all* of the things that are being purchased. Taking time to assemble this record of the types—and quantities—of things purchased by a museum or cultural institution is indispensable when drafting a museum-wide sustainable purchasing policy. By studying this list, one gets a sense of the high-volume purchases, in terms of both quantity and cost to the organization, as well as of other products that can be targeted for reduction or replacement.

Because a museum cannot change its purchasing practices overnight, it is helpful to start small. Something as simple as replacing a high-volume item, like paper towels, with a sustainable alternative can contribute immediately to a museum's effort to become more sustainable. Replacing paper towels with hand dryers is a change that will be experienced by essentially all of a museum's employees and visitors, which gives a sustainability initiative added exposure. A museum might consider posting small signs that describe the environmental benefit of the new dryers, so it is understood why this change is being made. (For a comparison of the environmental impacts of hand dryers and paper towels, see Koerner 2008.) Despite the environmental benefits of hand dryers, recent studies have shown that paper towels are more hygienic than hand dryers, so museums may wish to keep them in their facilities (Petri 2012). If museums choose to keep paper towels in their washrooms, they might consider composting them rather than throwing them away, which American University has recently begun doing on its campus as a part of its Zero Waste Policy (Raman 2011).

Museums can also identify products that have relatively easy-to-come-by, more sustainable alternatives. Examples of these alternatives might be recycled-content copy paper or energy-saving light bulbs. Note that items, such as energy-saving light bulbs, that will be used around collection objects should be approved by an institution's conservator prior to being purchased and installed.

When beginning to pursue environmentally preferable products, it can be helpful to keep an eye out for products that have been certified by a nonprofit "ecolabeling" program, like Green Seal. In order for a product to become Green Seal certified, it must first meet rigorous environmental standards. Green Seal's standards are developed "using a life-cycle approach to ensure that all significant environmental and social impacts are considered in the development of [the] standard, from raw materials extraction through manufacturing to use and disposal" (Green Seal 2013). Green Seal's website, www.greenseal.org, features a searchable database of certified products, organized into categories like construction materials and equipment, institutional cleaning products, paints and coatings, and hand soaps and cleaners.

While Green Seal is a helpful resource, it is not the only certification program available to help identify environmentally preferable products for cultural institution facilities. Among others are

- EcoLogo, which is similar to Green Seal and certifies products and services that meet its own rigorous environmental standards;

- GreenGuard, which certifies products that have low chemical emissions;

- Green-e, which certifies companies selling renewable energy; and

- Fairtrade International, which certifies that producers are fairly compensated for their products and that their products were produced to certain environmental standards.

This list represents only the tip of the iceberg in terms of existing ecolabeling programs. Nonetheless, it's important to keep in mind the growing trend of "greenwashing," the practice of misrepresenting products or services as being environmentally friendly when they have not been properly reviewed by a legitimate certifying program. Sometimes companies will even apply deceptive ecolabels to their products that advertise that products are "green," when in actuality the products have never been vetted against any environmental standards. For this reason, museums should make sure that they perform due diligence to verify that the ecolabels on products they purchase are from legitimate ecolabeling programs.

While considering products purchased in-house is important, it is also necessary to consider products that are purchased in fulfillment of contracted or outsourced services. For example, if a museum contracts with a cleaning service, it should consider the types of cleaning products that its contractor uses. If a museum is working with a contractor on a remodeling project, it should consider the building materials used by this contractor. Eventually, as a part of its sustainable procurement policy, it may make sense for a museum to integrate sustainable procurement requirements into its contracts with outside vendors. Setting sustainable purchasing standards for vendors that are similar to those of in-house purchasers reinforces an institution's commitment to sustainability. This is especially true when applied to large construction contracts. If executed sustainably, these contracts can make an appreciable difference in a cultural institution's environmental impact (New South Wales Environment & Heritage [NSW] 2011).

As with implementing the sustainability policy, rolling out a new sustainable procurement policy gradually, by applying it to just a few products in the beginning, can be a good way to earn buy-in over time. This allows for the policy to be introduced without overwhelming staff members by implementing sweeping changes all at once. This gradual rollout also allows for a trial period during which time the policy can be adjusted, if necessary, before being applied to the entire organization's purchases (NSW 2011). In addition to gradually implementing the policy, several other strategic approaches can aid in its implementation. For example, requiring that purchases be made or approved by a staff member who is thoroughly familiar with the sustainable procurement policy can help insure that purchases cohere to the requirements (Brophy and Wylie 2008).

If purchases are made by staff members from throughout a museum, it is important that these individuals are properly trained with respect to the new policy and its significance, as well as knowledgeable about resources for making procurement decisions in light of the policy's stipulations. That is to say, merely sending out an e-mail announcing that there is a new procurement policy and expecting sustainable purchases to quickly and easily follow suit are not enough. A training component is essential to communicating the changes the policy brings about, why employees should care about the policy, and how the policy will be implemented over time. In addition to educating employees about the new policy, it can also be helpful to work with suppliers when developing and implementing a sustainable procurement policy. Getting suppliers involved early on can "help reduce anxiety about changes that could affect their business . . . and give them lead time to prepare for implementation of the policy" (NSW 2011). It is possible that suppliers will be able to provide helpful feedback regarding a sustainable purchasing policy, though their feedback should be considered somewhat cautiously.

Many universities have begun adopting sustainable procurement guidelines and sharing them publicly. For this reason, if a museum is looking for good examples, an online search of university sustainable procurement, or purchasing, policies will yield many results. As an example, consider Duke University's well-organized "Environmentally Preferable Purchasing (EPP) Guidelines." Duke's EPP guidelines describe environmentally preferable procurement activities as organized within six areas of focus: Source Reduction, Recycled Content Products, Energy and Water Savings, Landscaping, Toxics and Pollution, and Forest Conservation. Though this policy is applied to university-wide purchasing, its areas of focus apply to facility management procurement, making this a particularly helpful policy to reference as a museum begins developing its sustainable procurement policy (Duke University, Financial Services 2013).

Sustainable Facility Management Practices in Cultural Facilities

This section provides an overview of some current practices in sustainable museum facility management, but it should not be considered an exhaustive listing of all of the sustainability strategies currently available to museums. Keep in mind that the conversation surrounding sustainable best practices in museums and cultural institutions is constantly evolving. To this end, organizations like the International Association of Museum Facility Administrators (IAMFA), the AAM, and the International Facility Management Association's Museums/Cultural Institutions Council (IFMA–MCIC) are continually seeking ways to help cultural institutions operate more sustainably. Taking an active role in one or more of these professional organizations puts the facility manager in touch with like-minded professionals and, ultimately, helps the museum stay on the cutting edge of best practices in cultural facility management.

Sustainable Operations and Maintenance

Pursuing operations and maintenance (O&M) strategies that balance environmental, economic, and social concerns requires continuous evaluation and adjustment. By committing to proactive O&M, a museum is likely to have happier occupants who benefit from improved indoor air quality and are absent less frequently. The museum will also generate less pollution and waste, and its equipment and building materials will last further into the future. Facility upgrades, like high-efficiency HVAC systems or LED lighting, are only effective if they are properly maintained over time; in other words, "A good maintenance program will enable a sustainable design to deliver on its promises." When maintenance is instead deferred, a number of issues, including reduced efficiency, poor air quality, insufficient fire safety, and structural problems, may arise. By implementing a proactive maintenance program, the facility manager increases the likelihood that the facility will continue to operate sustainably (Kennedy 2011). See chapter 5 for more information about developing a comprehensive maintenance program.

Carefully selecting maintenance supplies, like low-toxicity paints, adhesives, solvents, and sealants, helps reduce occupants' exposure to hazardous materials (Coombs Bobenhausen 2010). The National Building Museum (NBM) in Washington, DC, makes a conscious effort to use paints and sealants that have little or no VOCs. VOCs can discharge toxic compounds for long periods—even years—after a paint or sealant is used. By switching to low- or no-VOC products, the National Building Museum is investing in better indoor air quality, and its visitors also have fewer complaints about paint fumes. The National Building Museum has also opted to use medium-density fiberboard (MDF), rather than sheetrock, in its galleries. MDF can be reused time and again, rather than thrown away, when the gallery space must be changed. When a particular piece of MDF is no longer suitable for use in the galleries, it is further repurposed as subflooring or exhibition pedestals (NBM 2008).

Building service work, or housekeeping, is another area in which careful management can make a contribution to sustainability. Choosing cleaning products that are less toxic or using fewer cleaning products altogether contributes to a healthier museum environment. As discussed earlier, nonprofit "ecolabeling" programs, like Green Seal, GreenGuard, and EcoLogo, certify environmentally friendly products. These programs can be helpful when identifying sustainable products for use in the museum. Properly measuring concentrated cleaning solutions is another way to reduce the amount of potentially toxic cleaners in the facility. Simple strategies, like using walk-off mats to reduce the amount of dirt tracked into the facility, can also contribute to cleanliness and help improve air quality. Outside, cleaning can be made more sustainable by simply sweeping paths rather than using water to hose them off (AZA 2011). Training is important when introducing any new "green cleaning" practices or policy. The Boston Children's Museum (BCM-MA), for example, emphasizes the importance of training its cleaning staff with respect to the correct use, storage, and disposal of its approved cleaning products (BCM-MA 2013).

In an effort to reduce the use of cleaning chemicals, some facilities have begun purchasing cleaning equipment that "ionizes" tap water. This ionization process is supposed to increase the acidity of the water and, in theory, give it the ability to clean surfaces without any added chemicals. This is a novel concept; however, this technology is still very expensive, and some scientists caution that sufficient research does not exist to support the safety and effectiveness of using ionized water as a cleaning agent (Johannes 2012).

Cultural institutions that must use ice-melting products during the wintertime should use products with potassium or magnesium chloride instead of those with sodium or calcium chloride. Though large quantities of chlorides can be unsafe for plants, those with potassium or magnesium are less harmful. In addition, potassium and magnesium chloride are less destructive to concrete, hard-surface flooring, and carpeting, and can be less toxic to animals. The use of ice-melting chemicals can also be reduced if snow is removed before it has a chance to melt and freeze into ice (Green Seal and Siemens 2011).

In addition to implementing a comprehensive maintenance program and carefully selecting maintenance and cleaning supplies, museums can pursue a number of other sustainable strategies. Among the strategies discussed in the following sections are benchmarking and energy and waste management. These tools help museums to continually track their environmental impact and refine their practices over time.

Sustainable Cultural Institution Facility Performance

Prior to ramping up sustainable initiatives in a museum, it is important to understand the current state of its triple bottom line. That is to say, how is the facility currently performing with respect to profit, people, and the planet? Museum and cultural institution sustainability pertains to more than just its facility management, so an assessment of the triple bottom line in a museum can be done holistically. Such a holistic assessment involves staff from all over the museum in order to assemble a broad picture of current performance *throughout* the organization. Sometimes, due to time or financial constraints, it may not be possible to dedicate the resources necessary to complete such an organization-wide assessment. If this is the case, focusing first on facility management-related sustainability may help to build the excitement necessary to pursue organization-wide sustainability in the future.

By getting a handle on existing facility management practices and outcomes in a museum, it becomes possible to set specific sustainability goals moving forward. Benchmarking exercises, audits, and waste stream analyses are three of the many ways that facility-related performance can be measured to provide a baseline. Comparing an institution's practices to those recommended in professional association guides like the AZA's "Green Guide," or checklists like the MA's "Sustainability Checklist" (see box 7.2), also helps a museum get a sense of where its future sustainability efforts can be focused.

BOX 7.2.

SUSTAINABILITY CHECKLIST

The three main aspects of sustainable development are social, environmental, and economic. This checklist helps you consider:

- What are the key features of your museum's approach to sustainability in these three areas?
- How have you gone about building sustainability into your long-term plans and day-to-day operations?
- How do you monitor and assess the extent to which you are achieving your objectives and targets?

General approach

- ❏ Do you have a written environmental or sustainability policy setting out your museum's aims and objectives?
- ❏ Has the policy been formally adopted by the governing body? Is it supported by senior managers and explained to staff as part of the induction process? Is the policy regularly reviewed and updated?
- ❏ Do you measure your progress against sustainability targets?
- ❏ Do you require staff to take account of sustainability in day-to-day decision making?
- ❏ Are all staff trained in environmental awareness and green practices?
- ❏ Is a working group or individual responsible for making improvements and monitoring progress?
- ❏ Do you have champions or reps to help change behavior and promote sustainable practices among their colleagues?
- ❏ Does your collections policy take account of sustainability? Do you know how much you spend in money and energy on maintaining collections?
- ❏ Do you assess the environmental and social impact of your projects at the planning stage?
- ❏ Do you write requirements for sustainability into contracts with consultants, designers, and contractors?
- ❏ Do you set out to make sure your organization is seen to be sustainable?
- ❏ Can you say how well you are meeting targets?
- ❏ Do you compare your performance on sustainability with other museums and organizations?
- ❏ Do you publicize your sustainability achievements?

❑ Do you explain and promote the principles of sustainability through your displays, exhibitions, and use of your collections?

Social

❑ Do you use local or Fair Trade suppliers and contractors (e.g., for shop and café supplies)?

❑ Do you work with other community organizations and local groups?

❑ Do you consult and involve local people over museum work and activities?

❑ Are your displays and programming accessible and inclusive?

❑ Do you make the museum buildings available for community uses such as meetings and local exhibitions?

❑ Do you advertise jobs locally and encourage recruitment of local people?

❑ Do you provide volunteering opportunities?

❑ Do you provide training, work experience, and skill-sharing opportunities?

❑ Do you set out to reach new users and disadvantaged groups (e.g., through outreach)?

❑ Do you aim for diversity among staff and volunteers to reflect the local community?

Environmental

❑ Have you carried out an environmental audit of your organization and its buildings?

❑ Have you calculated the carbon footprint resulting from day-to-day operations?

❑ Do you monitor the amount of energy you use, and where?

❑ Have you set targets for reducing energy and water use, and reducing waste?

❑ Have you reviewed or changed your standards for environmental control or collections care with a view to saving energy or reducing dependency on air conditioning?

❑ Do you try to strike a balance between the needs of collections, staff, and visitors and the museum's impact on the environment?

❑ Have you invested in plants and equipment that will reduce your environmental impact?

❑ Do you use energy-efficient lamps and lighting wherever possible?

❑ Do you choose recycled materials where they are available?

❑ Do you recycle as much as you can?

❑ Do you encourage visitors and staff to walk, cycle, or use public transport rather than private cars?

❑ Do your IT (information technology) systems allow your staff to work from home?

❑ Do you provide secure storage for bicycles?

❑ Are bus stops and stations clearly marked on your website and marketing materials?

❑ Do you have a green purchasing policy for the products and materials you buy for day-to-day operations?

❑ Do you try to source goods locally to reduce transport carbon emissions?

❑ Do you minimize the number of flights staff have to make?

❑ Do you check out the green credentials of consultants, contractors, and suppliers?

❑ Is there a green space surrounding your museum? If so, do you care for it in a green way?

❑ Do you encourage biodiversity in the area surrounding the museum?

Source: Printed with permission of the Museums Association, www.museums association.org/sustainability.

If an institution is interested in pursuing green certification, such as Leadership in Energy and Environmental Design for Existing Buildings (LEED-EB) certification, it makes sense to invest in a certification guidebook to use when establishing a baseline. For example, the U.S. Green Building Council's *Reference Guide for Green Building Operations and Maintenance* (2010) can help the museum take stock of its current practices and gain an understanding of what needs to be done on the road to accomplishing LEED-EB certification. As Brophy and Wylie (2008) point out, whether or not there are plans for a museum facility to pursue certification, the LEED *Reference Guide* can be a valuable assessment tool.

A number of benchmarking opportunities also exist, with options ranging from the free federal Energy Star Portfolio Manager program to the more specialized, fee-based IAMFA program (discussed in greater detail in chapter 5). Benchmarking alongside similar facilities allows a museum to compare its facility's data and practices to those of comparable facility management organizations. Ultimately, this comparison gives a museum a sense of what it is doing well and where it can make improvements in its performance.

Several years ago, participating in a benchmarking exercise spurred a comprehensive energy conservation project at one prominent museum on the West Coast. The museum's benchmarking report revealed that, despite having some of the lowest energy rates, it had one of the highest energy bills among the cultural institution facilities participating in that particular exercise. This directed the museum's facility managers to look for ways to significantly reduce its energy use by pursuing aggressive facility improvement measures. As a result of these improvements, the museum now expects to see over $100,000 per year in utility cost savings.

Energy Audits

Energy audits help to identify areas in which the museum facility can achieve greater energy efficiency. The purpose of an energy audit, or assessment, is to document the condition of a facility and how it is being used. Afterward, opportunities for enhancing energy efficiency can be identified (Deru et al. 2011). Energy audits vary in terms of cost and intensity, from simple walk-through audits that a museum can complete in-house to more complex audits that might be completed by a local utility company or a contractor. Ideally, whether completed in-house or by a contractor, an audit of the museum facility's performance should be performed each and every year so that year-after-year performance can be analyzed, trends in energy use can be identified, and, ultimately, adjustments can be made.

Local utility providers often offer free or discounted energy audit services to their customers, so, before hiring a third party to conduct an energy audit of a facility, make sure to inquire as to whether the museum's utility provider offers free or reduced-cost audits. If a museum does hire an external auditor, it should make sure that the auditor will cohere to commonly accepted energy audit standards, like those established by the American Society of Heating, Refrigerating and Air-Conditioning Engineers (ASHRAE).

As outlined in their guidebook, *Procedures for Commercial Building Energy Audits*, ASHRAE endorses three, increasingly more sophisticated energy audit levels: ASHRAE Level 1, Level 2, and Level 3 (Deru et al. 2011). The ASHRAE Level 1 audit, also known as a "walk-through survey," is the simplest of the ASHRAE audits and is a prerequisite for LEED certification. The walk-through audit generally entails a review of the facility's energy bills and a short on-site survey of the facility. It leads to general suggestions for the facility and recommendations for additional analysis. The Level 2 audit, the "energy survey and analysis," is more thorough than the Level 1 audit. The Level 2 audit provides the information necessary to understand the benefits of any recommended energy efficiency measures (EEMs) resulting from the audit in terms of their cost and efficiency. Completing a Level 2 audit can help a facility earn credit toward LEED certification. The Level 3 audit, the "detailed analysis of capital-intensive modifications," entails collecting and analyzing the detailed data necessary to predict the costs and savings associated with large-scale capital improvements (Kelsey and Pearson 2011). For a summary of the ASHRAE audit assessment tasks for each level, see table 7.1.

ASHRAE recommends that energy audits be undertaken by an integrated building assessment team that includes the energy assessment provider, or auditor; members of operations and maintenance staff; and the building manager. Including all of these individuals on the audit team ensures that the audit's energy efficiency measures are financially feasible and that staff can be taught the necessary skills to operate and maintain the facility in keeping with the proposed measures. Put another way, "Without [the assessment team's] cooperation and future stewardship, energy saving measures installed during the process will be at risk after the assessment team completes their work at the site" (Kelsey and Pearson 2011, p. 378). Working together, the building assessment team can evaluate a museum facility and make a plan for improving energy efficiency that works within the museum's budget and is achievable by its maintenance personnel and/or contractors.

If a museum does not have the resources necessary to hire an energy assessment provider, a less sophisticated audit of the museum facility can be completed in-house. While many of the free, "do-it-yourself" energy audit guides available online are geared to homes and commercial spaces—and not museums—these guides nonetheless provide helpful starting points. For example, the City of Houston's Green Building Resource Center (GBRC) has made its "Do-It-Yourself Home Energy Audit" available online. This four-page, quick-start guide presents steps for completing a cursory evaluation of insulation, air leaks, heating and cooling equipment, lighting and appliances, windows, and plumbing. (Please see the bibliography for the link to the GBRC guide.)

Table 7.1. Summary of Energy Assessment Tasks for Levels 1, 2, and 3 (ASHRAE Audits)

	Level		
Process	1	2	3
Brief walk-through survey	•	•	•
Detailed on-site survey		•	•
Identify low-cost and no-cost recommendations	•	•	•
Identify capital improvements	•	•	•
Review mechanical and electrical (M&E) design and condition		•	•
Measure key parameters		•	•
Analyze capital measures (savings and costs, including interaction)		•	•
Meet with owners and operators to review recommendations		•	•
Additional testing and monitoring			•
Detailed system modeling			•
Schematic layouts for recommendations			•
Report			
Estimate savings from utility rate change	•	•	•
Compare energy use intensities (EUIs) to those of similar sites	•	•	•
Summarize utility data	•	•	•
Estimate savings if EUIs met target	•	•	•
Detailed end-use breakdown		•	•
Estimate low-cost and no-cost savings	•	•	•
Estimate capital project costs and savings		•	•

© ASHRAE, www.ashrae.org. *ASHRAE Transactions*, Vol. 117 (Part 2), 2011. Reprinted with permission of ASHRAE.

At the other end of the spectrum of free, do-it-yourself energy audits are more detailed manuals, such as the Washington State University (WSU) Energy Program's *Energy Audit Workbook*. The 54-page WSU workbook aids in the documentation of key building characteristics, such as annual utility costs, building occupancy, and the types of heating and cooling equipment in use, and it identifies important, energy-saving maintenance that can be performed. The WSU audit requires a higher level of technical expertise to complete than the GBRC audit, but it helps to tailor each aspect of a facility's upcoming maintenance and updates in order to achieve increased energy efficiency. Remember, before making any changes to a facility that may impact the well-being of its collections, such as altering thermostat set points, it is essential to confirm that these changes will not compromise the care of collections.

Plug load audits are one relatively simple way to identify opportunities to reduce energy use. The plug load is the energy that is drawn by a piece of equipment when it is plugged into an electrical socket. A vampire load, sometimes known as a phantom load, is the energy that is drawn by a piece of equipment that is turned "off" or in standby mode (Rivas 2009). These unnecessary vampire loads can account for between 6 and 20 percent of a facility's annual energy consumption (GreenCityBlueLake Institute [GCBL] 2013).

By auditing its plug loads, a museum can see how much energy is being used or wasted by devices in the facility. With this knowledge, the museum can then educate staff with regard to unplugging devices that are not in use and making smart decisions when acquiring new equipment. It may also be prudent for the museum to invest in "smart" power strips that cut power to devices when they are in standby or when no motion is detected (Chandler 2009).

When the sustainability branch of the Cleveland Museum of Natural History, the GreenCityBlueLake Institute, undertook a plug load audit throughout the museum, it identified some clear areas for energy use reduction: vending machines, water coolers, and coffee machines. A vending machine in the museum's employee lunch room was using 3,652 kWh of energy annually, at a cost of $365.29, while *one* coffee maker cost the museum over $120 per year in electricity. Several freezers that had been donated to the museum each cost over $100 per year to operate. To address the cost of powering its vending machines, the museum is investigating Energy Star alternatives and motion sensor technology, and it removed the light bulbs from one machine. The museum is also weighing whether it makes sense to accept donated freezers and refrigerators, considering how much it costs to power these pieces of equipment over time (GCBL 2013).

Sustainable Energy Management

Once a museum has a clear sense of its existing facility management practices and outcomes, it can set specific goals and identify the methods that will help it operate more sustainably in the future. After performing an energy audit, one of the most common next steps is to have the facility retrocommissioned, if it was never commissioned before, or recommissioned, if it was previously commissioned but operations and maintenance procedures could benefit from further adjustment. What is commissioning? Commissioning is a rigorous quality assurance process that confirms that the building and its systems work as they were intended. As a part of the commissioning process, the building's staff is also properly trained with the skills they need to keep the building's systems in good operating condition (Lawrence Berkeley National Laboratory [LBNL] 2013).

Retro- and recommissioning can be thought of as "tune-ups" of a building, much in the same way that people periodically have their cars tuned up. In the words of Wayne Robertson, "A building is, after all, a machine with moving parts intended to work together as a system and after a time, systems deteriorate if left alone" (2011). By periodically assessing the way a building is operated and maintained, facility managers can make targeted adjustments to their equipment and to their operations and maintenance procedures in order to improve efficiency. Several indicators that a facility is a good candidate for recommissioning include if it has been more than five years since it was commissioned or last recommissioned (or if it was never commissioned to begin with), if its energy use has increased without explanation, if renovations have occurred without an accompanying assessment of the building's HVAC systems, or if the building's systems appear to be outdated (Robertson 2011).

What sort of energy-saving results can recommissioning produce? Let's look at the Canadian Museum of Civilization's (CMC) recommissioning as an example. The CMC was originally commissioned in 1989, but was not recommissioned until more than ten years later. When the museum was audited and recommissioned between 1999 and 2000, the CMC slightly adjusted its temperature set point by just one degree Celsius and fine-tuned its central plant and controls software. Together, these adjustments led to a 5 percent annual reduction in the museum's electricity consumption. Five percent may not sound like a lot, but, for the CMC, it meant $70,000 per year in savings. With savings like that, it becomes much easier to justify investment in the recommissioning process (Larocque and Keeley 2002). For additional examples of specific energy efficiency measures, see the "Energy Efficiency Improvement Checklist" in box 7.3.

Museums can also work with energy service companies (ESCOs) to implement energy efficiency projects in their facilities. Not only do energy service companies identify and install the improvements, but also the ESCOs finance these projects. Over time, the facility repays the ESCO using

BOX 7.3.

ENERGY EFFICIENCY
IMPROVEMENT CHECKLIST

Boilers, Steam and Electric Generation

❏ Time, temperature, turbulence and oxygen balanced for optimum efficiency
❏ Co-generation to optimize fuel use
❏ Steam/electric load vs. capacity balance optimized
❏ Boiler feedwater treatment optimized
❏ Annual tube check/cleaning, boiler re-insulation completed on schedule
❏ Annual pressure relief valve checks/rebuild per schedule
❏ Steam pressure optimized/no leaks
❏ Economizers optimizing heat recovery
❏ Boiler blowdown timing/amount as recommended
❏ Steam/condensate piping insulation inspected/repaired annually
❏ Condensate return recovery percent
❏ Traps/strainers cleaned/checked
❏ Condenser tubes cleaned per annual schedule
❏ Electrical distribution/contacts checked with thermal imaging and cleaned annually
❏ Motors blown out per schedule
❏ Premium motors used
❏ Power factor optimized by metering and adjustable capacitors
❏ Sub-metering employed to identify high energy areas
❏ Net-metering sell-back program used to optimize energy costs

Building Heating, Ventilating and Air Conditioning

❏ Insulation adequate
❏ Window/door seals working
❏ Proper air supply/exhaust balance
❏ Proper air-volume change rate
❏ Proper thermostat settings used
❏ Building automation-systems control resets
❏ Proper filter maintenance scheduled annually
❏ Sunny-side window shades closed
❏ Zones/heating/cooling not competing
❏ Economizers returning seasonal hot/cold air temperature
❏ Use of variable air volume, variable-speed drives instead of dampers

- ❏ Peak-demand reduction opportunities checked annually
- ❏ Chilled water system operating efficiently
- ❏ Cooling towers/spray nozzles cleaned per annual schedule
- ❏ Refrigeration system lines/valves properly insulated
- ❏ Ice storage used for peak-demand optimization
- ❏ Pumps/motors/blowers/drives checked with vibration analysis
- ❏ Belt drives are tightened, belts replaced per annual schedule
- ❏ Water sub-metering used to optimize water use
- ❏ Hot water temperature set optimally
- ❏ Hot water tanks/lines insulated
- ❏ Water heaters off when not needed
- ❏ Special purpose areas; for example, kitchen, lab, cold storage optimized for HVAC and R control

Compressed Air

- ❏ Compressor cycling optimized per baseline
- ❏ Lines and valves checked, and leaks fixed
- ❏ Pressure regulators/filters/oilers cleaned/checked per schedule
- ❏ Condensate blowdowns completed per schedule
- ❏ Air tools cleaned, no line leaks, and operating efficiently
- ❏ Multi-compressor systems cycling most efficiently

Lighting

- ❏ Lighting levels optimal for space use per standards
- ❏ Replace incandescent with compact fluorescent lamps
- ❏ Clean fixtures for high efficiency per annual schedule
- ❏ Optimal use of natural light, occupancy sensors
- ❏ High-efficiency lamps used in high-bay areas
- ❏ Wall/ceiling coatings optimize reflectance

Other

- ❏ Facility-wide annual lube program optimizes lube quality/quantity/frequency
- ❏ Annual PM/PdM (preventive/predictive maintenance) system coverage and schedule compliance > 95 percent
- ❏ Total lifecycle management practiced.
- ❏ Compare alternative purchases using
- ❏ Lifecycle Cost Analysis
- ❏ Investigate renewable energy sources;
- ❏ e.g., solar

Your facility-specific checkpoints:

_____

_____

_____

_____

_____

Source: Quoted from Westerkamp (Summer/Fall 2010). "Facility Managers Lead the Move to Green with Improvements in Energy Efficiency." *Papyrus: A publication of the International Association of Museum Facility Administrators* (11)2: 33. Available at www.iamfa.org.

the money saved from increasing its energy efficiency (U.S. Department of Energy [DOE] 2011). Recently, the Honolulu Museum of Art (HMA) worked with an ESCO to replace its five unconnected chillers with a new, integrated HVAC system and controls. This retrofit project allowed the HMA to see a 28 percent reduction in energy consumption, which adds up to $250,000 in yearly energy savings (DOE 2012).

In addition to considering ESCOs, be sure to check into state and local government programs that may be available. For example, the Brooklyn Children's Museum (BCM-NY) facility in New York was able to finance its energy-saving systems through two state energy organizations—the New York State Energy Research and Development Authority (NYSERDA) and the New York Power Authority (NYPA). The BCM-NY facility received $250,000 from NYSERDA to invest in photovoltaic panels, and it accepted $500,000 from the NYPA to purchase its geothermal mechanical system and other performance-enhancing equipment. Altogether, savings of nearly $100,000 per year are expected due to these measures (BCM-NY 2013).

Other museums, like the Children's Museum of South Dakota, have received cash rebates from their local utilities to invest in energy efficiency measures. The Children's Museum of South Dakota (CMSD) collected over $16,000 in incentives from its local utility to use to install a more efficient chiller, motors, and food service equipment, as well as demand-controlled ventilation (South Dakota Municipal Electric Association 2011). If the occupancy in a museum varies widely depending on the time of day, a museum may want to consider a demand-controlled ventilation (DCV) system, like the CMSD's. DCV works by monitoring carbon dioxide (CO_2) levels and, if the CO_2 levels are found to have exceeded a predetermined set point, increasing the rate of ventilation. That is to say, if more people are present, more CO_2 will be detected and, in turn, the rate of ventilation will be increased. With a DCV system, outside air is heated, cooled, and dehumidified on an as-needed basis, rather than at a fixed rate based on an assumed occupancy (LBNL 2013).

"No people, no lights" describes the Brooklyn Children's Museum's lighting strategy, where occupancy sensors are used to control lighting in the museum's offices, classrooms, and restrooms on an as-needed basis (BCM-NY 2013). Many museums and cultural institutions are also updating their lighting systems to save energy and reduce maintenance costs. In most buildings, lighting represents a significant proportion of total energy consumption. It might be surprising to learn that lighting typically accounts for between 20 and 50 percent of a business's electricity use. Simple strategies, like installing occupancy and daylight sensors that react to changing conditions, can help make immediate headway toward reducing energy use in a museum.

As discussed in chapter 4, the types of lamps used in a museum—whether incandescent, fluorescent, halogen, or LED—help determine how efficient its lighting system will be, but there are other factors to consider as well. For example, the type of fixture and ballast, as well as the location of each fixture, should be taken into account when updating a lighting system (Energy Star). In a museum, where different types of collections have particular light sensitivities, involving members of conservation staff along with a lighting professional is particularly important when planning lighting upgrades.

Among popular options for museums seeking efficient lighting are T8 and T5 fluorescent lamps and LED lamps. The Ringling Museum of Art in Sarasota, Florida, recently worked with a lighting consulting firm to upgrade the lighting throughout its expansive property. After installing a combination of LED, T8 fluorescent, and halogen lamps, as well as occupancy sensors, the museum saw an improvement in the quality of its lighting and saved nearly $100,000 per year on energy costs. In turn, the museum used these savings to pay for the upgrades (Stones River 2013).

Though results vary from project to project, LEDs can show a return on investment in them in as little as two years (Vaughan 2012). As a part of its Energy Action Plan, the British Library in London has been converting its lamps to LEDs in stages over the past few years. Through its lamp replacement program, the library has seen a 50 percent reduction in lighting-related carbon dioxide emissions in its King's Library location, which holds the precious collections of King George III. As an added benefit, the high-security collections environment is now disturbed less frequently for lighting maintenance, because LEDs last longer than the fluorescent lamps used previously (Dixon 2011).

As addressed in chapter 4, museums continue to debate the merit of flexing their humidity and temperature requirements, including making seasonal adjustments to temperature and humidity set points in order to achieve greater efficiencies. If it is possible to reduce the amount of time that the museum's heating and air conditioning systems must operate, a museum can operate much more sustainably. Many conservators approach this idea cautiously because of the potential risks posed to sensitive collections objects. Nonetheless, it is worth it for facility managers to meet with conservators to discuss the possibility of relaxed standards, while assuring them that the primary concern is ensuring appropriate conditions for the collections.

Facility managers and conservators have begun searching for middle ground on this topic, and some institutions, like the Indianapolis Museum of Art, have had success with expanding their acceptable temperature and humidity ranges. The Smithsonian Institution recently held a two-day "Summit on the Museum Preservation Environment." This summit provided Smithsonian facilities and collections staff the opportunity to work collaboratively toward developing environmental standards that address both the conservation of collections and environmental sustainability (Smithsonian Institution 2013). Collaborative meetings, like the Smithsonian's summit, help facility and collections staff identify mutually agreeable environmental conditions that work from the perspectives of both conservation and sustainability.

Waste Stream Audits

While an energy audit helps a museum get a handle on where energy can be saved in its facility, a waste stream audit shows where opportunities exist to reduce a museum's contribution to landfills. Waste stream audits normally involve collecting or sampling waste from a facility over a 24-hour period and sorting it into predefined categories (e.g., metal, glass, plastic, paper, and food waste) so that the waste can be analyzed. Analyzing each of these categories, in turn, helps determine what types of waste can be targeted for diversion, like recycling, composting, or reuse (Natural Resources Defense Council [NRDC] 2013).

Waste stream audits can also provide museum facility management with the concrete numbers necessary to make a compelling argument for pursuing recycling and composting initiatives. For example, in 2010, a group of students at the University of Kansas (KU) performed a waste audit of the Spencer Museum of Art, located on the KU campus. The students found that over 65 percent of the museum's waste stream, by both weight and volume, was comprised of recyclable materials. At the time that the students' report was published, the museum had plans to implement office paper, newspaper, and bottle recycling, and these plans were well supported by the results of the audit (Keith et al. 2010).

A waste audit can be performed by museum staff and volunteers or with help from a specialized consulting firm. If a museum decides to perform its audit without the help of a consultant, there are free step-by-step resources available to walk its staff through the process. For example, nonprofits, including Keep America Beautiful (KAB) and the NRDC, have posted guides to conducting waste audits on their websites.

Cultural institutions in the United States, like the Museum of Science in Boston, Massachusetts, have also become partners in the WasteWise program offered by the U.S. Environmental Protection Agency. A free, online waste-tracking tool, WasteWise helps facilities collect and analyze information about their waste generation and set future waste diversion targets. WasteWise partners can also call the toll-free helpline to get support over the phone, and they have access to press-release templates that help publicize waste reduction successes. For links to the KAB, NRDC, and WasteWise auditing tools, please see the bibliography.

Integrated Solid Waste Management

After completing a waste audit of its facility, a museum can develop an integrated solid waste management plan. This plan specifically targets the types of waste revealed during the audit through, in order of priority, (1) source reduction, (2) reuse, (3) recycling and composting, and, as a last resort, (4) disposal (Department of Environmental Quality, 2013). Source reduction means preventing waste from being created in the first place. For example, many organizations are now asking staff members to think carefully before printing e-mails and to set printers to print double-sided pages automatically. In restrooms, it is also possible to install air dryers instead of paper towel dispensers to reduce paper waste. While it may seem that paper towels have a lower environmental impact than electric hand dryers, this is not the case. One comparison found that recycled paper towels have an energy expenditure of 460 kilojoules per use, while standard hand dryers have a net expenditure of 222 kilojoules per use (Koerner 2008).

Reusing items also keeps them out of landfills. To find a new home for those things that staff members no longer need, a museum can establish a "swap board" in a common staff area, like the break room, or on the museum's intranet to advertise these items' availability. If the museum cannot rehome the items internally, it can try to donate them to charity or even share them on an online swap board, like Craigslist—it is surprising what people are interested in reusing!

In addition to targeting waste for reduction and reuse in their facilities, many museums, like the Science Museum of Minnesota (SMM) in Saint Paul, have begun aggressive recycling campaigns. The SMM has invested in a recycling program that has the museum on track to increase its recycling rate from 18 percent to 75 percent over a two-year period. How is the SMM achieving such dramatic results? The museum kicked off its recycling initiative, Project No Waste, with a waste management assessment performed by a local, third-party sustainability consulting firm. The assessment showed that, of the 500,000 pounds of waste generated by the museum annually, fewer than 100,000 pounds were recycled. Ultimately, a plan was made to target paper, plastic, metal, and construction waste from all areas of the museum facility for recycling and composting. In the first six months of implementing the plan, the museum had already increased its recycling rate from 18 percent to over 50 percent (SMM 2012).

Like the Science Museum of Minnesota, after conducting a waste audit of a museum, staff will have an understanding of what types of recyclable waste is being generated and where in the facility this waste is normally thrown away. This data will help plan where recyclables should be collected, how often these items must be picked up, and where they can be stored before being hauled away. In terms of locating the collection sites, convenience is a key consideration. For example, if the recycling bins are set immediately next to trash bins, people are much more likely to recycle. If possible, setting a small paper recycling bin next to each desk, copy machine, and printer will also increase the overall rate of recycling.

Recycling bins must be easily accessible to building service workers or other staff members who will be collecting the recyclables, and they must be visible to staff and visitors. The bins and their locations also need to cohere to applicable fire codes. The museum can have the bins and locations reviewed by the local fire marshal prior to investing in a particular type of bin or becoming set on certain locations.

Some museums have had difficulty finding locations for recycling receptacles that fall in line with the museums' aesthetic standards. Suffice it to say, sometimes recycling receptacles are just not pretty, and they can take up a great deal of space. Recycling bins that collect beverage containers can also attract pests, like yellow jackets. For these reasons—and more—a compromise may be necessary between the green team coordinating the placement of recycling bins and the museum stakeholders who have aesthetics in mind. Nonetheless, it is important to remind anyone who wants to place the bins in less prominent spots that the bins are less likely to be used if they cannot be easily seen.

Keep in mind that there will likely be an adjustment period during which time the museum will have to try out recycling bins in different locations and add or remove bins before finding the optimal placement and number of bins. Even then, things may change over time, and the same spots that worked for bins this year may not be the best places for them next year. One way to keep track of what is or is not working is to periodically check in with the staff or volunteers who empty the bins—they will provide helpful feedback on how best to adjust the pickup process.

In addition to determining where bins should be located, a location for the recyclables to be held after they have been collected and before they are hauled away for processing must be identified. Because a truck will be picking up the recyclables, it is ideal to identify space near the loading dock for consolidation. If this is not a possibility, a fenced, outdoor location that is easily accessible by both the building service workers collecting the recycling and the truck hauling it away is a possibility. If neither of these options works, it may be necessary to have the recycling hauled away each day.

When identifying the consolidation location and collection frequency, a museum should take into account the actual volume of recyclables it expects to collect each day, as well as how much space is available to store recyclables before they are hauled away. If it can allocate a larger space, the museum will not have to pay to have its recycling hauled away as frequently. Before settling on a space and investing in bins, a museum should consult with the recycling collection service to ensure that the type of bins it plans to use will work within their pickup routine and that their trucks are compatible with the museum's pickup location.

If the museum needs help selecting a collection service, it can start by asking the local department of public works for a list of preferred vendors. Detailed guidelines for establishing contract language with the recycling collection vendor, as well as other helpful hints related to establishing a recycling program, can be found in the comprehensive *College and University Recycling Manual*, which is published online by the University of California, Davis and the California Collegiate Recycling Council (UCD–CCRC).

While working on collecting common recyclables, like paper, plastic, metal, or glass, a museum may also consider composting its carbon- or nitrogen-rich waste, either on-site or through a vendor that hauls away its compostable materials. Waste that is composted yields nutrient-rich humus, which can be added to soil to improve its quality and enhance nutrient levels. Not only does composting divert organic material from landfills, but also, by generating compost on-site, a museum can cut down on its purchase of chemical fertilizers (U.S. Environmental Protection Agency [EPA] 2009).

Cultural institutions have been cultivating successful composting programs for years. Zoos have the especially unique opportunity to compost their animal waste, and some zoos even sell their compost. For example, the Louisville Zoo in Louisville, Kentucky, holds its "ZooPoopyDoo Compost and Mulch Sale," where it sells its compost for $40 per scoop (Louisville Zoo 2013). At the Woodland Park Zoo (WPZ) in Seattle, Washington, the manure compost is so popular that the WPZ holds a "Fecal Fest Lottery" twice yearly to determine who will be allowed the opportunity to purchase its compost. All told, the WPZ generates almost 1 million pounds of compost per year, while saving $60,000 per year in disposal costs (WPZ 2013).

Other examples of composting at cultural institutions include the Children's Museum of Pittsburgh, which works with a local vendor to compost its suitable kitchen and public waste (CMP), and the Experience Music Project (EMP) Museum in Seattle, Washington, which uses composting to manage its special events waste. To accomplish this, the EMP caterer has opted for 100 percent compostable eventware, including dishes, straws, silverware, and cups. This means that special event attendees at the museum can put all of their event-related waste into one of the EMP's green bins marked for compost. To streamline the process, the EMP purchased a trash bin cleaning machine, which means that they do not have to purchase compostable bin liners. Instead, when they are full, the cans are emptied into one of the composting containers onsite, then washed and reused. Considering that over 100 compostable bin liners, costing 40 cents each, might otherwise be needed during a large special event, the EMP's bin cleaning machine is both a sustainable—and cost-effective—purchase (Richardson 2012).

As with implementing any new policy or program in a museum, it is important to have buy-in from throughout the entire organization for a recycling or composting program. From the staff and visitors who will recycle their waste to the building service workers who will be collecting it to the museum leadership who will be promoting and funding the program, it is crucial to have everyone on board. Members of the green team can help by introducing the program and its benefits at staff meetings, new employees should be familiarized with the program during their orientation, and awards programs can be held to reward those whose recycling efforts are particularly effective. Museums might also kick off their recycling efforts and periodically renew interest in them during nationwide recycling and waste reduction events. Participating in events like Earth Day and Clean Your Files Day, held each April; Compost Awareness Week, held each May; and America Recycles Day, Use Less Stuff Day, and Buy Nothing Day, held each November, can help promote recycling and waste reduction in museums and their communities (UCD–CCRC 2013).

After implementing integrated waste management, museums should continue to evaluate their waste streams and track the costs and savings related to the program over time. If they do not continue to analyze their waste streams, they will not know if their waste management plans are effective, and it will be difficult to identify additional areas for improvement. By contrast, if a museum can demonstrate measurable progress toward its waste diversion goals, while showing that the overall savings outweigh any costs associated with the new program, it will be much easier to build a sense of pride and gain support for future initiatives (AZA 2011).

Sustainable Water Management

Carefully managing water is crucial to reducing the environmental impact of a cultural institution. Not only does careful water management help keep local rivers and streams clean, but also it cuts down on energy consumption. The NRDC (2009) provides this powerful illustration of the connection between water use and energy consumption:

> The collection, distribution, and treatment of drinking water and wastewater nationwide consume tremendous amounts of energy and release approximately 116 billion pounds of carbon dioxide (CO_2) per year—as much global warming pollution each year as 10 million cars. (p. 1)

People know that using water carefully is important, but how many museum staff members know how many gallons of water are used by their cultural institutions each day? When the Cleveland Metroparks Zoo (CMZ) began monitoring its water use in 1992, it discovered that it was using over 1 million gallons per day. Consider one year's worth of water at that rate—it would add up to over 360,000,000 gallons! What's a zoo to do in this situation?

By keeping tabs on water use, a cultural institution can establish a baseline, make a plan toward managing water use, and document its progress toward reduced usage over time. The Cleveland Metroparks Zoo did just that. After establishing its baseline, the CMZ began improving its aging water distribution lines and infrastructure. In addition to updating these elements, the zoo also paid special attention to its exhibit pools. By installing submeters in strategic locations, like the bears' and wolves' pools, the zoo was able to isolate and repair underground leaks. Ten years later, the zoo evaluated its water use again, added several more submeters, and implemented a daily water-use tracking system. As part of this tracking system, water meter readings were recorded two times each day and analyzed for trends over time. Analyzing these data allowed the zoo to respond immediately when water use changed unexpectedly in a particular location. As an added benefit, water use data were also aggregated quarterly and shared with staff and visitors to create awareness of water use at the zoo. Through these efforts, the zoo was able to reduce consumption from an average of over 1 million gallons per day to a daily average of 572,000 gallons (CMZ 2012).

The CMZ case illustrates the benefit of submetering as a means to identifying and repairing leaks and, in turn, using less water. A faucet leaking at a rate of one drip per second wastes about 3,000 gallons per year (EPA 2012). Other common ways that cultural institutions are using less water include installing waterless urinals, dual-flush toilets, motion sensor faucets, and faucet aerators. Some museums, like the Brooklyn Children's Museum in New York and the Golisano Children's Museum of Florida, are harvesting rainwater for use when toilets are flushed. The Canadian War Museum in Ottawa, Canada, took advantage of its location near the Ottawa River to provide river water to its toilets and urinals, rather than using potable water. At first, some guests were uncomfortable with the natural color of the river water in the toilets. The museum headed off future complaints by posting signage explaining that the water came from the river and that the color was normal (Harding 2006).

Increasingly, cultural institutions are seeking ways that water can be used more sustainably in their landscaping through strategies like planting native plants and reusing water in their facilities. The Bowdoin College Museum of Art (BCMA) in Brunswick, Maine, and the Children's Museum of Pittsburgh (CMP) are two facilities that have selected hearty and native plant species that can survive on naturally occurring moisture and that require less tending.

If existing landscaping requires an irrigation system, installing a rain sensor can help cut back on unnecessary water use. The Golisano Children's Museum uses graywater for its irrigation. Note that graywater is water that has been drained from "cleaner" fixtures like sinks or dishwashers, but not from toilets. Toilet water is called black water and requires additional treatment prior to being reused.

Sustainable water management also means working to reduce runoff to keep pollutants from entering local water systems. Runoff is precipitation that moves over impermeable surfaces, like parking lots, sidewalks, or streets, gathering up pollutants. Eventually, the runoff and its pollutants make their way into the storm sewer system or into nearby bodies of water. If the polluted runoff flows into the storm sewer system, that does not mean it gets treated; instead, it is likely released back into local water sources (EPA 2013).

Rainwater harvesting is one way that cultural institutions can reduce runoff. For example, the Boston Children's Museum collects rainwater from its roof to be used for irrigation and toilet flushing. Collecting rainwater has reduced the BCM-MA's demand for potable water by 77 percent, while decreasing the facility's runoff into the Fort Point Channel by 88 percent (BCM-MA 2013). Managing parking lot drainage is another way to reduce runoff. The Yellowstone Art Museum in Billings, Montana, has installed a recycled glass parking lot that is able to absorb up to four inches of rainwater in half an hour. Following absorption, a built-in filtration system removes pollutants, like oil, before the rainwater soaks back into the ground (Lutey 2009). Using organic fertilizer, cutting back on the use of toxic pesticides, and finding alternatives to salt for melting ice are three additional ways to lessen the impact that runoff has on water quality. Staff should also be trained with regard to cleaning up hazardous spills, not only for their own safety but also to keep these hazardous substances from entering the water supply (AZA 2011).

Integrated Pest Management

As discussed in chapter 5, integrated pest management (IPM) is a preventative, less toxic way to limit pests in a facility. Whereas traditional pest management practices rely heavily on the application of chemicals (Museum Conservation Institute [MCI] 2006), IPM relies on strategies for preventing entry into a given facility, as well as continual detection and monitoring.

Sealing off openings through which pests may enter is one of the most important deterrents. To detect pests, for example, sticky traps can be placed strategically throughout the facility, and staff can be trained to report pest activity that they notice in the facility. In addition, materials that will be brought into the museum can be inspected for pests prior to entering the facility. Keep in mind that the museum environment will attract pests if it is not regularly cleaned, if trash is not regularly removed, and if the temperature or humidity levels are high. As a part of its IPM program, the Peabody Museum of Archaeology and Ethnology at Harvard University takes care to limit food and drinks to certain locations in its facility and advocates keeping food in closed containers (Peabody Museum of Archaeology and Ethnology 2013).

It is necessary to identify what constitutes an infestation for particular types of pests and when action should be taken to reduce their presence. If pests are present at levels that exceed the acceptable "threshold," pests can then be removed using nontoxic strategies. For example, the Peggy Notebaert Nature Museum introduces ladybugs, mealybug destroyers, and wasps to its garden as a part of its IPM plan. In turn, these helpful insects target various pests found throughout the garden (Wunschel 2013). For more information about IPM at the Nature Museum, see box 7.4.

Sometimes, the most sustainable practices are also the most time tested. For example, the ancient practice of falconry works to regulate damaging bird populations, like pigeons, by making them feel unsafe nesting in ar-

BOX 7.4.

INTEGRATED PEST MANAGEMENT IN THE BUTTERFLY HAVEN AT THE PEGGY NOTEBAERT NATURE MUSEUM

By Andrew Wunschel, Assistant Horticulturalist

I'll be honest with you, folks. There's just no way I can keep every greenhouse pest out of the Judy Istock Butterfly Haven. And you want to know something else? I don't particularly intend to.

Now I'm not rolling out the red carpet for aphids here. At least not compared to the hero's welcome they get just by us stocking the Haven with all their favorite foods and a perfect breeding climate. If they were easy to keep out, they wouldn't be called pests. Aphids, whiteflies, mealybugs, and scale insects can lay waste to thousands of dollars' worth of plants in no time, and then all we'd have is hungry butterflies and some sticks covered in bug poo.

Mealybug Destroyers

I could run around in the off-hours spraying chemicals. I don't because 1. Toddlers (et al) will put anything, including leaves coated in poison, directly into their mouths and 2. Butterflies, being insects, react unfavorably to insecticides. Also, I'd have to get here even earlier in the morning.

But more important than my alarm clock is the fact that we, as an institution, have adopted Integrated Pest Management (IPM) as our strategy for all pests. One part of IPM means using the least harmful means of control first. That would be prevention most of the time. I check plants for infestations before I plant them in the Haven. I monitor the plants already there to catch outbreaks at early levels, and then a little soapy water works miracles. But the true secret, the one that has me smugly unconcerned while hordes of mealybugs roam the streets, is that every now and then I release MORE bugs into the Haven.

We order the workhorses of the Butterfly Haven from Beneficial Insectary in Redding, CA. Ladybugs (*Hippodamia convergens*) devour most soft-bodied plant pests, and do so as adults and as larvae. This is also true for the similar-looking *Cryptolaemus montrouzieri*, which goes by the more pronounceable and colorful common name 'mealybug destroyer.' I also release three wasps into the Butterfly Haven—all of them completely harmless to humans. In fact, they are all smaller than the stinger of the wasps commonly associated with fear and pain. Being so small I guess they are not worthy of cool common names, but they answer to *Aphidius colemani, Aphytis melinus,* and *Encarsia formosa* and they parasitize aphids, scale, and whiteflies respectively. Parasitic wasps lay their eggs inside living hosts, sometimes paralyzing them first, and let their newly-hatched young eat their way out. Some people think that's gruesome, some think it's awesome, some think it's both.

Our Workhorse, the Ladybug

Notice how I mention these helpers as adults and as larvae. If I were somehow, magically, able to remove every single 'bad bug' from the Haven, my beneficial buddies would have no food, and therefore couldn't breed and maintain a population. One aphid or scale (both of which can reproduce asexually, which is far creepier to me than the parasitic wasp thing) could turn into millions nearly overnight. Instead we aim to keep the pests at an 'acceptable' level, which is another tenet of IPM. Then our beneficial insects have more likelihood of breeding and remaining in the Haven to greet incoming pests with something a little less like paradise.

To them, that is. All this goes on at the smallest limits of human perception. At scales more in line with our everyday experience, the Haven remains the tranquil sanctuary we have come to expect. There might be an aphid or two in there, but don't worry. I'm hardly working on it.

Source: Wunschel (2013). "Integrated Pest Management in the Butterfly Haven," Peggy Notebaert Nature Museum. Available at www.naturemuseum.org/the-museum/blog/integrated-pest-management-in-the-butterfly-haven. Printed with permission of the Peggy Notebaert Nature Museum.

eas that are patrolled by birds of prey. At the British Museum in London, falconry has been used to reduce pigeon populations around the museum. A raptor is released two days per week at the British Museum in order to encourage pigeons not to roost on the property (Wittig 2008–2009).

While there are many benefits to IPM, there are several potential downsides. It can be time consuming to put an IPM plan into place, and, for it to be successful, staff from throughout the museum must be invested in the plan. In addition, during the early implementation phase, IPM can be more expensive than traditional pest management. There is no one-size-fits-all approach that can be used when implementing IPM; it must be tailored to meet the needs of each cultural institution (MCI 2006). Despite the resources required to implement IPM, it is worth considering for any cultural institution interested in lessening its environmental impact.

Sustainable Transportation

Transportation to, from, and around a museum campus can also be evaluated and adjusted in order to become more sustainable. In keeping with this idea, the motto of the Smithsonian Institution fleet program is "You can't manage what you don't measure." The Smithsonian fleet program tracks the performance of each vehicle in its fleet so it can be evaluated against carefully identified standards, including fuel economy, maintenance requirements, and greenhouse gas emissions. Taking a proactive approach to developing a more sustainable fleet, the Smithsonian recently converted its diesel fuel site to renewable biodiesel, opened a compressed natural gas refueling site and electric charging station, and began using hybrid electric shuttle buses, electric motorcycles, and electric cargo vans as part of its fleet (Smithsonian Institution 2012).

Even if a museum does not manage a whole fleet of vehicles, there are ways to contribute to sustainable transportation practices. If the museum provides sufficient bicycle parking, people will be more likely to bike, rather than drive, to the museum. It helps to have a locker room with showers that staff can use after they bike to work. Carpooling can be encouraged through incentive programs; for example, carpool matching programs that help staff members identify people with whom they may carpool. The use of public transportation can be supported by providing transportation passes to staff (Brophy and Wylie 2008). Some facilities also make preferred parking areas available to those who drive hybrid or electric vehicles. If the museum is relocating to a new site, proximity to public transportation should be considered when selecting the new location.

Summary

Sustainability initiatives will be most successful if they are tied to the museum's mission and clearly articulated in a policy that is approved by museum leadership. Particular attention should be paid to the goods and services purchased by the museum and to the development of a policy that helps support "green" purchases. In addition, implementing a maintenance plan that keeps the facility's assets in good working condition will contribute to the museum's overall sustainable performance. Facility management practices can be made more sustainable through ongoing benchmarking and auditing of waste management and energy and water use. These metrics help the museum make targeted adjustments that reduce waste and increase efficiency. Taking such an integrated approach to sustainability requires an initial investment of staff time and money, but it has the potential to yield long-term savings, happier staff and visitors, and a healthier environment. For an example of a cultural institution that has taken an integrated approach to sustainability, see box 7.5, which describes the extensive sustainable practices utilized by the Missouri Botanical Garden.

BOX 7.5.

CONSERVATION IN ACTION: THE MISSOURI BOTANICAL GARDEN

Above: An electric car charging station at the Missouri Botanical Garden.

The Missouri Botanical Garden invests significant resources in developing and sharing new discoveries in plant science and using that knowledge to help manage those ecosystems here and around the world. The Garden is equally committed to inspiring and educating all members of our local region about the benefits of being good environmental stewards and establishing sustainable communities through conservation, ecological restoration, and responsible use of natural resources.

From our very successful plastic pot recycling campaign to our use of renewable energy to our improved storm water management, we strive to make the most sustainable choices throughout all our facilities and at all our sites.

Employee Engagement

The Garden's Green Team includes representatives from all Garden buildings and from our off-site locations: the Shaw Nature Reserve, the Butterfly House, and the Litzsinger Road Ecology Center. Meeting monthly, the Green Team works collectively to implement sustainable office operations throughout the

Garden. The team also hosts periodic lunch-and-learn and field trip opportunities, cultivating a broad sustainability knowledge base that Garden employees can apply in all working areas.

In 2010, the Green team launched the Green Today Greener Tomorrow campaign, which celebrates successes in sustainable operations while at the same time promotes ways to improve. From single-stream recycling, food waste composting, and energy reduction strategies, the Green Team strives to engage employees and volunteers in continually advancing the Garden's green practices.

Built Environment

The Garden is committed to designing, constructing, and operating all Garden facilities in compliance with Leadership in Energy and Environmental Design (LEED) green building standards. In February 2010, the Garden's Monsanto Center officially earned silver certification under the LEED for Existing Buildings: Operations & Maintenance rating system, while the Commerce Bank Center for Science Education earned Energy Star certification in June 2011.

The Garden's parking lot provides demonstrations of storm water best management practices utilizing porous pavements and a rain garden (bioretention). This type of parking lot significantly reduces runoff, flash flooding, soil erosion, and water pollution.

Horticulture

Horticulture displays are the number one reason people visit the Garden, providing excellent opportunities to demonstrate sustainable gardening strategies. These strategies include the following:

- Composting (and reusing on site) nearly 100 percent of the Garden's plant waste
- Washing and reusing plastic and clay pots
- Using some propane-powered mowers
- Utilizing eco-friendly fertilizers
- Installing rain sensors on irrigation systems
- Promoting and using native and adapted plants in horticulture displays
- Providing sustainable gardening educational displays and resources for homeowners and the nursery industry
- Operating the most extensive public garden recycling program in the nation: the Plastic Pot Recycling program, which collected a record 138,000 pounds of horticultural waste in 2010. To date, the program

has saved over 980,000 pounds of plastic garden pots, cell packs, and trays from landfills.

Energy

Energy efficiency:
- In 1996, the Missouri Botanical Garden's Board of Trustees established an energy policy resolution confirming energy efficiency in its facilities to be a major capital and operating priority.
- The Garden has invested in energy efficiency through improvement of lighting technology, upgrade of heating and cooling systems, and ongoing maintenance of existing systems.
- From 2000 to 2005, the Garden increased building area by 11 percent while reducing annual energy usage by 22 percent as a result of implementing energy efficiency measures.

Renewable energy:
- In 2009, solar panels were installed in the Kemper Center for Home Gardening to offset the power demand of the floral clock, a temporary display installed in honor of the Garden's sesquicentennial anniversary.
- In 2010, a 25 KW photovoltaic solar system was installed atop the Commerce Bank Center for Science Education, offsetting approximately 5 percent of the building's electrical needs.

Energy use reduction:
- In 2011, the Garden initiated the Turn it Off Campaign to encourage employees to turn off lights, computers, and other equipment when not in use. The goal of the campaign is to reduce the Garden's carbon footprint by 10 percent in one year.

Recycling and Waste Reduction

The Garden operates one of the most extensive public garden recycling programs in the nation. From office operations to visitor services, over 80 percent of nonorganic solid waste collected at the Garden is recycled.

- Single-stream recycling is collected throughout the Garden and at all public events.
- Over 90 percent of the construction waste from recent Garden projects was repurposed or recycled, including the Spink Pavilion renovation and the Shaw Nature Reserve Edgar Anderson Center construction.

- Used visitor maps and tickets are collected for reuse and/or recycling.
- All outdated electronics, batteries, and lamps are directed to specialized recycling facilities.
- All copy paper is 100 percent postconsumer recycled content.
- All boxed lunch waste is composted.

Janitorial and Cleaning Supplies

The Garden was an early adopter of green cleaning practices.

- All cleaning products are Green Seal certified.
- All janitorial paper products contain postconsumer recycled content.
- Microfiber cleaning cloths have replaced disposable rags.
- Motorized cleaning equipment is certified by the Carpet & Rug Institute.

Recycling

From office operations to visitor services, over 80 percent of nonorganic solid waste collected at the Garden is recycled.

- Single-stream recycling is collected throughout the Garden and at all public events.
- Used visitor maps and tickets are collected for reuse and/or recycling.

Take Back the Tap

In 2009, the Garden initiated the Take Back the Tap campaign, educating our visitors on the environmental impact of the bottled water industry and the savings associated with drinking tap water. Refillable water bottles are sold at the Sassafras Cafe, the Children's Garden, and the Garden Gate Shop. Now four hydration stations have been installed throughout the Garden, making it easier for visitors to refill water bottles.

Sassafras

In 2008, the Garden's restaurant, Sassafras, became the first restaurant in the State of Missouri to be certified by the Green Restaurant Association. Green practices include the following:

- Reusable plates and utensils
- Napkins and cups with recycled content
- Recycling and waste reduction
- Composting of food waste and disposables
- Water saving features
- Fair Trade Organic Coffee
- Use of natural light
- Visitor education about green achievements

Electric Vehicle Charging Stations

The Missouri Botanical Garden's charging stations, located in the west parking lot of the Ridgway Visitor Center, are equipped to charge four vehicles at one time.

Fully charging an electric vehicle (based on recovering 40 miles of electric driving range) at 240 volts can take between 4 and 5 hours. There is no charge for the use of the Garden's charging stations.

Garden Gate Shop

The majority of Garden visitors stop by the Garden Gate Shop to purchase high-quality gifts that are also eco-wise. In addition to offering a wide variety of merchandise made from recycled content, all shopping bags and packing tissue used in the shop are 100 percent recycled content. In addition, the Garden Gate Shop provides incentives to reuse shopping bags and participates in the Eco-Libris program.

Publications

First we ask, "Do we need to use paper to achieve our goal? Can we fulfill our communication goals electronically?" Therefore:

- All copy paper is 100 percent postconsumer recycled content.
- Most printed publications are printed on 100 percent postconsumer recycled content paper.
- The majority of class catalogs are now only available electronically.

Source: Reproduced with permission from the Missouri Botanical Garden.

RISK MANAGEMENT AND SAFETY IN CULTURAL INSTITUTION FACILITIES

At that time, it was the largest disaster ever experienced by a major research library. . . . We were pioneers in addressing a disaster of this magnitude, and we orchestrated a recovery program designed to create a library to take us into the future.

—Julie Wessling, assistant dean of Colorado State
University Libraries (Miller 2007)

On July 28, 1997, a disastrous rainstorm hit Fort Collins, Colorado, and led to tremendous flooding all across the city. By nightfall, many buildings in the city had sustained damage, including Colorado State University's (CSU) Morgan Library. CSU's Emergency Management Team (EMT), whose emergency operations center had also been wiped out by the flood, had to quickly set up a new command center and get to work. Among the first things the EMT leader did was to get in touch with EMT leaders at two other universities that had recently suffered natural disasters to find out how they had been remediated. At the same time, a CSU facility manager began coordinating the pumping of 5 million gallons of water from campus buildings (Hansen 2007), and pumps and fans were running constantly. Over 100 people quickly gathered to pack up almost 70,000 boxes of books to be sent to a Fort Worth, Texas, facility where the books could be flash-frozen with liquid nitrogen and, eventually, restored. Though the University ultimately lost over 500,000 books, these swift actions allowed many texts to be saved (Dimas 2007).

Cultural institution environments, like that of the Morgan Library, are expected to safely house valuable collections and human occupants. Accomplishing this requires careful risk management and the implementation of safety policies, procedures, and training. This chapter introduces these concepts, but should not be seen as an exhaustive listing of the many resources available to cultural institutions to aid them in developing their safety and risk management strategies. Safety and risk management are complex disciplines, and each cultural institution must identify safety considerations and risk management strategies that address its unique circumstances.

Risk Management in Cultural Institution Facilities

Risk management aims to recognize and limit the possibility of potentially harmful future events, and it should be "proactive rather than reactive" (Cullen 2012). For museums, it is important to implement risk management in order to safeguard people, collections, and facilities. When managing risk, cultural institutions must first work to identify their risks through a risk assessment. After conducting a risk assessment, it is necessary to implement policies, procedures, and training necessary to address the risks that have been identified.

Conducting a Risk Assessment

Risk management first involves conducting a risk assessment. A risk assessment takes stock of a museum, its collections, and life safety with respect to the variety of scenarios that could affect each of these elements. For cultural institutions that are interested in conducting their risk assessment in-house or that are unable to hire a third party, the National Institute for Conservation (also known as Heritage Preservation) provides a comprehensive "Risk Evaluation and Planning Program" checklist on its website that can serve as a thorough starting point (www.heritagepreservation.org).

Examples of the scenarios that might be assessed during a risk analysis include weather-related emergencies, such as hurricanes, and facility emergencies, such as sewage leaks. Other common risks to museum collections that should be considered during a risk assessment are

- Physical forces [earthquakes, physical damage from staff, vibrations from drawers, and repair work]
- Fire [flame and soot]

- Water [floods, and plumbing or roof leaks]
- Criminal [robbery, isolated theft, and vandalism]
- Pests [rodents and insects]
- Contaminants [dust and gases]
- Light and UV radiation
- Incorrect temperature
- Incorrect relative humidity
- Custodial neglect [data loss, misplacement, and sample mixing]. (Quoted from American Museum of Natural History)

As indicated by the above list, careful facility management plays an important role in both the prevention and mitigation of risk. Several of these issues can be mitigated by applying facility management best practices, including regularly inspecting plumbing and roofs, implementing an integrated pest management plan, assembling and following a building service (housekeeping) plan, and carefully filtering undesirable light from lamps and windows. For information about reducing air pollution and managing light exposure, see chapter 4, "Managing Cultural Facility Systems." Integrated pest management, temperature and humidity management, and building service plans are further described in chapter 5, "Managing Cultural Facility Maintenance and Operations."

Risk Management Policies, Procedures, and Training

It is important to distinguish between what is a policy and what is a procedure. We can think of a policy as the formalized guidelines that are required in order to coordinate and carry out activities in an organization. By extension, procedures are the actual operational processes that are necessary in order to execute policies (California Polytechnic State University 2013). Museums should draft appropriate risk management policies, implement effective procedures, and provide training to all staff. To oversee this process, a member of the museum's staff should be appointed to assess risks and deploy these effective policies, procedures, and training. It is possible that the museum's facility manager will serve in this capacity; if not, the facility manager can certainly assist the on-staff risk manager in identifying and mitigating risks. The risk manager can also seek the help of members of the local fire and police departments, insurance risk managers, security experts, and government risk managers, such as representatives of the U.S. Federal Emergency Management Agency (FEMA) (Adams-Graf and Nicholson

2000). By inviting a diverse array of people to participate in a cultural institution's risk management, the institution is more likely to find ways to reduce or eliminate risks (Croft and Sherman 2005).

A member of the in-house staff should be responsible for overseeing risk management, though the risk assessment can be conducted by a third party that specializes in conducting this type of study. This third-party vendor should conduct a thorough analysis of the facility and the museum's assets and, in turn, provide a summary of its findings. This summary is useful for the museum, because the museum's risk-related policies, procedures, and training can then be tailored to addressing concerns that are flagged in the risk assessment summary.

The Minnesota Historical Society (MHS) suggests that policies, procedures, and training should be focused around prevention and response: "First, develop systems and procedures to lessen and *prevent* the threat of accident, fire, crime or disaster. Second, develop systems and procedures that will provide for the most comprehensive, rapid and effective *response* to any accident, fire, crime or disaster" (Adams-Graf and Nicholson 2000, p. 4). To simplify prevention and response strategies, the MHS proposes programs that attend to eight discrete aspects of a cultural institution:

- A Building and Grounds Program
- A Lock and Key Program
- A Collections Management Program
- A Guard Program
- A Visitor and Staff Security Program
- A Fire Protection Program
- An Emergency/Disaster Program
- An Insurance Program

As collections management does not normally fall under the purview of facility management, it is not discussed in detail here. That said, it is important for collections staff to include a facility management representative in their discussions of and planning of collections recovery initiatives. Each of the other programs likely requires attention—if not oversight—from the cultural institution's facility manager.

For each of the risk management programs listed above, the cultural institution should work to develop policies and procedures that realistically address the areas of concern identified in the risk analysis. For example, the Building and Grounds Program should clearly describe the weaknesses of the museum campus's facilities. Procedures that this program might entail include ensuring visibility by keeping the exterior of the building free of plant material that might disguise intruders or hazardous materials, ensuring appropriate lighting of all entrances and parking areas, and putting locks on doors and windows. Motion sensors are also helpful near entrances and windows. It may also be helpful to arrange for police or contracted security personnel to periodically maintain a presence outside the facility.

While a museum's Building and Grounds Program addresses securing the facility from the exterior, the Lock and Key Program works to secure interior spaces for the purpose of controlling access to collections. Written procedures should be formalized that describe how and to whom keys or key cards will be issued. All keys should be labeled "Do Not Duplicate," and a process should be put in place for retrieving keys from staff members who will no longer be employed by the museum, prior to their departure.

A Guard Program that dovetails with the facility management program is critical to the institution's safety. Because guards are frequently on duty around the clock, they may often be the first people to notice something awry with the facility. For this reason, they should learn the correct procedures for reporting facility emergencies, such as poorly functioning air conditioning or broken windows. Guard staff should also be trained to make a full patrol of the building and its perimeter when the museum opens and closes and taught what their role is in an emergency or in the event that criminal activity is detected. Depending on the structure of the museum staff, the guards may also be made responsible for issuing back-of-the-house passes to nonstaff and for tracking, storing, and collecting keys for the facility. It is also important that packages shipped to the museum be inspected, and this task may be assigned to the guards per museum policy.

The Visitor and Staff Security Program establishes policies and procedures related to keeping people safe and, in the event that safety is compromised, how to respond to certain types of emergencies. Examples of procedures that might be a part of this program include keeping emergency phone numbers posted on or near all phones and keeping "emergency response flipbooks" near phones. Emergency response flipbooks normally detail first response steps for different types of injuries, criminal activities, and fires and natural disasters. Regular drills and practice responses for various types of emergencies should be conducted, so that employees have the opportunity to practice, evaluate, and adjust their emergency response procedures. See box 8.1 for a description of a major accident response exercise (MARE) at the National Zoological Park in Washington, DC.

A museum's Fire Protection Program is critical to ensuring life safety and the preservation of collections. It is imperative that the museum has installed alarms that detect and react to heat, flames, and smoke. In addition, automated fire suppression systems and handheld fire extinguishers should be strategically placed throughout the facility. All employees should be thoroughly trained with respect to the use of fire extinguishers and should regularly practice evacuating the building so they know how best to exit the facility, where to meet, and how to account for missing persons in the event of a fire. The museum can invite a representative of the local fire department to review the facility for fire safety concerns, and, during this review, a museum staff member can point out which areas of the facility hold the most important collections. A lock box that holds keys to the facility can be installed outside of the building in order to give emergency responders access to the building in the event that a member of the staff is unable to do so (Adams-Graf and Nicholson 2000).

The museum's Emergency/Disaster Program, or emergency action plan (EAP), is a set of policies and procedures that are approved by the museum's governing board, and it must be reviewed and updated on a regular basis. Over the last several years, museums have demonstrated that they must be prepared to face a wide variety of emergencies in order to ensure the safety of human life, as well as precious collections. These emergencies can be sudden, like earthquakes, fires, tornadoes, bomb threats, or chemical spills. In other cases, there may be time to prepare for emergency events, like hurricanes, floods, civil disturbances, or droughts (Mitchell 2011). Whether an emergency occurs suddenly or is known to be approaching, the Emergency/ Disaster Program should clearly describe each staff member's role, as well as the tools and supplies that are needed in order to respond to each type of emergency (see box 8.2 for a description of the building systems supervisor's role in the event of an emergency). For example, if delicate paintings need to be moved during an emergency, staff members who do not normally handle

BOX 8.1.

EMERGENCY MANAGEMENT DECISION-MAKING UNDER PRESSURE

By Meredith Beers, MPH, PhD student, Tulane University School of Public Health and Tropical Medicine, Department of Global Environmental Health Sciences

In an emergency situation, the emergency manager is the person everyone turns to for guidance, so the pressure is on the emergency manager to make the best decision, sometimes with a limited amount of information. In today's world of news media, social media and smart phones, every move is seen and tweeted and captured on camera and sent out for the world to watch and judge. This adds to the pressure that emergency managers face during emergencies.

Emergency managers now have to work in what feels like a goldfish bowl, knowing that every decision is subject to real-time criticism from persons not involved in the situation. How can emergency managers learn how to make the best decisions in the high-pressure, critical moments?

Lessons Learned from an Internship Project

While interning at the Smithsonian Institution National Zoological Park in 2011, my internship project was to update the National Zoo's Emergency Response Guide (ERG). As I worked on the ERG, I kept thinking about how planning is essential to a smooth response.

At the end of my internship, we ran a Major Accident Response Exercise (MARE) to test the ERG and see if people knew their roles and responsibilities. The MARE did its job: it highlighted the strengths and exposed the weaknesses of the ERG.

This exercise showed zoo leadership the areas that needed improvement, so that in the event of an actual emergency, the decision-making process and response would be muscle memory instead of a first run. The MARE also taught me that while planning is essential, exercises are critical.

In any emergency, whether you are in charge of a zoo, an airport, a school or a city, the pressure is on to make sure that in the critical moments you and your staff know what to do and how to do it. What I learned is that exercises are critical because they are the best way to practice roles and responsibilities as well as decision making.

A few weeks after I returned home to New Orleans, my boss at the National Zoo e-mailed me to tell me about the emergency situation they had just been in: the Aug. 23 (2011) 5.8-magnitude earthquake. Everything went well, and everyone was fine. However, as they were still debriefing from the earthquake, they were starting to ready the zoo for Hurricane Irene.

While I lamented not being there to help ready the zoo for the approaching storm, I knew that the lessons observed during the MARE and then later in the response to the earthquake were now lessons learned. My boss told me about the changes they were implementing based on the MARE as well as on the earthquake. This made me think about the difference between lessons learned and lessons observed.

Lessons Observed Aren't Always Lessons Learned

In the aftermath of disasters, as hot washes and debriefings are being conducted, lessons learned are being recorded. However, how frequently are these lessons being applied? How often are plans changed and exercises run to practice the new method?

More often than not, I think that we observe lessons but we do not learn them, as frequently the same mistakes are made over and over. A lesson cannot be called "learned" until we change our practices. The best ways to ensure that a change has been made and the lessons are really learned is to:

- Update your plan.
- Teach your plan.
- Practice your plan.

Conclusion

We are all at risk of being in an emergency situation. In these situations, the pressure is high and smart decisions need to be made. With practice through exercises, emergency managers will learn how to quickly make the best decisions in high-pressure situations. With practice, lessons observed can also be turned into lessons learned.

When a real emergency situation is upon you, if you and your team have done exercises and practiced your emergency plan, everyone will know their roles and responsibilities—and decision making in the high-pressure situation will be second nature.

Source: Beers (2011, p. 12). Printed with permission from Meredith Beers, MPH, PhD candidate, Tulane University School of Public Health and Tropical Medicine, Department of Global Environmental Health Science.

artwork may be called into service. These staff members should be trained to handle the artwork before the emergency, so that they can work quickly and safely during an unexpected event. For tips on training staff to handle this potentiality, see the Getty Conservation Institute's guidebook, *Building an Emergency Plan: A Guide for Museums and Other Cultural Institutions*, which includes a helpful section on the handling of different types of art in emergency situations (Dorge and Jones 1999, pp. 252–256).

Similar to the emergency response flipbook, a listing of all applicable contacts and resources for particular disasters should also be compiled and shared with each staff member as a part of the disaster planning process. Examples of information that might be included in this resource list include the contact information for partner institutions, for emergency personnel, and for expert conservators in disaster management. It may also include a listing of facility management staff members who are assigned to each area of the facility or who have the expertise necessary to assist with remediation. Duplicates of important disaster-related documents, such as facility floor plans, disaster management procedures, and insurance policies, should also be kept off-site so that they can be accessed in an emergency situation.

When it is not possible for a risk to be avoided, it is likely necessary for a museum to purchase insurance that covers damage or harm to its collections, facilities, and occupants. Development of the museum's "Insurance Program" can involve insurance underwriters (Adams-Graf and Nicholson 2000). These underwriters should be invited to inspect the facility and its assets on a yearly basis. This walk-through inspection gives underwriters an opportunity to propose ways in which the museum's facility or its operations

BOX 8.2.

IN AN EMERGENCY: BUILDING SYSTEMS SUPERVISOR JOB DESCRIPTION

Building Systems Supervisor

RESPONSIBILITIES: Maintains maximum functioning of all physical plant systems. Reduces or eliminates risk to people, buildings, and objects through repair work and anticipation of structural, electrical, mechanical, and other problems.

REPORTS TO: PROTECTIVE SERVICES MANAGER

LINE OF SUCCESSION:
1. Maintenance Superintendent
2. Maintenance Engineer
3. Chief of Security

ACTION CHECKLIST:
___ Quickly gathers information and develops initial strategy on personnel available and the nature of the emergency.
___ Receives the Building Systems Supervisor's Emergency Supply Kit and a portable radio from protective services.
___ Assembles and directs a team of workers, primarily from Engineering Department, to immediately conduct initial structural, systems and utility damage assessments. Reports location(s) and severity of problems to Protective Services Manager.
___ Provides emergency power. Coordinates use of emergency generator(s) with Equipment and Transportation Supervisor.
___ Directs necessary emergency shutdown procedures for heating, ventilation, air conditioning, water, and electrical systems.
___ Shuts off water heaters and gas supply lines as necessary.
___ Restores and maintains essential services.
___ Repairs emergency equipment by priority.
___ Inspects and clearly marks hazards and hazardous areas.
___ Constructs emergency facilities as needed, in coordination with Safety and Welfare Supervisor.
___ Provides mechanical maintenance as necessary.

Source: Originally appeared in the Seattle Art Museum's *Emergency Planning Handbook* (Seattle: Seattle Art Museum, 1994). Reproduced with permission from the Seattle Art Museum, www.seattleartmuseum.org.

might be adjusted in order to reduce risk. Prior to purchasing insurance, each museum needs to decide how much risk it is willing to assume on its own, at what point a given risk is significant enough to require insurance, and the deductible it is able to afford for each type of insurance that is purchased. By increasing the deductible, the museum is able to pay a lower premium for insurance, and this is a good strategy for risks that are not seen as likely to occur. It is also important for the museum to build sufficient financial reserves so that it can cover losses that are not covered by its insurance policies or pay the deductible for losses that are covered (Croft and Sherman 2005).

While this multiprogram risk management approach is grounded in the MHS's guidelines, there are certainly other approaches available to cultural institutions. For example, the Northern States Conservation Center (NSCC) offers a detailed interpretation of the risk assessment and management process on its website, www.collectioncare.org (Schindel 2012). Another valuable guide is "Emergency Planning," chapter 10 in the *Museum Handbook* published by the U.S. National Park Service (O'Connor 2006, pp. 10:1–75). This chapter provides detailed information about developing an emergency operations plan (EOP) as well as a sample emergency response checklist. The Northeast Document Conservation Center offers a free, online disaster-planning tool, dPlan. An institution can input its own data into the dPlan program, found at www.dplan.org, and a disaster plan will automatically be generated based on that information.

As with any element of cultural institution facility management, it is critical that an institution's risk management strategy aligns with its particular circumstances. Prior to putting any risk management or disaster planning strategy into practice, the cultural institution should undertake a collaborative process with input from staff from throughout the organization, as well as from trained risk management professionals, to ensure that all of its bases are covered.

Disaster Assistance for Cultural Institution Facilities

Each year in the United States, the Heritage Preservation organization sponsors MayDay, an event that builds awareness of and encourages preparation for disasters that affect cultural institutions. As part of this event, cultural institutions are encouraged to take one step during the month of May to increase their levels of disaster preparedness. For example, in May 2012, the Utah State University Museum of Anthropology assembled its first-ever disaster plan and the Indiana Historical Society in Indianapolis reviewed its disaster plan, took inventory of its disaster supplies, and trained staff on proper steps to take when faced with an emergency (Heritage Preservation 2013). All museums that participate in MayDay are asked to submit a description of their MayDay-related disaster preparation activities to Heritage Preservation, which in turn shares these accomplishments online. Not only does Heritage Preservation sponsor MayDay, but also its website, www.heritagepreservation.org, is a storehouse of free resources for cultural institutions preparing for natural disasters.

In the event that a disaster does occur, a number of assistance programs are available to aid cultural institutions during the recovery process. For example, FEMA offers assistance to certain types of nonprofit organizations, including museums. This aid can be applied to the removal of debris, to taking emergency protective steps, and to the repair, replacement, or restoration of facilities that have been damaged by a disaster. Eligibility information for this program, as well as general information related to disaster preparedness, is available on the FEMA website, www.fema.gov.

Even if a cultural institution facility already has a clear disaster management plan in place, when an emergency strikes, navigating the process can be overwhelming. Luckily, organizations like the Northeast Document Conservation Center (NDCC; see www.nedcc.org) and the Conservation Center for Art and Historic Artifacts (CCAHA; see www.ccaha.org) are passionate about preserving documents, art, and artifacts. Both the NDCC and the CCAHA offer 24-hour emergency assistance over the phone for cultural institutions requiring immediate support. This support can be invaluable in terms of guiding institutions as they take their first steps toward rescuing their collections in an emergency. For an example of how the U.S. National Park Service Museum Emergency Response team responded to Superstorm Sandy in New York City, see box 8.3.

Safety in Cultural Institution Facilities

The Children's Museum & Theatre of Maine in Portland, Maine, truly exemplifies what rigorous safety standards might look like in a cultural institution facility. For example, all public areas of the Children's Museum & Theatre are cleaned and disinfected each evening, and all toys are washed at least once per week. In an effort to remove hazards, the Children's Museum & Theatre

BOX 8.3.

HOW ELLIS ISLAND'S IMMIGRANT ARTIFACTS WASHED UP IN MARYLAND

By Emily Berman

While many homeowners in the New York area are still struggling to deal with the flooding from Superstorm Sandy, so are two of the city's iconic islands: Liberty Island (home of Lady Liberty) and Ellis Island, the historic gateway to the United States for millions of immigrants at the turn of the twentieth century. Liberty Island is set to reopen this summer to tourists, but Ellis Island still has a long way to go.

During the storm, a large wave went over the backside of Ellis Island, knocked out lower level windows and doors and flooded the basements of the island's main buildings.

Diana Pardue, the Chief of the Museum Division at the Statue of Liberty and Ellis Island, explains all the HVAC, boilers and electrical lines need to be redone. Salt water and wiring don't mix.

Most of the museum's collection was on upper floors, away from the water. But everything below the water line was covered in silt.

Sending in the "Museum Doctor"

At times like this, the National Park Service calls in Bob Sonderman. For most of the year, Bob Sonderman manages a museum storage facility in Prince George's County. But when duty calls, he can be on the road in a matter of hours.

"I pack my van full of everything I can possibly think of," he says. "I have big blower fans, I have a generator." He even brings his own gasoline, which, in times of disaster, can be difficult to buy.

Sonderman is head of the National Park Service's Museum Emergency Response Team. And basically what an EMT does in a medical emergency, Sonderman does in a museum emergency. They've rescued artifacts after Hurricanes Isabel and Ivan, Katrina and the Gulf Oil Spill.

When Sonderman got to Ellis Island, he was shocked at the damage. "The initial response is Holy Cow! I didn't realize it was going to be this bad. All these museum objects were covered in gook and salty, ookey water, and they're still in the exhibit cases."

A display case of medical equipment used to examine incoming immigrants was knocked on its side, and filled with silt. The artifacts were metal, and would soon begin to rust. Sondermen ran out to his van, took out the crowbars, and cracked open the display cases to get these objects out.

"We're the best break in crew you've ever seen!" Sonderman brags, chuckling. "The longer you wait, the more in jeopardy the collection can become."

Moving to Maryland

The team sent the medical instruments to metals conservators in West Virginia. They froze all the wet documents, to stop mold growth. And everything else needed to be put by a fan to dry off. But, the island—and actually, a lot of New York City—didn't have power. In order to preserve the artifacts, they'd need a dry, stable environment—in other words, Sonderman's facility in Landover, Maryland.

More than a million items were painstakingly packed and shipped down on seven semi-trucks. Some of the most fragile things, like tape of oral histories, videos and X-rays of passengers as they came off the ships are in a different room. All the items are organized by the way they were exhibited or stored in the museum on Ellis Island, to make the return trip north as easy as possible. Sonderman says it will all go back someday.

Someday, but not anytime soon. At the end of January [2013], President Obama signed the Sandy Recovery Act, designating $234 million to national parks impacted by the storm. There's still no running water, and no electricity on the island, and Diana Pardue says the museum will be closed for renovations through the rest of this year.

In the meantime, Sonderman says, the island's collection will stay in Maryland, until the job is done.

Source: Originally published March 8, 2013. Reproduced with permission from WAMU 88.5, www.wamu.org.

has installed child-safe electrical outlets that prevent children from inserting their fingers or other objects into the sockets. Regulated thermostats keep the water in the visitors' restrooms cool enough to prevent burns. A member of the Children's Museum & Theatre's staff is always on hand in play areas to check for any hazards that may arise during the day and to address guest concerns. Anytime that a liquid spill occurs, it is cleaned using procedures for cleaning hazardous waste. All Children's Museum & Theatre staff members are certified in first aid and cardiopulmonary resuscitation (CPR) for both children and adults, as well as trained in the use of automated external defibrillators (AEDs). Children's Museum & Theatre staff members also wear uniforms that make it easy for visitors to identify them, should a visitor need help. In addition, these staff members are all prepared to follow the Children's Museum & Theatre's emergency evacuation plan, leading visitors to their designated meeting place.

As the Children's Museum & Theatre of Maine illustrates, safety in a cultural institution must be integrated throughout many aspects of the institution's operations. Facility management personnel can play a key role in ensuring the safety of staff and visitors. In order for an institution to have a strong culture of safety, a member of its staff should be appointed to serve as the museum's safety officer. The safety officer's job is to ensure that the museum is operating in compliance with its safety policies and procedures. Please note that if the museum has not yet established safety policies and procedures, it is important for these to be clearly and carefully defined as soon as possible. Once safety policies and procedures are defined, the safety officer can periodically inspect the facility, check into any safety-related complaints, and assess incidents that occur on the museum campus (Genoways and Ireland 2003).

It is important that the facility be inspected on a regular basis and that there be a process in place for documenting safety deficiencies and for noting corrective actions as they are taken. If a museum is regularly inspected and properly maintained, chances are that many of its hazards are removed right away. Staff from throughout the facility can get involved in the inspection process. Involving staff members who may not normally carry out safety inspections is helpful, because when they return to their regularly scheduled work, they have a new appreciation for spotting potential hazards and what it takes to keep the museum environment safe (Hankins 2013).

It is also crucial for regular maintenance to be carried out on equipment, especially equipment that visitors and staff regularly use, including escalators and elevators. Even if they are maintained regularly, escalators can be very hazardous to persons wearing sandals and can present fall hazards to families who place children in strollers on them. Consider placing signage near escalators reminding guests to be careful near the ends of the escalator and to remove children from strollers prior to boarding the escalator. Other critical equipment, especially fire detection and suppression systems, should be regularly inspected and maintained.

Material Safety Data Sheets (MSDSs), which describe characteristics and handling procedures for hazardous substances, need to be available to those who work with or near these substances. Each MSDS should be kept both in the work area in which the substance will be used and in a master file that collects all MSDSs relevant to the facility. Staff who work with these substances should be required to review an MSDS for each substance they work with and, in turn, initial the sheet to acknowledge that they have read and understand its contents.

In the museum environment, hazardous materials might be found in specimen jars—for example, formaldehyde—or come in the form of artifacts, such as artillery shells. Still other hazardous materials are as commonplace as cleaning supplies and copy machine toner. In addition, biological waste materials, such as bodily fluids, animal waste, and organic waste from cafeterias, can be found in and around many museums. It is crucial that appropriate procedures be established for each type of waste, that employees have a clear understanding of the risks and requirements associated with handling this waste, and that it is properly disposed of using accepted standards (Genoways and Ireland 2003). For more information about disposing of hazardous waste, see OSHA's website, www.osha.gov/SLTC/hazardouswaste.

If an incident occurs that causes an injury or damage to property, it is important for the incident to be documented. The cause of the incident should be determined, and corrective actions should be taken in order to prevent it from occurring again. In addition, the safety officer should follow up on corrective actions to be sure that they offered the correct solution to the problem. It is also important that staff be notified of these incidents as they occur. Roger Hankins, supervisory safety manager in the Smithsonian Institution's Office of Facilities Management and Reliability, suggests setting up a safety alert program to share safety-related information with staff and, hopefully, avoid a repeat incident. For additional safety tips from Hankins, see box 8.4.

Slips, trips, and falls are among the most common workplace injuries—second only to motor vehicle accidents in the United States—and

BOX 8.4.

SAFETY PRIORITIES IN
MUSEUM ENVIRONMENTS

By Roger Hankins, supervisory safety manager for the Smithsonian Institution Office of Facilities Management and Reliability

Above: Facilities staff at the National Portrait Gallery in Washington, DC, demonstrates proper use of safety equipment and personal protective gear.

1. *Conduct monthly training sessions on how to best perform tasks, and ensure the training is tracked and maintained consistently.* Know what type of training each employee or job requires and tailor your program to meet those needs. Require all employees, including supervisors, to participate in these training events and make the information as understandable and interesting as possible. Be creative in developing these classes! You can't expect staff to work safely if they are not trained in the proper way to perform their tasks.

2. *Implement a Facility Safety Inspection program for all facilities.* Document any deficiency, and ensure corrective actions are taken and that the issues have been resolved. Having different groups of employees

participate is a great way to show what we do and why; they will then take that knowledge with them to their own areas. If the facilities are maintained to a high degree, then the majority of hazards are removed from the area.

3. *When events occur that cause either injury or damage, perform detailed incident investigations to determine cause, corrective actions needed and a review process to determine the effectiveness of those actions.* Communication of these events to the staff is very important! Use some type of Safety Alert program to get this information to the facilities in a timely and effective manner. Sharing this knowledge may very well prevent another occurrence.

4. *Develop a thoughtful, proactive approach to making the areas safer by listening to new ideas, looking at past areas of concern and developing strong relationships with the employees and staff.* It is in everyone's interest to keep both the employees and the museum safe and protected. Use this approach to build trust among all the staff.

5. People often look at "safety" as a separate step that must be done to meet a standard. *But the reality is that safety is an integration of activities into a process to ensure hazards are controlled.* This becomes second nature when approached correctly and implemented properly; it should be a seamless act when performing any action. (Such as putting on your seatbelt as soon as you enter your vehicle.) This is a long-term process, but the most effective method to truly develop the culture needed in any environment.

Source: Text printed with permission of Roger Hankins. Photo reproduced with permission from the Smithsonian Institution Office of Facilities Management and Reliability, www.facilities.si.edu.

these injuries are caused by mistakes like incorrect usage of ladders, uneven surfaces, and simply not paying attention when walking. Training museum facility management and building service staff to take precautions to avoid slips, trips, and falls—such as avoiding carrying items that make it difficult to see where you are walking and wearing nonslip footwear—can help reduce injuries significantly. When working in particularly high-elevation locations, facility management staff members need to be trained and required to use personal protective equipment (PPE), such as harnesses (Positive Promotions 2005). In addition, staff members should be provided with and trained with respect to the use of the PPE necessary to safely perform their jobs. Examples of PPE that might be required, depending on the job, include goggles, steel-toed boots, respirators, and latex gloves.

Additional training for museum facility management personnel is discussed in chapter 10. However, it is important to reinforce the benefit of training with respect to increasing safety. Museums can hold safety-training sessions each month in order to make sure that each employee knows the optimal way to carry out each task. A process for documenting this training for each employee should be developed and utilized. This documentation is often necessary to demonstrate compliance with applicable regulations, like those of OSHA (Hankins 2013).

Summary

Cultural institutions are dynamic places. With so much going on in and around them—from hosting special events and temporary exhibitions to completing renovations and responding to severe weather—it is necessary for cultural institution personnel to look for ways to effectively manage risk and improve safety considerations at all times. As with many aspects of cultural facility management, an institution's ability to manage risk and ensure safety is enriched through collaboration. By looking to other facilities' risk management plans and safety policies, procedures, and previous experiences, as well as drawing on the knowledge and experience of in-house staff and outside experts, cultural institutions can position their facility management operations to successfully reduce risk and improve safety.

SPECIAL EVENTS IN CULTURAL FACILITIES

Special events are an especially effective fund-raising method that help museums reach a broad range of contributors. They also can be expensive and time-consuming undertakings. Before embarking, it is important to analyze the cost/benefit ratio to ensure the event will be profitable. Time and effort of numerous staff and volunteers will be needed to attend to countless details, time necessarily taken away from other museum functions. Careful planning is essential.

—Hugh Genoways and Lynne Ireland (2003, p. 136)

Museum and cultural institution facilities are often sought-after locations for special events—whether for corporate holiday parties or weddings, nonprofit fundraisers or children's birthday celebrations, museums have to be ready to smoothly host a variety of events. Because hosting these special events means that the facilities will be used in ways outside of their normal day-to-day operations, the facility manager plays a key role in making the facility work for each event, while also keeping the collections safe and ensuring that "business as usual" can be carried out by staff and visitors before, during, and after the event.

For this reason, in many cultural institutions, especially in smaller museums that do not have a dedicated special events department, many aspects of special event management fall under the purview of the facility manager. For example, at the Fred Jones Jr. Museum of Art in Norman, Oklahoma, the director of facilities is the same person who serves as the director of special events *and* as the director of museum security. Especially when juggling so many responsibilities at one time, it is important for cultural institution facility managers to have a very organized and transparent process for streamlining special events in their facilities. Included in streamlining this process are clear special event guidelines, a carefully assembled facility use agreement, and well-defined strategies for accessibility and emergency planning.

Special events, especially those hosted by parties from outside the museum, present a number of opportunities and challenges to cultural institutions and their facility managers. For example, special events are great opportunities to showcase the facility and the museum's mission for people who might not normally find themselves in the museum. Hosting special events gives a museum valuable face time with event guests who may not have known about the museum or who may not have taken time to visit prior to receiving an invitation to the event. In turn, by truly shining during the special event—for example, by providing good customer service, clean restrooms, and an overall sparkling and engaging environment—the museum is cluing event attendees into how wonderful the museum, its facility, and its people are. This can, in turn, pique guests' interest in returning during regular business hours to visit the collections, host their own special events, and, perhaps eventually, contribute their money, time, or talents to the museum's mission.

In addition to helping to spread the word about a museum, special events can provide additional revenue from rental fees and catering income. If the museum gift shop stays open during special events, revenue at the shop can see an increase from such an event. It has even been suggested by one museum that "couples who get married in the museum are more likely to think of us fondly and remember us in their wills" (Merritt 2005, p. 35). With the variety of benefits observed when renting out museum space, it is easy to see why so many museums offer this option. That said, with space rentals come added foot traffic, as well as outside food, drinks, decorations, and more that present challenges when trying to keep both the collections and the facility in their best condition. It is important to remember the added wear and tear that special events often have on facilities. Frequently, these events are set up and torn down very quickly by third-party vendors, resulting in haphazard work that bangs up corners, dents walls, and scratches floors. During the event, something as seemingly innocuous as red wine can cause lasting damage to carpeting with even the slightest spill. In addition to the potential for physical damage, special events can disrupt the experience of museum visitors and the ability of staff to accomplish their work.

To reduce the potential for damage to a facility and for disruption to staff and visitors, as well as to make sure that those renting the space are not using it in a way that goes against the museum's mission, it is important to utilize event guidelines and a facility use agreement to protect a facility before, during, and after an event. Taken together, the event guidelines and facility use agreement act as a museum's roadmaps when deciding to whom its facility can be rented, how much special-use liability insurance to require outside venders to furnish, which hours the facility will be available, and many other important details that affect both the museum's operation and the facility's condition. To further simplify special event planning, if an organization internal to the museum is hosting an event, for example, if the museum's development office is hosting a membership event, similar special event guidelines and agreements can—and, we would argue, should—be applied to the internal special event planning process.

Establishing Special Event Guidelines

Developing special event guidelines allows the facility manager the opportunity to get to know the facility, its potential, and its vulnerabilities in new ways, while also setting clear expectations for those who will be renting or using the facility. The facility manager will begin to consider each space not just in terms of how staff can use it to get their work done or how it keeps collections safe, but also in terms of how it can accommodate unique events and the challenges posed by the events possible within the space. Museum staff will need to familiarize themselves with the maximum occupancy of their facilities, and of each room, and consider whether tent space will be allowed on their grounds in order to accommodate overflow during especially large events. Staffing is another concern—how will a museum keep its bathrooms clean and its collections secure during special events that may be happening during off-hours? Considering these issues will help lay the groundwork for a solid set of special event guidelines and, in turn, successful special events that reflect well on the museum and its facility.

One item that must be addressed upfront by museum administration—and, subsequently, made clear in special event guidelines—is who will be allowed to host an event in the facility. For example, some museums choose not to allow special events unless the museum itself is a host or co-host of the event. That policy, however, appears to be the exception, as a majority of museums open their doors to special events hosted by outside parties. Among the museums that rent space out for special events, there are some differences in terms of the types of events allowed. According to a 2005 survey of U.S. museums, 65 percent of museums would rent to political groups and 85 percent would rent to religious groups; a greater number of museums indicated that they would rent to corporate groups (90 percent) and non-religious nonprofit groups (95 percent; Merritt 2005, p. 80).

In any case, to whom the museum does and does not rent its facilities can affect publicity and word of mouth pertaining to the museum, so this is a decision that should not be taken lightly. Museums and cultural institutions that receive federal funds, such as the Smithsonian Institution and the National Archives, are explicitly prohibited from discrimination, as per Title VI of the Civil Rights Act of 1964. For this reason, the National Archives states within its space use guidelines that its "facilities shall not be made available to any organization that practices or advocates discrimination based on race, color, religion, sex, national origin, age or condition of handicap" (National Archives). Ultimately, as Merritt states, a museum's policy about who may rent space should be "based on a museum's mission and values, and is a cornerstone of building a communications plan for answering questions like 'Why would you rent to them?'" (2005, p. 35).

When an individual or an organization is interested in hosting an event in the museum's facility, they will approach the museum with a number of questions so they can be sure that the space will suit the needs of their event. Having a pre-prepared special event brochure or packet assembled that lists details about the space, as well as the basic event guidelines, will ease the selection process for potential renters and save staff from the redundancy of answering the same questions over and over again. Many cultural institutions are beginning to post these brochures and guidelines online, so prospective renters can review them prior to making contact with the institution to inquire about renting space.

As an example of providing special event guidance online, the Matagorda County Museum (MCM) in Bay City, Texas, posts a listing of around 35 key considerations for those interested in hosting a special event at their facility on its website. The MCM's considerations are easy to understand and provide clear guidelines and information for prospective renters. One of these considerations, labeled "The 10 Steps," establishes, in chronological order, the ten basic tasks involved in coordinating a special event at the facility. An easy-to-navigate, thorough online listing of guidelines, like that of the Matagorda County Museum, helps prepare prospective renters, some of whom may not have experience planning special events, for their initial contact with the museum. This is especially important, because more and more people planning events are beginning the process by doing online research. By providing clear, easy-to-understand information about the facility and the special event process online, the museum can instill confidence in prospective renters that the museum is organized, experienced, and ready to host a great event.

Posting this information online is a sound approach from the perspectives of marketing and efficiency; however, there are several things to keep in mind when doing so. First, because rental pricing can vary so much from event to event (i.e., in terms of how large the event is, what time of year the event will be held, and special requests that are made), museums may not want to post pricing online. It can become confusing for the renter when one price is quoted online and yet another is quoted when the time comes to put down a deposit and sign the contract. Regardless of how much information the museum decides to post online, it is probably a good idea to include a note on the website that makes it clear that any information posted is subject to change without notice. Be sure to provide current contact information on the site (e.g., that of the facility manager or the special events coordinator) and ask that interested parties contact the museum to learn more about how their specific requests can be met. Including this note on the website is especially important because sites are not always updated each time facility or events-related details change. Without this disclaimer, people who rely on online research to make their plans can become frustrated when options represented online are not actually available.

Those interested in having an event at a cultural institution would likely appreciate the opportunity to tour the facility with a knowledgeable guide. This tour will provide the opportunity for a guide, likely the facility manager and/or special events coordinator, to showcase the available spaces and answer any questions the prospective renter has about the space, logistics, and policies. Some institutions provide online forms so that people can request a tour on the museum's website. If the museum is not going to provide an online form, it is especially important to include contact information for the facility rental point of contact on the website.

Prospective renters will want to know the square footage available for special events and whether any areas of the facility are off-limits. Knowing what is available will help interested parties assess how well the space can accommodate the special needs of their event—for example, whether there is room for stage setup, buffets, tables of different sizes, overflow, and so on. It is also helpful to have a list of event types the cultural institution has hosted in the past, as well as the sizes of these past events. Taking time to photo-document how events of different types, styles, and sizes look in the facility when they are all set up and, in turn, compiling these images in a "look book" helps prospective renters get a feel for the events the facility is able to host.

Many cultural facilities point out in their guidelines and facility use agreements that exhibitions and interior arrangements of spaces are subject to change prior to the event. It is possible that prospective renters will tour a space when one exhibition is on display, but, when the date of the event arrives, a different exhibition will be on display in that same space. This change has the potential to surprise and, possibly, upset renters who may not have considered how the museum's rotating exhibition schedule could affect their event. To inform renters of this possibility, museums, like the San Diego History Center (SDHC), often include language in their guide-lines that describes this possibility. For example, the SDHC guidelines state, "All exhibitions and displays are subject to change without further notice and may not be moved, rearranged, or altered for the event." Trans-parency about the possibility that exhibition content may change helps prevent last-minute panic on behalf of the renters. Museums do not want renters realizing on the day of the event that the aesthetics or arrangement of the space will be different from what they had originally expected. It is much better for renters to be prepared for this change in advance, especially if the new exhibition content is controversial and may have the potential to alarm event attendees.

It is also important to let prospective renters know, in advance, whether there are any restricted dates—for example, holidays like Thanksgiving or New Year's Day—that the facility is not available to host special events. Many cultural institution facilities also restrict the times that special events can occur in order to avoid interfering with the regular schedules of visitors and staff, as well as a minimum rental period (e.g., three hours). For example, some facilities specify that special event setup may begin only after the museum has closed to the public for the day. To address their concerns about special events interfer-ing with regular activities, the National Archives Southeast Region Facility (2013) includes this language in its special events guidelines:

As a matter of National Archives policy, co-hosted private events should not interfere with the normal public access to National Archives exhibit spaces, public use areas, and facilities. While events may be held during normal business hours, the events shall not impede facility access for non-event patrons, researchers, and staff. (p. 1)

Many facilities also specify a particular time by which events must end and by which all cleanup must be complete. Establishing these times in advance helps keep expectations clear, so that hosts and vendors can plan the event schedule accordingly, and museum staff who must be present for the event have a reasonable expectation in terms of when their shifts will end.

To help with scheduling, it can be useful to require that rental requests and/or applications be submitted well in advance, for example, at least one month prior to the event. Some cultural institutions, like the San Diego Natural History Museum, allow a date to be held for a set period of time as a courtesy to the first party to request the date. Doing so gives the first prospective renters who show an interest in a particular date the first right of refusal should another party attempt to schedule an event at that same time. While some institutions offer to hold the space for free, others require a deposit—for example, 50 percent of the quoted rental fee—and a signed facility use or rental agreement before a date will be held. In either case, it is a good idea to be up front about the museum's reservation policy beginning with the initial discussions with a prospective renter.

In terms of assigning a rental fee for the facility, there are several factors to take under consideration, including any discounts that may be offered to particular groups. Some cultural institutions offer a courtesy discount (e.g., a discount of 10 percent) to nonprofits wishing to rent their space. Other cultural institutions require those who wish to rent the space to become museum members as a part of the rental agreement. If the museum offers special discounts or has membership requirements, these are both items that will need to be included in the guidelines packet that is posted online or handed out to potential renters. It is also important to inform renters, especially in the facility use agreement, that any damage or abuse resulting from the event that requires cleanup, repair, or replacement of the museum's property must be paid for by the renters. To help ease this process, some museums require that renters put down a damage deposit prior to the event. For example, the Bowers Museum in Santa Ana, California, asks that renters provide a valid credit card that the museum can hold until after the event. If any damage occurs, the credit card will be charged to cover the damage, and an itemized description of the damage-related charges will be sent to the renter (Bowers Museum 2012).

Any time a facility manager or other museum staff member must ask a renter to pay for damage, it can make for an uncomfortable conversation. There can be disagreement over whether the damage was preexisting or whether it truly occurred during the event. To help prevent any disagreement, it is a good idea for both the facility manager and the renter to formally acknowledge the condition of the facility in a condition report prior to the event. This report, which notes the condition and cleanliness of the facility, should always be kept updated and on file by a designated staff member. Prior to an event, the renter can inspect the facility and revise the condition report, if necessary. Both the renter and the facility manager can then sign the condition report to mutually acknowledge the condition of the facility before the event. This report will, in turn, become an important addendum to the facility use agreement. After the event, the facility manager will reference the report, noting any repairs or additional cleaning requirements necessary to return the facility to the condition it was in prior to the event. With the report on hand, disagreements over the condition of the facility before the event are more easily resolved.

In addition to having a clear policy for documenting the condition of the facility and any necessary damage deposits, it is also important to have clear guidelines that outline when final payment for the event is due. Some cultural institutions require full payment in advance of the event (e.g., a minimum of five full business days before the event) and will cancel the reservation if payment is not received by this deadline. Still others are comfortable with sending an invoice to the renter afterward. In either case, the forms of acceptable payment, to whom payment should be remitted, and by when is all information that should be discussed with the prospective renter early on and clearly outlined in the facility use agreement.

Because the renter or cultural institution may cancel the event after the use agreement has already been signed, it is necessary to have a clear policy for handling the cancellation process. It is helpful for this policy to be embedded in the use agreement, so the renter will have formally acknowledged it in advance of a potential cancellation. The cancellation policy should consider whether any portion of the rental deposit is refundable should the renter choose to cancel the event. There are a number of other considerations when determining the cancellation policy, such as whether the museum requires the renter to give a certain number of days' notice (e.g., five business days) in order to receive a full refund of the deposit and whether the museum requires the renter to reimburse any direct costs incurred by the museum in anticipation of the event. The cancellation policy should also outline under which conditions the museum, itself, is able to cancel the event—for example, when the renter does not cohere to the facility use agreement or other rental policies and guidelines.

In addition to considering how to handle cancellations, it is also important to consider how to handle renters' requests to change the agreed-upon parameters of the event. It is common for museums to require notice in advance (e.g., a minimum of several business days before the event) if any changes, such as additional lighting, moving services, or audiovisual equipment, are necessary. Weather-related changes to the event also need to be taken into consideration. For example, if the event is scheduled to take place outdoors on the museum's property, will the museum make contingency spaces available indoors in the event of rain or severe weather so that the event will not have to be cancelled? If applicable, these weather contingencies should be clearly articulated in the guidelines and, possibly, in the use agreement.

Many facility use agreements require the renter and any event vendors, such as caterers, to furnish proof of liability insurance prior to the event. Frequently, the minimum policy required is $1 million, with the museum being listed as an "additional insured" (and the renter or vendor listed as "primary insured") for the entirety of the event. Sometimes, museums compile a list of preferred vendors that have acquired and filed proof of this insurance with the museum in the past. In this case, museums may require that renters work exclusively with these preferred vendors for the sake of simplicity or, alternatively, offer this list to renters as a starting point. It is important to establish a date within the facility use agreement by which proof of insurance must be furnished (e.g., one month in advance of the rental date). It is also common to include a liability release statement in the facility use agreement. This statement establishes that the renter will not hold the museum or its employees accountable for damages resulting from the facility rental. As an example, in its special events guidelines, the National Archives Southeast Region Facility (2013) has very specific language to this effect:

> Organizations shall indemnify and hold harmless the United States and the National Archives, their agents and employees, against any and all damages, claims, or other liability due to personal injury or death, or damage to, or loss of, the property of others, arising out of its use of National Archives facilities. All organizations will sign the attached Facility Use Indemnification Form. (p. 6)

A carefully worded release statement such as this may help protect the museum in the event of an accident on the property.

One additional concern is protecting the museum's brand. Because the event will be held at the museum, the museum will be represented in some form or fashion on event invitations, in event announcements, and in other types of communication about the event. Before the event host sends out any invitations or press releases about the event, it is common practice for the museum to reserve the right to review these communications. Having the opportunity to review and approve these communications prior to distribution helps the museum ensure that its brand, including its name, logo, and mission, is being accurately reflected in event communications. Cultural institutions also consider how their brand is reflected *during* the event. Some institutions, like the Museum of Chinese in America (MOCA) in New York, New York, implement guidelines that address press coverage and visibility of the museum's logo during the event. The MOCA includes these brand-related items among its restrictions: "For corporate events, no organizational logo may cover a MOCA logo (on signage, podium, etc.); all displays, decorations and logo usage must be approved by the Museum"; and "The Museum reserves the right to approve all press releases and on-premises press coverage" (MOCA 2013). While this level of brand management may seem beyond the scope of what many cultural institutions have time to oversee, it is nonetheless important to keep in mind how renters choose to represent the institution and its mission when marketing and holding events on the museum's property.

It is also necessary to consider the appropriate number of museum staff, including security personnel, building service workers, and so on, that must be present for each event. Illustrating the challenge of staffing and setting up for special events, Christy Jellets, facilities operations manager at the Atlanta Botanical Garden, says,

> My team is responsible for all setup for internal meetings or events as well as those not set up by a caterer. Additionally, my staff works every event managing trash, facility care, etc. The biggest challenge is getting detailed information in time to schedule staff and complete the set-up. Often details are left until a day or two before the event. (Jellets 2012)

If the facility manager is not the primary contact for those renting the facility or planning an event, it is important that the primary contact passes event-related information along to the facility manager as soon as possible. This allows staffing to be scheduled and setup to be planned well in advance. How many staff members are present will, of course, depend on the size of the event. It must also be decided beforehand which staff members' presence will be included as part of the facility rental fee and which staffing levels may cost extra. For example, some museums may provide the staff necessary for an event as a part of the regular rental fee, but, for especially large events, require an additional fee to provide the extra staff necessary to support the event.

One additional staffing consideration comes in the form of docent-led tours. These tours may be included as part of the facility rental fee, but some museums may choose to charge extra to make docents available during the event to lead tours. In either case, it is important to make clear how much notice the museum will require if the renter would like docents to be present and how much this service will cost, if anything. By extension, it is necessary to decide beforehand whether event guests will have access to exhibits for free or, alternatively, whether a fee will be charged to cover the security costs necessary to give guests access to the exhibits.

Catering Guidelines

If catering is allowed in the museum facility for special events, there are a number of elements that must be considered prior to working with prospective renters. Clear catering guidelines, such as what types of food and beverages are allowed in the facility, acceptable food-heating methods, and whether kitchen space will be made available to caterers, can prevent last-minute surprises. Some questions that might be asked when preparing catering guidelines include the following:

- Will the cultural institution have a list of preferred caterers? Does the museum charge an extra fee for those who deviate from the preferred vendor list, if this is allowed?

- Will the museum require caterers to take a walk-through tour with a member of the facilities or security staff prior to the event?

- Will the museum allow alcoholic beverages in its facility? If so, which beverages, and who may dispense them? Is a permit required?

- Does the museum have kitchen space that will be made available to caterers before and/or during the event?

- Where, exactly, are food and beverages allowed in the museum? How will the museum make this clear to event attendees?

- If the museum has its own catering service, will catering fees be billed separately from museum facility charges? Are renters required to use this service if they desire a catered event?

- Are open flames for cooking banned from the facility? If they are allowed, is a fire permit required?

After museum staff has identified the parameters for catering within the museum, it is a good idea to compile these guidelines into one document that is shared with the caterer of each event early on in the planning process. It is common for institutions to require that caterers sign a copy of these guidelines to acknowledge that they have read the guidelines and that they agree to the terms.

Many institutions also list basic catering pointers on their websites. For example, the Morris Graves Museum of Art's (MGMA) facility rental policy concisely states the following catering-related information online:

> Our culinary center on the lower level provides ample room for food service and is easily accessible by the loading dock. The culinary center is not designed for cooking, however, only warming of items in hot box [sic] and/ or microwaves, to prevent excessive food smells from impacting the art. Building users are to provide their own food preparation supplies (utensils, serving trays, etc.). Alcohol may be served according to regulations of Alcoholic Beverage Control. (Humboldt Arts Council 2013)

Note how the MGMA rental policy points out that the culinary center is accessible from the loading dock. Clearly identifying the best places to deliver food and supplies, as well as the easiest and safest routes for moving these goods through the facility, helps prevent confusion upon the caterer's arrival. Before the event, it is a good idea to have both the renter and the caterer complete a walk-through of the facility with the facility manager, allowing time to coordinate logistics, such as delivery, setup, and cleanup.

Delivery, Setup, and Cleanup Guidelines

Successfully coordinating delivery, setup, and cleanup first involves determining guidelines that govern when, where, and by whom each of these tasks must be completed. Some questions that might be asked when preparing delivery, setup, and cleanup guidelines include the following: Is there any storage space available for event materials prior to the event? If so, how far in advance may these materials be delivered, and how far in advance must these deliveries be scheduled? Which elements of the museum space can be rearranged in preparation for the event (e.g., desks, stanchions, and kiosks), and who is allowed to move these items (e.g., the facility manager or vendors in coordination with the facility manager, etc.)?

Museums sometimes provide staff to help with the setup and teardown of special events, and, in these cases, the museum needs to determine whether there will be an additional fee for this service. It is also important to consider whether there is a certain time frame within which vendors may begin setting up for the event (e.g., no earlier than two hours before the event) and whether teardown must be completed within a certain timeframe following the event (e.g., teardown must be completed within one and one-half hours following the scheduled end time). For an additional fee, some facilities will allow more time for setup and/or teardown. Of course, each cultural institution facility will have its own unique set of parameters, and the list above merely serves as a starting point when assembling or reevaluating these guidelines. In any case, clearly defining special event delivery, setup, and cleanup parameters and ensuring that a member of the museum staff goes over them with the renter will make any event more successful.

Decoration, Prop, and Equipment Guidelines

In addition to considering delivery, setup, and cleanup guidelines, it is also important to establish parameters for the types of decorations, props, and equipment allowed into, or available from, the facility. Because materials that are brought in from outside have potential ramifications on the condition of museum collections, there are a number of questions to begin considering when establishing guidelines for special event decorations, props, and equipment. For example, high-intensity lights are banned by some facilities because these lights may induce fading of certain types of collections.

Working as a team, with staff members ranging from conservators to members of facility management, the museum will need to decide how its spaces can be prepared for events. Among the questions this team might consider include the following:

- Are there any specific restrictions, such as for burning candles, torches, lanterns, or lamps; for fresh plants and flowers; or the like? Will LED tea lights be offered or suggested as an alternative to candles?

- Are high-intensity light sources banned, because of their potential for damage to collections? Are there certain areas (e.g., nonexhibit areas) where this lighting is allowed?

- What types of signs, banners, placards, and decorations are allowed in the museum?

- Can signs, decorations, or displays be attached to parts of the facility, such as walls, doors, floors, railings, or furniture?

- Does the museum have any stands available for the display of event signage?

- Are tape, staples, nails, and/or other attachments allowed as a part of event setup? (Generally, the answer is "no.")

- What types of props and equipment (e.g., stages, risers, chairs, tables, and coat racks) are allowed? Are any of these available to rent directly from the museum?

- If there will be dancing, is the renter required to rent a dance floor to prevent damage to the museum's flooring?

Because keeping people, collections, and the facility safe during the event is a priority, the types of items that the facility use policy allows into the museum from outside are very important to consider. Generally, restrictions are placed on candles, torches, and lanterns, and, frequently they are also placed on fresh flowers. For example, the Cincinnati Art Museum (CAM) allows floral arrangements, both fresh and dried, that have been supplied by a professional florist, but prohibits live potted plants, fresh-cut garden flowers, and asparagus ferns (CAM 2013).

Some museums, like the Sam Noble Oklahoma Museum of Natural History (SNOMNH), extend their decorating restrictions to include an even broader array of potentially hazardous materials, many of which may seem harmless to prospective renters. For example, SNOMNH *excludes*, among other things:

All organic materials, including items such as fresh flowers, live plants, soil, sand, grasses, feathers, moss, branches, bark, potpourri, rice, birdseed, oatmeal, straw, hay, mats or baskets woven of natural material, bouton-nieres, corsages, and bouquets constructed, in part or in whole, of natural materials, [and] centerpieces. (SNOMNH 2011)

Traditional wedding flowers are not allowed in this particular facility. While this is a potential challenge for wedding parties and others rent-ing the facility, it can be creatively overcome given adequate notice. To provide an additional layer of protection, SNOMNH also asks that the special events coordinator approve of all decorations a minimum of two weeks prior to the event. Having a member of museum staff review and approve of setup and decorations well in advance is yet another way that a museum can protect its facilities and collections, while helping the event to run smoothly.

Audiovisual (A/V) and Information Technology (IT) Guidelines

In addition to considering decoration guidelines, it is also important to consider the types of audiovisual and information technology services that the museum can offer during an event, how much will be charged for these services, and which equipment may be brought in from outside. Some facili-ties simply choose to make basic equipment available for use during events and do not charge an additional A/V or IT fee. By contrast, others offer a menu of A/V and IT services and charge fees according to how many menu items are selected for the event and the staff time required to manage these services during the event. What follows are a number of questions to con-sider when beginning to formulate A/V and IT guidelines:

- What type of sound equipment is permitted? Does the museum have sound equipment available to rent?

- Does the museum allow outside sound systems to be plugged into its local public address system?

- Does the museum require that audiovisual or lighting contractors take a walk-through with the facility manager so each piece of additional lighting and any projectors, screens, speakers, micro-phones, or other equipment can be approved?

- Will the museum make audiovisual staff available during the event? Is there an extra fee for this? If not, does the museum require that a particular third-party audiovisual contractor fulfill A/V requests?

- How far in advance should audiovisual requests be made? For example, "Audiovisual requests must be made to the facility manager at least five business days prior to the event."

- How much notice is necessary for changes to be made to an audiovisual request? For example, "Changes to audiovisual requests must be made at least 48 hours in advance of the event."

- Will renters have access to wireless internet in the museum? Is there a use fee for this access?

- Is videoconferencing available? Is there a fee for this service?

As with the catering guidelines, once parameters for A/V and IT have been determined, it is helpful to compile a document that lists these specific guidelines for renters. These guidelines should be provided to them prior to their signing the facility use agreement. Then, when renters sign the facility use agreement, they can also sign to acknowledge that they have received and will abide by these guidelines, as well as the catering guidelines.

One example of how these types of audiovisual considerations manifest in real-world museum rental policies comes from the National Cowboy and Western Heritage Museum (NCWHM) in Oklahoma City, Oklahoma. The NCWHM includes a section titled "Audio Visual Options & Charges" in its space rental policy document. Within this section, the NCWHM describes how the fees for its technical package, which includes cued lights, sound, audio or video tapes, wireless microphones, or other special equipment, change depending upon how much notice is given:

> At least two weeks' notice must be given for the Technical Package. If there is less than two weeks' notice, time and a half will be charged for technicians. If less than 72 hours['] notice is given, double time will be charged. (NCWHM 2011)

This policy not only helps enable the museum to schedule A/V staff members and prepare for setup of the required equipment well in advance, but also paves the way for the NCWHM to charge a premium for those who wait until the last minute to request this service. While not all institutions may be as specific as the NCWHM with respect to notice required and fees charged, the NCWHM audiovisual policy nonetheless illustrates the high degree of specificity that a facility can choose to pursue within its guidelines.

Additional Special Event Guidelines to Consider

In addition to establishing guidelines for catering and setup and tear-down, it is important to consider other guidelines that will apply *during* the event. For example, will filming or photography be allowed in the museum during the event? If it will be allowed, is it allowed everywhere or only in certain areas that do not house collections? Some facilities that allow photography require that permission be obtained in advance from a designated staff member. To ensure that light-sensitive collections are safeguarded, whether or not photography is allowed, and where, specifically, it is allowed should be discussed with the museum's conservator. Some cultural facilities also choose to include guidelines that mandate that the equipment used during an event, such as lighting, cameras, or sound systems, must not interfere with the temperature or relative humidity of the space. It is also a good idea to consider whether smoking will be allowed anywhere on the museum property during a special event. If so, where, exactly, it is allowed should be specified in the guidelines and clearly marked with signage.

The renter will also need to be informed of parking availability for event attendees. If the facility has parking spaces available, is there a fee associated with this parking? Will the museum be willing to reserve spaces for the event? Be ready to suggest nearby parking facilities that the renter can work with to reserve parking spaces as well as public transportation options for traveling to the museum. In addition to considering parking and transportation, storage of personal items during the event should also be considered. Will there be lockers available to securely store personal items? Will the museum provide a coat check?

Sometimes, a cleaning fee will be added to the facility use fee, in anticipation of the additional foot traffic through the facility. A cleaning checklist is often provided to the renter, and, if the facility is returned in clean condition, the cleaning fee is refunded. For example, the Warhawk Air Museum (WAM) in Nampa, Idaho, provides a basic cleaning checklist that must be signed by both the renter and a member of the museum staff after the event concludes. With respect to cleanup, the WAM checklist states the following:

> It is expected that the facilities are left in the same condition found upon arrival. Please use the following checklist for assurance:
>
> - All food is removed from premises
> - All floors/spills are cleaned
> - Garbage is bagged and removed by renter
> - Tables and chairs are cleaned and stacked neatly
> - Kitchen is cleaned
> - Additional materials brought in for the function are removed from the premises. (Quoted from WAM 2013)

To ensure that items on this checklist are completed, WAM retains a $500 reservation and cleaning deposit that is refunded after the event if no repairs or additional cleaning is necessary (WAM 2013).

An example of a cleaning and setup checklist particular to caterers can be found in the Morris Museum of Art's (MMA) facility rental packet. Note that the MMA's catering checklist, shown in box 9.1, requires initials from a member of security, a member of museum staff, and a representative of the catering organization both before and after the event. Before the event, these three parties must provide their initials to acknowledge that eight specific tasks have been completed. After the event, these same three parties must initial acknowledging that five postevent tasks have been completed. Though this document requires additional time for these three individuals to complete, in the long run it is easy to see how both time and money are saved by ensuring that these crucial tasks are completed before and after the event.

The Facility Use Agreement

Many of the special event guidelines identified above will be important enough that they should be incorporated into the facility use agreement or rental contract—the document that the renting party will sign, acknowledging what is required of them before, during, and after the rental period. When preparing a use agreement, it is a good idea to review agreements from other cultural institution facilities, keeping in mind that particular characteristics of a museum's collections and facilities may require attention in its facility use agreement that other museums' agreements may not reflect. For

BOX 9.1.

SAMPLE CATERING CHECKLIST: MORRIS MUSEUM OF ART

MORRIS
MUSEUM of ART

Catering Checklist

EVENT NAME _____

EVENT DATE _____

BEFORE EVENT

Staff member on duty_____
Security_____
Caterer_____

Please initial completed requests before event.

Staff   Security Caterer

_____ _____ _____ 1. Event setup form has been completed and turned into security and curatorial staff.
_____ _____ _____ 2. Catering checklist and setup form are at security desk for event.
_____ _____ _____ 3. Tables are setup and wiped down before caterer arrives.
_____ _____ _____ 4. Furniture in museum is dusted and clean.
_____ _____ _____ 5. Trashcans are available in the service hallway for food prep and around the facility.
_____ _____ _____ 6. Tray stands and trays are setup.
_____ _____ _____ 7. Rented equipment is setup before caterer arrives.
_____ _____ _____ 8. Appropriate gallery signs are in place for event.

AFTER EVENT

Staff member on duty_____
Security_____
Caterer_____

Please initial completed requests after event and sign at the bottom.

Staff   Security Caterer

_____ _____ _____ 1. All trash has been taken from trashcans around museum, kitchen, and service hallway to the dumpster.
_____ _____ _____ 2. If kitchen was used, it has been thoroughly cleaned.
_____ _____ _____   Floors swept and mopped
_____ _____ _____   Counters and tables cleaned with provided counter cleaner
_____ _____ _____   Refrigerator emptied and cleaned
_____ _____ _____ 3. If service hallway was used, it has been thoroughly cleaned.
_____ _____ _____   Floors free from food and litter
_____ _____ _____   Tables free from food and wiped down
_____ _____ _____ 4. If museum equipment was used, it has been cleaned thoroughly.
_____ _____ _____   Warming oven
_____ _____ _____   Tray stands/trays
_____ _____ _____   Microwave
_____ _____ _____   Carts/dollies
_____ _____ _____   Chafing dish
_____ _____ _____   Coffee pot
_____ _____ _____ 5. If floral prep room was used, it has been thoroughly cleared of materials and cleaned.
    (*For museum staff only.*)

_____   Signature   Date
Please PRINT Staff on duty Name

_____   Signature   Date
Please PRINT Security Name

_____   Signature   Date
Please PRINT Caterer Name

1 Tenth Street, Augusta, Georgia 30901-0100   **706.724.7501**   **www.themorris.org**

Source: Reproduced with permission from the Morris Museum of Art, www.themorris.org.

example, the Denver Firefighters Museum (DFM) rental contract includes the stipulation "The event shall be terminated immediately for any individual attempting to or actually sliding down any of the firehouse poles" (DFM 2012). The firehouse pole is certainly an element that the Denver Firefighters Museum must address that other museums likely do not have to think about. Each museum should consider what the "firehouse pole" might be in its facility; in other words, what unique elements of the facility must be specifically addressed in its use agreement?

It is ultimately up to each individual cultural institution as a whole to decide what should be included in its facility use agreement, and every museum's agreement will be unique to its particular circumstances (see box 9.2 for a sample of the Fred Jones Jr. Museum of Art's guidelines). Because of the variety of interests at stake when bringing special events into a facility, it is valuable to make the creation of special event guidelines a collaborative process that involves members of the museum's administration, curatorial staff, and facility management, as well as others from throughout the institution. In any case, remember that the purpose of this agreement is to establish in writing that each party—both museum and renter—is aware of and agrees to a mutual set of expectations.

As the museum considers possible special event guidelines—for example, its cancellation policy, whether to require a deposit, and the amount of liability insurance required of vendors—make note of which of these guidelines or policies the renter should formally acknowledge in the facility use agreement. As discussed earlier, it is often desirable for renters and vendors to sign a copy of the institution's special event or facility use guidelines to formally acknowledge that they have read and agree to these policies. Having their acknowledgment in writing not only reinforces the facility's policies in the eyes of the renter and vendor, but also provides the cultural institution with a written record of their acknowledgment of these policies, should the institution require proof of this acknowledgment to settle a dispute at a later date. To ensure that the museum is properly articulating its special event guidelines and facility use agreement, it is always a good idea to have these documents vetted by an attorney prior to putting them to use.

Developing a Special Events Reservation Form

A facility reservation form, also known as the facility use application or special events checklist, is an indispensable tool for the facility manager as

BOX 9.2.

SPECIAL EVENTS AT THE FRED JONES JR. MUSEUM OF ART

Above: The Fred Jones Jr. Museum of Art's Sandy Bell Gallery is set up for a special event.

The Fred Jones Jr. Museum of Art, located in Norman, Oklahoma, requires that special event setup plans be approved by its facility manager in advance of each event. To safeguard its facilities, its special event guidelines stipulate that any decorations used during an event must be freestanding.

Source: Photo reproduced with permission from the Fred Jones Jr. Museum of Art, The University of Oklahoma, www.ou.edu/fjjma.

he or she helps arrange the facility to safely and successfully accommodate special events. This form gathers information from the prospective renter that can be used to evaluate whether the facility is a good fit for the event, whether the event poses any hazards, and what will need to be done to prepare the facility for the event. This form can then be filed as documentation of the prospective renter's request to rent the facility, along with a note as to whether it was accepted or declined. Gathering this information up front ensures that everyone understands what the renter's expectations are for the event, while helping the facility manager and other museum staff host the event to the best of their ability. It is important to note that, if a member of the museum's staff other than the facility manager collects and files the reservation form, information from the form should be shared with the facility manager soon after it is received.

The specificity of these forms varies—some institutions' forms will simply ask for a bit of information, such as who will be renting the venue, as well as their contact information, when they would like the event to take place, how many people will be present, and what type of event will occur. By contrast, others' forms collect much more detailed information about the event. Additional information that might be requested includes a listing of the activities that will occur at the event, as well as catering-related details, such as whether alcoholic beverages will be consumed. If so, the name and contact information of the vendor providing the alcohol are often requested, as well as whether the alcohol will be served or sold, who will be serving or selling the alcohol, and whether the sponsoring organization has obtained any required permits and alcohol servers' liability insurance coverage. It is also common to ask whether food will be served, and, if so, the name and contact information of the vendor providing the food may also be requested. Collecting these vendors' names up front, as well as documenting what they will be serving, is helpful in several respects. First, it gives the facility manager the ability to schedule pre-event walk-throughs with the vendors, as well as to coordinate deliveries. Second, it allows any special needs for food or beverages (e.g., heating or chilling requirements) to be identified and planned for early on.

In addition, museums often ask prospective renters to identify their setup needs at the time the reservation form is submitted. This allows these details to be accommodated—or renegotiated, if necessary—from the very beginning of the planning process. Among the setup elements that might be covered on the reservation form are the following:

- Whether any particular kind of setup is needed. If so, the names of the persons completing setup may be requested, along with a diagram of setup.

- Whether a tent will be set up. If so, the name and contact information of the vendor providing the tent and setting up the tent may also be requested, along with the date and time of setup, the date and time of teardown, and the location of the tent.

- If the event is to be held outdoors, is a severe-weather plan in place?

- Whether any special effects are planned (e.g., foam, fog, water, balloons, pyrotechnic materials, etc.). If standby emergency medical and/or fire suppression personnel is necessary, the names and contact information for this personnel may be requested.

- Whether there will be entertainment or amplification of any kind.

- Whether the event includes professional entertainment.

In addition to inquiring about setup, some facilities' reservation forms also ask how admission to the event will be controlled and whether there will be any cash transactions at the event. If there will be cash transactions, it is a good idea to ask how security will be provided for incoming money. This reinforces for the renter that keeping their incoming money safe is their responsibility and that they must have a plan for doing so.

Though this is not an exhaustive list of all the pieces of information that a cultural institution may request from a prospective renter, it demonstrates the types of information that a museum may want to ask for up front so that it can streamline its special event preparations. In some cases, such as when high-risk special effects are listed on the request form, a museum may need to renegotiate this element of the event with the renter or decline to make the facility available for the event. It also helps to start collecting contact information for vendors with this form. If this information is not yet available, the form can require that it be provided by a particular date in advance of the event. Having vendor contact information on hand can prove valuable. As mentioned earlier, the museum will be able to schedule deliveries and walk-through tours with the vendors at its convenience, rather than waiting for these vendors to contact the museum at the last minute.

Special Event Management Tracking

As discussed earlier, identifying and, in turn, following a clear set of special event guidelines is crucial to facilitating successful events in a cultural institution. Cultural institutions are dynamic places whose schedules are often packed full of events being hosted by parties from both inside and outside the institutions. Whether hosting educational sessions or film screenings, weddings or fundraisers, museums not only have to identify appropriate event guidelines for their facilities but also must have a system for precisely scheduling events in a way that provides each event with appropriate levels of space, privacy, and support staff.

At some cultural facilities, like the National Gallery of Art (NGA) in Washington, DC, special events are held so often that an entire office is dedicated to organizing them. Additionally, many other offices and departments hold events that require facility management support. To support these requirements, the NGA's facility management team has several staff members that work closely with the special events and other Gallery offices to ensure that both the facilities and the setup needs are seamlessly coordinated. Because the NGA hosts over 800 various events a year, scheduling and setup are not easy tasks. Even after events are scheduled, there are usually changes that must be communicated to and implemented by NGA staff from multiple offices. It is challenging to get such information out to everyone in real time so accommodations can be made. To aid in scheduling, the Gallery is currently considering an in-house software application for computers and mobile devices that tracks special event scheduling and logistics. This "app" would allow key staff to retrieve this information on handheld devices and maintain control as details and special requests evolve (Samec 2012).

While some museums, like the National Gallery of Art, develop their own event management software, there are a number of off-the-shelf software solutions for tracking events in cultural institution facilities. We do not endorse any of the following options; however, we provide them as examples of the types of software available to help with special event management in cultural institutions. One software option that is widely used by cultural institutions is Artifax Event (Artifax Event [2013a]). Artifax Event stores detailed information for each event and allows information about events to be easily shared across museum departments, while also helping to automate administrative tasks related to special events. In addition, Artifax Event offers modules for purchase that supplement the basic event package, including a module that aids in scheduling staff, a module that makes event information available online in a standard web browser, and a module that presents event information in a format that is appropriate to share with visitors on foyer monitors (Artifax Event [2013b]).

Among other software options is Ungerboeck Software International's (USI) package for museums, zoos, and other cultural attractions. USI bills its package as an "end-to-end solution" that handles up-front tasks, like room scheduling and registration, as well as postevent tasks, like invoicing and internal billing. Examples of activities the USI package can handle are catering, financials, and document and supplier management, as well as conference planning and registration. Software options that integrate event management into a larger package that tracks nearly all of a cultural institution's activities, like collections, conservation, research, and exhibition management, are also available. For example, Zetcom's MuseumPlus software has modules that track each of these core mission-related elements, as well as event management details. Among the event management support services offered by MuseumPlus are room and equipment reservations, contact storage, and the ability to generate a daily program. MuseumPlus also supports invoicing for room and service rentals (Zetcom).

For some cultural institutions, the solution may actually be found in a software program that is readily available and already familiar to staff members. For example, the Baltimore Museum of Art's (BMA) staff has had success implementing a museum-wide master calendar using Microsoft Outlook. This shared calendar tracks all special events and is made available digitally to each and every staff member on the Museum's server. Every week, "detail sheets" that provide information about upcoming events are also handed out to staff. As Alan Dirican (2012), deputy director for operations and capital planning at the BMA, describes,

> We've been pushing for a Master Calendar for a long time. Finally, it took off, and everybody lives by it now. [Microsoft] Outlook has turned out to be perfect for that. Getting everyone's buy-in to use the calendar is important. Now, we're trying to include projects on the calendar, so if contractors are going to work in an area nearby, [special events] will know when the work will take place while they are planning the events—we're cross-checking. And I will look and see if there is an event on the calendar when planning work in the area and work around that schedule.

The last point that Dirican makes is particularly important—if facility-related work is scheduled, such as floor care work or painting walls, it is crucial that this information is shared so that the work does not conflict with special events and vice versa. Sharing this facility-related information as soon as it is known, with all parties involved in the planning of events, simplifies the event scheduling process and lowers the potential for last-minute planning disasters. In addition to ensuring that the information gets shared with all parties early on, making certain, as Dirican said, that the museum gets "buy-in" from those who need to use the calendar is critical to its success as a special event tracking and planning tool.

Special Event Accessibility

As mentioned in chapter 6, finding ways to accommodate people with disabilities to ensure their enjoyment of the special event or exhibition is not only the right thing to do but also mandated by federal and many state laws. Disabilities are physical or mental impairments that affect "one or more major life activities," like seeing, hearing, or mobility. Working together, the facility manager and staff members coordinating museum events can make sure that everyone attending events in the facility is able to participate. As the Cornell University (2013) *Guide to Planning an Accessible Event* asserts, "A well-planned event ensures the participation of all" (p. 7).

The first step when planning an accessible event is to select a space for the event that can be easily accessed by a person using a wheelchair or other mobility device. All areas of the facility that will be used during the event must be able to be reached by a person in a wheelchair, and an accessible restroom should not be further than 200 feet from the event setting. It is also important to consider how people will arrive to the event, where they might park, and the route they will take into the facility. Be sure that people requiring mobility devices can arrive to the facility and make their way to the event location without difficulty. If this is not possible, and the event will be held in a space that cannot be made easily accessible, a clear plan must be made in order for people with disabilities to reach the event space, and, in turn, this plan must be communicated to these participants. It is also a good idea to include information about reaching the event location in publicity leading up to the event. In publicity for the event, people requiring accommodations should be directed to contact a representative of the museum. The date by which the accommodation request should be made should also be included in event publicity (Cornell University 2013).

Staff responsible for setting up event furniture should leave sufficient space for people using mobility devices to move easily within the space. Dedicated locations for persons using wheelchairs can be reserved throughout the seating area, for example, at the front, center, sides, and rear of the space. If there are audiovisual cords that obstruct the walkways, they should be covered. Keep in mind that cable covers with thicknesses over half-an-inch are difficult for wheelchairs to cross. It is also important to keep in mind that event presenters themselves may require accommodations; for example, if the presenter uses a mobility device, a ramp and adjustable lectern will need to be provided.

When setting up the event space, be sure that sign-language interpreters, if they will be present, will have the lighting necessary to do their job. In addition to considering lighting for sign-language interpreters, lighting in general should also be considered. For example, is there glare coming from windows that may affect attendees' ability to see during the event? Pay attention to the sound quality in the room as well, especially how it is affected by the ventilation system or by any sounds coming from nearby rooms.

Signage is another important consideration, as it helps to orient people as they arrive to the event. The name of the museum, as well as its street address, should be clearly marked and identifiable from the street. Sometimes, a museum's primary entrance is not wheelchair accessible; in this case, signage identifying where the accessible entrance is located should be positioned at the primary entrance. Additional signs that identify the locations of accessible restrooms, elevators, and so on should also be displayed. If Braille directional signs are not available, consider how blind attendees will be directed throughout museum.

Providing disability-awareness training to all staff helps prepare them to create a welcoming environment for all visitors by teaching them how to make accommodations for guests before and during an event (Watson Hyatt 2009). Staff should be trained to do their best to accommodate all requests that can be reasonably met. Training can also prepare staff to communicate sensitively with people requiring accommodations. For example, some phrases, like "wheelchair bound" or "handicapped," are obsolete and should be avoided. Staff present during the event, including facility management staff, should be prepared to answer frequently asked questions regarding accommodations. For example, staff should be able to direct attendees to the nearest accessible restroom or drinking fountain or assist guests in locating a wheelchair (Cornell University 2013).

While emphasis in this section is placed on accommodating attendees who use mobility devices, bear in mind that all attendees are unique and carry with them particular requirements that must be met in order for them to enjoy a given event. Planning ahead to meet each and every guest's needs can be challenging, but providing guests the opportunity to communicate their needs before and during the event helps make the event a success. By working together, facility management and special events staff can meet the needs of all museum guests through clear communication, careful consideration of all event spaces, and a readiness to attend to any issues that may arise.

Special Event Emergency Planning

Special events require additional planning order to keep everyone safe during the event. Two important concerns are the facility's maximum capacity and ensuring expedient evacuation. It is important that the number of people attending the event does not exceed the maximum capacity of the space or facility. One way to prevent overcrowding is for staff at the entrances to use two clickers—one to count guests as they enter and another to count guests as they exit.

When the event is being set up, it is important that exit doors, hallways, and stairways are not obstructed. Aisles leading to exits should be at least four feet wide and should never be blocked. In addition, exit signs need to be plainly visible and cannot be blocked by event decorations. If the museum needs to be evacuated, it is important that all museum staff and volunteers are aware of the exit routes and how to direct guests during an evacuation. As the event begins, an event host should review the evacuation plan with guests (Massachusetts Institute of Technology 2010).

It is helpful to evaluate and adjust special event safety procedures in light of accidents, injuries, or emergencies that have occurred during special events at the facility over the past year. This is only possible if careful records of such incidents are kept throughout the year. For further guidelines and resources related to emergency planning, please see chapter 8.

Summary

Managing successful special events in cultural institution facilities requires clear communication between special event staff, facility management staff, event hosts, and vendors. The museum can ensure that all parties have a mutual understanding of how a special event will proceed by establishing clear guidelines that pertain to catering, deliveries, setup, cleanup, and technical requirements. In addition to developing special event guidelines, it is important that the museum be prepared to offer an enjoyable and accommodating experience to people with disabilities who attend each event. Emergency planning that takes into account how staff and guests will be apprised of safe evacuation routes during each event is also crucial. Special events can be time-consuming to plan and execute, but these events are becoming increasingly important as museums seek new ways to connect with their communities while adding to their bottom lines. By working together, special event and facility management staff can simplify the process for hosting these events, while keeping people, the collections, and the facility safe for years to come.

CHAPTER TEN
TRAINING CULTURAL FACILITY PERSONNEL

In times of change, learners inherit the earth, while the learned find themselves beautifully equipped to deal with a world that no longer exists.

—Eric Hoffer (1902–1983)

The learning that is encouraged by many museum and cultural institutions' missions creates the ideal environment to support continuous learning and development by members of their facilities staff. The standards to which the facility will be managed create the requirements for staff to learn and understand *why* tasks need to be performed in specific ways. Training is generally a short-term cost that provides instruction as to *how* something should be done. The distinction between the *why* and the *how* is important for facility leadership and staff to understand, since the facilities make no distinction between whether those caring for them are in-house or contracted staff.

Taking the long view when investing in the development of high-performing facility management (FM) staff may provide significant cost avoidance to the museum. Often, training is one of the first things to be cut when budgets are tight, and cultural institutions are always seeking ways to utilize funds more efficiently. The decision to not provide adequate or appropriate training for facilities staff generally has a negative impact on the performance, longevity, and appearance of cultural facilities. The operating conditions and appearance of cultural facilities, particularly those that have high traffic, are significantly influenced by staff who are well versed in the latest information available relative to efficiency, sustainability, operations, maintenance, and other high-performance building initiatives.

Many of the buildings that house museums were not constructed to provide the taxing environmental conditions necessary for collections integrity. Nor were they intended to accommodate the volume of visitors or the special events that take place throughout the facilities. Frequently, facility management staff must determine ways to extend the useful life of equipment and systems. Marginally performing equipment stresses the built environment and requires that staff be able to manage their museums' facilities and grounds in ways that mitigate these stresses. In order to accomplish this, the facility management staff must be current in their knowledge of *why* and *how* to perform their work.

Identifying Performance Gaps

Identifying performance gaps is an effective process to determine the most productive place to invest in the development of facility management staff. Initially, this is done by establishing the desired performance standards of the facilities staff and then examining the current organizational performance. The difference between the desired standards (what an organization *wants*) and the current performance (what an organization *has*) is the performance gap. By looking at this gap, organizations can best leverage their resources to determine and address the areas that need attention.

In order to determine the training standards for the organization, it is critical to define the duties of the staff. To do this, it is important that current position descriptions are available for each staff member. Current position descriptions are used to identify the duties for the performance gap analysis. Once the key responsibilities and duties are identified, it then becomes easier to articulate the baseline expectations of knowledge and determine the appropriate sources of training that will provide the knowledge necessary to properly carry out facility management–related tasks.

Operations and Maintenance Training

Maintenance and operations skills training for facility management staff can be secured through a number of sources. Organizations that determine standards for the facility management profession, like the International

Facility Management Association (IFMA) and APPA, Leadership in Educational Facilities (simply known as APPA), are very good places to begin looking for educational standards and providers, and these organizations are often sources of valuable information regarding consultants, schools, or other sources of skills training. Local unions, vocational schools, community colleges, as well as other cultural facilities are excellent places to consult for advice about training and development offerings and initiatives for facility management staff. Often, vendors and manufacturers of equipment are also viable sources of training information for facilities staff.

While networking with these other organizations, facility managers should be sure to determine whether they offer or host ongoing classes that their staff can attend. Even better, they can ask if these organizations would like to partner with their cultural facility to secure training at a better value. As an example, the Smithsonian Institution's Office of Facilities Management and Reliability contracts with educational organizations, like the George Mason University Office of Continuing Professional Education, which offers courses leading to a professional certificate in facility management, and the Cleaning Management Institute, which offers custodial technician certification. The Smithsonian then invites professionals from outside cultural institution facility management organizations to join their classes. These outside organizations must pay for their own staff at the going rate that the vendor charges for the training; however, this way of crowdsourcing enrollment provides scalability for those organizations sending students and helps them avoid having to meet minimum thresholds required to conduct classes internally.

Specialized Training

Specialized education for facilities professionals encompasses more than skills training for operations and maintenance. Leadership in cultural institutions requires that specific roles in the facility organization receive specialized education in order to best fulfill their responsibilities. Examples of the roles requiring specialized education include facilities supervisors, safety professionals, emergency responders, information technology specialists, and administrative staff. What follows are descriptions of some of the specialized training available to support cultural institution facility management staff.

Specialty Training for Supervisors

Supervising in the facilities environment requires knowledge of the technical aspects of the work supervised, but, more importantly, requires other skillsets that facilitate good organizational performance. Included in those skillsets are the perspective and judgment required to engage people, leadership skills, and a focus on results, prioritization, and scheduling work. It is also necessary to be able to persuade and negotiate, communicate well, treat people equitably, make decisions, and be genuine and consistent in all aspects of leadership. Supervising in the facilities arena is very different from in an office environment, and it requires specialized knowledge about how each facility management staff member fits into the larger enterprise.

Organizations, such as APPA and the Association for Facilities Engineering (AFE), provide training focused on supervision in facility management, while member associations, such as IFMA and the International Association of Museum Facilities Administrators (IAMFA), provide opportunities for supervisors to network and share information with each other. It is often a good idea to have facilities supervisors work with more senior facilities professionals in a mentoring capacity so they learn from high-performing facilities leaders. This ensures that protégées learn supervisory skills in a safe environment from colleagues who have been identified as successful supervisors.

Emergency Response Specialty Training

Facilities staff is generally among the first to respond to emergency situations that may occur in their facilities. Therefore, it is important that staff be aware of potentially serious or threatening situations as well as appropriate responses for those situations. The situation could be anything from a visitor's medical emergency to a failure of a building system that may create hazardous conditions to a potential terrorist event. While each of these events involves different responses, they highlight the importance of the facilities staff being aware of and prepared for a possibly hazardous or dangerous situation, and the need for each staff member to know how best to assess and respond to the circumstances. Emergency response personnel are generally found within the facility management organization; however, they must work with staff throughout the cultural institution to ensure the safety and security of all collections, visitors, and staff.

While emergency responses are important, it is also imperative that Business Continuity Plans are in place to ensure that the enterprise of the facility can either continue in place or be resumed quickly after a serious situation. A good source of additional information about emergency or business continuity training is the Federal Emergency Management Agency (FEMA) of the U.S. Department of Homeland Security (http://www.fema.gov/training). Additional, geographically specific information about emergency management and business continuity planning can be found on individual state emergency management websites. These websites generally include the contact information for state officials who are a valuable source of information for facilities staff. The Wisconsin Division of Emergency Management website, www.emergencymanagement.wi.gov, is an example of the types of well-rounded resources that are available at the state level.

Safety Specialty Training

The work of facilities professionals is filled with potentially hazardous and dangerous situations. The work may involve heights, or contact with chemicals, asbestos, or any number of other potentially threatening circumstances, and facilities professionals must be trained and, frequently, certified so that they know how to safely navigate these situations. A strong organizational focus on safety is necessary to ensure that facilities professionals remain safe so that the physical environment can be made safe—and remain safe—for all stakeholders.

An added dimension of safety training is that certain training is mandated by the Occupational Safety and Health Administration (OSHA) of the U.S. Department of Labor. While safety training can be outsourced, it is possible to conduct some of this important training in-house by using resources that are available online such as the OSHA eTools and Electronic Products for Compliance Assistance (www.osha.gov). These are interactive, Web-based training tools that address a variety of topics related to OSHA training standards, including confined space, asbestos, respiratory protection, and OSHA-compliant recordkeeping. Bear in mind that the mandatory nature of safety training will generally require administrative staff to keep detailed training records.

Administrative Specialty Training

In addition to the upkeep of training and compliance records, facilities administrative staff is often responsible for managing volumes of records that may relate to staff meetings, special events, inspection reports, and asset records and inventories. Administrative staff may also be responsible for preparing and executing budgets, providing customer service, managing personnel and staffing issues, writing reports, maintaining time and attendance, writing and enforcing policies, processing invoices, ordering supplies and materials, and researching and preparing papers and reports.

This is a broad array of mission-critical tasks, and facility administrative support staff requires specialized training in order to provide the level of service and support that cultural institution facility organizations must provide their customers. While administrative staff may have been reduced in recent years due to automation, software, or even computer-aided facility management (CAFM) implementation, it is important to note that these staff members provide a consistency of information and service in organizations that cannot be duplicated by automation. To help make the most of an investment in a full-time administrative staff, ensure that these individuals are properly trained to handle the varied, and sometimes complex, tasks for which they are responsible.

Developing Well-Rounded Employees

While the facilities staff in cultural institutions is focused on performing vital work, it is important to note the unique ways that facilities-related challenges can be addressed. Consider the demographics of the organization and the workforce, and recognize the value of the institutional knowledge of the staff. As organizational priorities change, the most successful cultural institutions seek to find ways to accommodate these changes. Often, looking inward to the current staff is a way to meet the challenges of the built environment while simultaneously providing learning opportunities for staff. Frequently, facilities staff members have the skills, insight, and interest in learning more about other facilities tasks. As a result, these employees are in a position to make greater contributions to achieving successful oversight and management of the cultural institution facility.

Providing the opportunity for current staff members to learn new skills is a very cost-effective way to address performance gaps in the facilities organization. The Smithsonian Institution facilities organization developed an organizational cross-training program entitled the Rotational Assignment Program (RAP). RAP is a competitive cross-training program in which supervisors identify opportunities where they have a need for additional support due to staff shortages or possible retirements. The Smithsonian program lasts one year, and it is only available to current employees. The supervisor for each RAP opportunity provides a description of his or her expectations of the program, and this information is shared throughout the organization. Interested employees must then apply for the opportunity and identify why their selection would benefit the organization. Once the supervisor considers the applications and interviews candidates, he or she works with the successful internal applicant and the applicant's supervisor to determine the work schedule and amount of time the employee will be able to participate in RAP, learning and performing new skills. All participants understand and acknowledge that their first priority is to meet the mission of the facilities organization, and employees may be needed to complete their assigned job before being able to work on their developmental opportunity.

By training in this manner, it becomes clear that there are opportunities for employee growth within the organization and that employees emerge from the program well placed to ensure the success of the facilities staff. The cost of this successful program is primarily in the management of resources by supervisors to ensure that all the required work continues to be done while the employee is participating in the RAP opportunity. Adjustments are required by the supervisors who are teaching the task and overseeing the "trainee's" work so that information is presented in an orderly way and supports the employee's and organization's success.

In the Smithsonian Institution's facility management organization, there are a number of examples of very successful employees who have been identified through RAP as having the ability, interest, and potential to move throughout the organization in a variety of roles. These individuals develop a valuable perspective related to the interconnectedness of the different parts of the organization that enriches their work and problem-solving abilities. These types of opportunities require minimal financial investment, yet they offer outstanding payback for the organization and the employee.

Independent Certifications

While employees can be trained in-house through peer mentoring and cross-training, professional certification programs also offer valuable training opportunities. To achieve professional certification, students are generally tested to ensure that they meet specific standards and are competent and qualified to perform a specific job or task. The benefit of certification is that it builds on the informal exchange of peer training that is often found in facilities organizations and provides a more comprehensive and informed perspective to the employee. Being certified is one way to ensure that the work performed by the employee is conducted to the highest, most professional level, thus benefitting the cultural institution.

A good place to begin seeking certification for employees is through associations and organizations that relate directly to the work performed. Professional associations can provide a good foundation for determining certification for the facilities staff in cultural institutions. See box 10.1 for a list of third-party FM training providers for cultural facilities personnel.

Cultural institutions can look for professional associations and organizations that relate specifically to their mission. These associations and organizations offer valuable resources that can help direct the training requirements for facility management personnel in order to address the strategic initiatives identified by museum leadership.

BOX 10.1.

THIRD-PARTY FACILITY MANAGEMENT (FM) TRAINING PROVIDERS FOR CULTURAL FACILITIES PERSONNEL

Although this listing is not exhaustive, the organizations listed below are good sources from which to secure FM training and information about training opportunities:

- International Facility Management Association (IFMA): www.ifma.org
- American Alliance of Museums (AAM): www.aam-us.org
- Association of Zoos and Aquariums (AZA): www.aza.org
- National Association of Power Engineers (NAPE): www.powerengineers .com
- APPA, Leadership in Educational Facilities: www.appa.org
- International Association of Museum Facilities Administrators (IAMFA): www.iamfa.org
- Cleaning Management Institute (CMI): www.cminstitute.net
- Association for Facilities Engineering (AFE): www.afe.org
- Society for Maintenance Reliability Professionals (SMRP): www.smrp.org
- The U.S. Green Building Council (USGBC): www.usgbc.org

Facility Management Internship Program

An internship program offers defined educational opportunities for academically successful students who work on projects that benefit both the students and the cultural facility. Many colleges and universities organize robust internship programs and offer academic credit to students whose internships meet certain educational requirements. A good way to find interns is by working with the career centers found on most university campuses or by working with specific university department chairs or faculty members. See box 10.2 for a checklist for developing and implementing a successful internship program. In addition, many cultural institutions are very familiar with hosting interns who complete valuable projects related directly to the museum's mission, so the facility management department may have access to an existing pipeline of potential interns already found in the museum's other offices. If the museum has a website, that is another great place to advertise internship opportunities and post deadlines and other information about the application process.

Many cultural institutions have not fully explored offering internship opportunities to support their facility management. The benefits of an internship program to the cultural institution are numerous; for example, internships can help ensure that facility initiatives receive specific attention from students who are beginning the transition from the role of student to that of an emerging professional. These students bring a fresh perspective to projects in addition to a high level of technological savvy and can often package and present information in a more interesting and concise way than can people who routinely work with the information. Interns can also focus on special projects that might otherwise fall by the wayside.

Museums facility managers should be careful not to limit their intern pool to students pursuing a degree in facility management. Often, good interns are those who have never given a thought to facility management, and FM internships present the opportunity to educate students about the importance of operating and maintaining the built environment. Whether they move on to work in a cultural institution, another nonprofit organization, or a corporate environment, the knowledge of the built environment gained during an FM internship will serve the students well in the future and support them throughout their careers.

Interns should be assigned clearly defined projects that support the mission and goals of the cultural institution and the facilities organiza-

BOX 10.2.

CHECKLIST FOR A SUCCESSFUL INTERNSHIP PROGRAM FOR YOUR FM ORGANIZATION

Above: Interns in the Smithsonian Institution's Office of Facilities Management and Reliability summer internship program take advantage of a back-of-the-house tour.

- ❏ List your organizational goals for having an internship program.
- ❏ Determine if it will be paid or unpaid.
- ❏ Create a list of potential responsibilities and objectives.
- ❏ Identify the supervisors.
- ❏ Write project descriptions (these will serve as the intern's position description).
- ❏ Advertise the internship opportunity (e.g., at universities and online—including on your organization's website).
- ❏ Review prospective interns and make selections.
- ❏ Notify the intern as soon as possible with a "Welcome Letter" containing logistical information.

- ❑ Identify and prepare a space for an intern.
- ❑ Orient and bring onboard the intern, in terms of
  - Policies
  - Expectations
  - Project description
  - Etiquette
  - Other issues such as security credentials, access, and attendance processes
- ❑ Seek ways to maximize collaboration between the intern and your organization.
  - Involve the intern early on in as many organizational experiences and practices as possible. Make sure you do not underestimate the complexity of tasks that the intern can handle.
  - Identify reasonably scaled projects that have been deferred due to budget cuts or other difficulties, allowing interns to take on these projects.
  - If you feel a project is beyond the intern's qualifications, identify portions of the project that the intern can complete.
  - Ask interns for his or her opinion about organizational practices. Oftentimes interns have ideas for simplifying protocol, completing projects more efficiently, and so on.
  - Try not to assign the intern mundane duties or ask that they perform secretarial work. Instead, try to immerse them in a range of organizational activities.
  - Conduct ongoing evaluation throughout the internship.
- ❑ Offboard the intern, making sure to do the following:
  - Ask for a project write-up and presentation.
  - Conduct a final evaluation.
  - Correspond with university if necessary for the intern to receive academic credit.
  - Conduct an exit interview.
  - Discuss the need for a letter of recommendation.
- ❑ Supervisor conducts an after-action review (AAR).

Source: Cupps and Olmosk (2008). Photo reproduced with permission of the Smithsonian Institution Office of Facilities Management and Reliability, www. facilities.si.edu.

tion. Projects should identify learning objectives for the intern, desired outcomes for the organization, and milestone dates. Intern projects might include benchmarking several years' worth of computerized maintenance management system data in order to identify equipment failure trends, researching environmentally friendly cleaning solutions, translating training materials and standard operating procedures into a second language, facilitating third-party certification of a facility, performing financial analyses for operations and maintenance, and proposing improvements to recycling initiatives. Other ideas for intern projects can come from a variety of sources, such as industry journals that identify current trends in facility management or data from CAFM systems. The museum's backlog of essential maintenance or its facility condition index (FCI) can also be good sources when identifying areas that would benefit from the closer look that an intern could provide.

No matter where the idea for the internship project originates, it is important that each intern is provided with the tools and resources necessary to complete the project and that he or she is given the opportunity to report on the outcomes when the project is finished. This reporting mechanism is essential to improving facility management processes and internship opportunities in the future.

Welcoming New Employees

Most organizations provide an orientation for new employees, and high-performing organizations welcome and engage new employees from the very beginning of their tenure. A museum's new employees may receive a traditional human resources (HR) orientation that contains some history of the institution and information about their pay, benefits, work schedules, and insurance. High-performing facility management organizations will go one step further and support the museum's basic HR orientation with a supplemental orientation that provides FM-specific information that helps the new employee understand more about the FM organization he or she has joined.

For cultural institution facility management organizations, orientation will help the employee understand what effective facility management practices look like in the museum and, thus, become productive more quickly. Remember that this orientation occurs in addition to the job-related training that this new employee will receive. This FM-specific orientation may

BOX 10.3.

SAMPLE TABLE OF CONTENTS FOR A FACILITY MANAGEMENT NEW EMPLOYEE ORIENTATION HANDBOOK

Cultural institution facility management organizations might consider including the following sections in their facility new employee orientation handbooks:

- ❏ Welcome
- ❏ The Institution's History
- ❏ The Institutional Leadership
- ❏ The Organizational Structure
- ❏ Facilities Leadership Photos
- ❏ Your Supervisor
- ❏ The FM Mission, Goals, and Values
- ❏ Institutional Code of Ethics
- ❏ The Facilities Organization (Description)
- ❏ Facilities Organizational Chart
- ❏ FM Work Areas
- ❏ FM Professional Affiliations (e.g., IFMA and IAMFA)
- ❏ Expectations of Staff Members
- ❏ Spotlight on Safety for FM Staff
- ❏ Career Development
- ❏ Personnel Matters—Payroll, Timekeeping, and Cost of Living
- ❏ Important Documents for Staff to Keep Track Of
- ❏ Sick and Annual Leave Requests
- ❏ Travel and Purchasing
- ❏ Getting Security Credentials and Access
- ❏ What to Do in Case of Emergency
- ❏ Computer Credentials and Policies
- ❏ Fitness Facilities
- ❏ Employee Discounts and Dining
- ❏ The Institution's Community Involvement
- ❏ Facilities Policies
- ❏ Map of the Immediate Area
- ❏ Frequently Dialed Phone Numbers
- ❏ Key Acronyms
- ❏ Equal Employment and Affirmative Action
- ❏ The Ombudsman, if applicable
- ❏ The Employee Assistance Program
- ❏ Labor Unions
- ❏ Index

include the history of the facilities organization; the opportunity to meet senior facilities staff; the mission, vision, and policies of the facilities group, as well as an overview of museum-specific levels of cleanliness and environmental conditions; the expectations that management has of them; and whom to contact if they have a question about anything relating to their job. All of this information can be packaged into a handbook that the employees take with them at the end of the training. See box 10.3 for a sample table of contents from a facilities new employee orientation handbook.

This small investment of time when employees are still new will provide them with invaluable information about their role as a part of a unique FM organization and help them understand the context in which they will be working. There is never a shortage of facilities work to be done in a cultural institution, and the sooner new employees are able to fully contribute, the better.

Once a new employee has been oriented and is ready to perform assigned work, it is a good idea to assign him or her to work alongside a high-performing employee for several weeks, at a minimum. This will allow the new employee to see the type of facilities and equipment that are currently in place, learn about the standards of the organization and the idiosyncrasies of the equipment, and get some valuable feedback from a person who models the standards to which leadership wants the new employee to perform. It is important that new employees be given every opportunity to be successful in the new organization, and this relationship provides an excellent opportunity for the transfer of knowledge from the seasoned veteran employee to the inexperienced new employee.

Ongoing peer mentoring helps to facilitate this successful transfer of knowledge and information to those who are new to the organization. Peer mentors are the people who *know* the standards, processes, practices, and information relative to their profession. The new people who *need to know* are referred to as apprentices, and the organization should give them every opportunity to learn what they need to know to become a model employee (Trautman 2007). The sooner that information exchange takes place and the apprentice becomes proficient at getting work accomplished, the more productive and successful the organization will be.

Summary

A strong facilities organization can be one of the best assets to any cultural institution. By carefully developing and implementing FM training programs, cultural institutions ensure that their facility management staff becomes familiar with the challenges of operating and maintaining a facility that supports their visitors, staff, and collections.

It is very important that the FM staff knows how to perform their work, and that these well-trained team members are able to take into account the ebb and flow of visitation and how it impacts the cultural institution over time. FM staff is often the best equipped to respond to unforeseen circumstances and events in order to ensure that their museums' facilities, collections, staff, and visitors remain able to relate more fully to their cultural institutions' missions.

Taking time to carefully orient new FM employees during their first days on the job is one invaluable way that these employees can be prepared to serve the museum. Performing a gap analysis for each member of the FM team—to identify where their current knowledge, skills, and abilities can to be supplemented so they can competently perform all aspects of their jobs—is critical. After that, a variety of training opportunities, available from professional associations, local universities and community colleges, third-party training providers, and in-house experts, can be identified in order to suit each employee's unique training requirements. As the museum's mission evolves over time, each employee's position description should be updated to reflect these changes. By extension, these employees must be provided the training necessary to support these changes.

Organizations that plan to continue performing the same work year after year will stagnate and become marginalized. Organizations that focus on performing the work that will be required in years to come will thrive and have greater impact and a more positive influence. The work of the cultural institutions of the future can be performed to exacting standards only if their employees are carefully trained. This training cannot be an afterthought; instead, it must be considered a necessary investment in the future success of the cultural institution.

RESOURCES

This annotated list of resources, including professional organizations, guidebooks, and websites, is offered to those interested in expanding their knowledge of topics covered in each chapter. We acknowledge that this is not an exhaustive list, and we do not endorse any vendor, author, or organization listed below. Instead, this list provides resources for cultural institution leadership and facility managers to compare, contrast, and consider as they continue to refine facility management practices in their museums or cultural institutions.

Chapter 1: An Introduction to Museum and Cultural Institution Facility Management

The International Association of Museum Facility Administrators (IAMFA) webpage
The International Association of Museum Facility Administrators works to meet the professional needs of museum facility administrators from around the world, focusing in particular on achieving "excellence and quality in the design, construction, operation and maintenance of world-class cultural facilities. " More information is available at www.iamfa.org.

The Museum and Cultural Institutions Council (MCIC) webpage
A council of the International Facility Management Association (IFMA).

The Museum and Cultural Institutions Council of the International Facility Management Association provides educational and professional development and networking opportunities to its members, which include facility management professionals in science centers, museums, performing arts centers, libraries, archives, historical sites, art institutes, theatres, and zoos. More information is available at http://mcicouncil.org.

The Smithsonian Institution Office of Facilities Management and Reliability (OFMR) webpage

The Smithsonian Institution is one of the world's most unique research, exhibition, and museum complexes, and the Office of Facilities Management and Reliability (OFMR) staff provides an environment that supports its staff and visitor experience. Each year, OFMR offers summer internship experiences to college students interested in careers in facilities management. OFMR also documents its museum facility management practices on its website. More information is available at http://facilities.si.edu.

Chapter 2: An Overview of Cultural Facility Management

American Alliance of Museums Ethics, Standards and Best Practices webpage
Published by the American Alliance of Museums (AAM).

This online resource lists standards and best practices that the American Alliance of Museums expects all accredited museums to achieve. Facilities standards are included in this listing. More information is available at www.aam-us.org/resources/ethics-standards-and-best-practices.

American Library Association Accreditation Standards, Policies, and Procedures webpage
Published by the American Library Association (ALA).

This online resource includes a list of accreditation standards for physical resources and facilities that are important for the library facility manager to understand and meet prior to an upcoming accreditation visit. More information is available at www.ala.org/accreditedprograms/standards.

Association of Zoos and Aquariums (AZA) Accreditation and Certification Materials webpage

This online resource provides information about AZA accreditation inspection standards, and it is a helpful resource for facility managers preparing their zoo facilities for accreditation or reaccreditation. More information is available at www.aza.org/accred-materials/.

Chapter 3: Cultural Facility Strategic Planning

The Manual of Strategic Planning for Museums
By Gail Dexter Lord and Kate Markert. Lanham, MD: AltaMira Press, 2007.

This text explains, for a museum-oriented audience, the entire strategic planning process from the initial stages to completion. Particular emphasis is placed on the significance of financial planning and working with limited resources.

Strategic Planning for Public and Nonprofit Organizations:
A Guide to Strengthening and Sustaining Organizational Achievement
By John M. Bryson. San Francisco: Jossey-Bass, 2011.

Geared toward public and nonprofit organizations, this text describes how these organizations can clarify their organizational missions and mandates, assess strengths and weaknesses, and identify stakeholders.

Team-Based Strategic Planning: A Complete Guide to Structuring, Facilitating, and Implementing the Process
By C. Davis Fogg. New York: American Management Association, 2010.

This classic strategic planning text, first published in 1964, helps an organization conceptualize its strategic planning process using six areas of focus—teams and teamwork, structuring and customizing the process, facilitating the process, managing and leading the process, gathering and organizing information, and cultivating organizational involvement.

Chapter 4: Managing Cultural Facility Systems

The American Society of Heating, Refrigerating and Air-Conditioning Engineers (ASHRAE) Handbook
Atlanta, GA: ASHRAE, 2009. In particular, see the "Museums, Galleries, Archives and Libraries" chapter.

Published by ASHRAE and updated every four years, this handbook provides technical information that is useful for understanding the unique temperature, humidity, and air quality requirements of museum, gallery, archive, and library spaces. It describes the reasoning behind existing standards, as well as strategies for limiting risk to damage caused by conditions with less than ideal temperatures, humidity levels, and air quality.

CIE Technical Report 157: Control of Damage to Museum Objects by Optical Radiation
Vienna: International Commission on Illumination (Commission Internationale de l'Eclairage [CIE]), 2004.

This report describes, in turn, the scientific processes that affect radiation-induced damage to museum collections, information that has been gathered that helps comprehend how these damaging processes can be abated, and useful methods for establishing and monitoring lighting displays. More information is available at http: //div6.cie.co.at/?i_ca_id=433.

Museum Handbook
Washington, DC: National Park Service, 2006. In particular, see the "Museum Collections Environment" chapter by Jessica Johnson.

The "Museum Collections Environment" chapter of the National Park Service's *Museum Handbook* provides in-depth descriptions of several environmental agents of deterioration, including temperature, relative humidity, light, and air pollution, that affect museum collections. It describes how each agent affects different types of collections objects, how their presence can be measured, as well as some strategies for reducing their impact on collections.
This text is available for free online at www.nps.gov/museum/publica tions/handbook.html.

The Plus/Minus Dilemma: The Way Forward in Environmental Guidelines
Washington, DC: The American Institute for Conservation and The International Institute for Conservation of Historic and Artistic Works, 2010.

This transcript of the 2010 joint meeting of the American Institute for Conservation and the International Institute for Conservation of Historic and Artistic Works provides several perspectives on recent moves to relax temperature and humidity standards in museums, including thoughts from leading conservators, scientists, and directors.

This transcript is available for free online at www.iiconservation.org/dialogues/plus_minus_trans.pdf.

Relative Humidity and Temperature Pattern Book: A Guide to Understanding and Using Data on the Museum Environment
By May Cassar and Jeremy Hutchings. London: Museums and Galleries Commission, 2000.

This manual emphasizes that, if the data on environmental conditions that museums collect are never analyzed, there is nothing to be gained from having collected it in the first place. To that end, it lays out guidelines for interpreting the temperature and humidity data collected in museum environments. In addition, it provides a comparison of the strengths and weaknesses of varying monitoring devices and how to improve their reliability. This text is available online for free at www.bartlett.ucl.ac.uk/graduate/csh/attachments/RH_pattern_book. pdf.

Chapter 5: Managing Cultural Facility Maintenance and Operations

Cultural Heritage Protection Handbook: Handling of Collections in Storage
Edited by Nao Hayashi Denis, Barbara Eggar, Helene Gipoulou, Nardjes Boudjemai, and Marie-Caroline Arreto. Paris: UNESCO, 2010.

This handbook describes best practices related to museum storage and the handling of collections in storage. It outlines how to develop appropriate storage areas for collections objects, why adequate storage conditions are important, and how staff members can work together to create these

conditions. This handbook is available for free online at http://unesdoc
.unesco.org/images/0018/001879/187931E.pdf.

Operations & Maintenance Best Practices: A Guide to Achieving
Operational Efficiency
By G. P. Sullivan, R. Pugh, A. P. Melendez, and W. D. Hunt. Washington,
DC: U. S. Department of Energy, 2010.

The U. S. Department of Energy provides this guidebook as a reference for facility personnel who oversee operations and maintenance
(O&M) and energy management activities in their facilities. Though this
guide is written particularly for those involved in the operation and maintenance of federal facilities, it is helpful for any organization looking to
streamline its processes related to O&M management, the integration of
technology into facility management, reducing energy and water use, and
cost savings. This text is available for free online at www1.eere.energy.gov/
femp/pdfs/omguide_complete.pdf.

The Society for Maintenance and Reliability Professionals (SMRP) webpage
SMRP offers workshops and networking opportunities focused on
its five bodies of knowledge: Business and Management, Manufacturing
Process Reliability, Equipment Reliability, Organization & Leadership,
and Work Management. SMRP also offers a Certified Maintenance &
Reliability Professional Program. For more information about SMRP, visit
www.smrp.org.

Chapter 6: Capital Improvement Planning and Implementation

Life-Cycle Cost Analysis (LCCA)
By Sieglande K. Fuller. National Institute of Standards and Technology 2010.

This is nonetheless a free resource that describes how a lifecycle cost
analysis can be carried out using the lifecycle cost formula. It also includes a

list of costs associated with building ownership and a list of relevant codes and standards. This guide is available from www.wbdg.org/resources/lcca.php.

Planning Successful Museum Building Projects
By Walter L. Crimm, Martha Morris, and L. Carole Wharton. Lanham, MD: AltaMira, 2009.

This book addresses museum building project management in terms of budgeting, conducting feasibility studies, managing capital campaigns, integrating key players into the process, selecting architects and builders, and communicating efforts. It also covers sustainability, codes, regulations, planning for operations, and a variety of other important capital project concerns.

ASHRAE (The American Society of Heating, Refrigerating, and Air-Conditioning Engineers) Guideline 0-2005: The Commissioning Process
Atlanta, GA: ASHRAE, 2005.

This ASHRAE guideline describes the commissioning process commonly used to ensure that a facility and its systems meet the standards set for a given facility project. This guide gives an overview of the process from the predesign stages to occupancy. It describes the key processes for each phase, how to document the process, and requirements for the training of personnel responsible for the operation and maintenance of the facility.

Chapter 7: Sustainable Cultural Facility Management

The Green Museum: A Primer on Environmental Practice
By Sarah S. Brophy and Elizabeth Wylie. Lanham, MD: AltaMira, 2008.

This text describes important practices for museums interested in starting or expanding sustainability initiatives. It covers how sustainability initiatives can be selected, organized, measured, implemented, and funded, and it includes a broad range of examples and case studies from a variety of cultural institutions.

The Zoo & Aquarium Green Guide: Suggestions for Beginning or Expanding
a Sustainability Program
Silver Spring, MD: Association of Zoos & Aquariums (AZA), 2011.

This guide clearly and concisely outlines seven, largely facility management–related areas in which zoos and aquariums can become more sustainable: energy, water, chemicals, waste, purchasing, awareness, and innovation. Though it is tailored to zoos and aquariums, any cultural institution can cull helpful strategies from this guide; these range from practical tips like when a facility's boiler should be replaced to ways to educate guests about sustainability efforts. This guide is available for free from www.aza.org/sustainable-practices.

College and University Recycling Manual
Davis, CA: University of California, Davis and the California Collegiate Recycling Council, n.d.

Helpful hints related to establishing a recycling program, including detailed guidelines for establishing contract language with a recycling collection vendor, can be found in this comprehensive guide. Though this guide was written specifically for an audience of colleges and universities, most of the pointers can be adapted to a museum or cultural institution setting. This guide is available for free online from http://sustainability.ucdavis.edu/local_resources/docs/recycling/manual.pdf.

Chapter 8: Risk Management and Safety in Cultural Institution Facilities

Building an Emergency Plan: A Guide for Museums and
Other Cultural Institutions
By Valerie Dorge and Sharon L. Jones. Los Angeles: Getty Conservation Institute, 1999.

This guide outlines the emergency planning process for museums and cultural institutions. It includes multiple case studies as well as descriptions of the roles of the museum director, emergency preparedness manager, departmental team leaders, and facility management (buildings and maintenance) personnel when preparing for emergencies. It is available for free online at www.getty.edu/conservation/publications_resources/pdf_publi cations/pdf/emergency_plan.pdf.

Museum Handbook
National Park Service: Washington, DC, 2001. In particular, see the "Emergency Planning" chapter.

The "Emergency Planning" chapter of the *Museum Handbook* covers why it is important for museums to plan for emergencies; resources available to help with planning; key considerations for different types of hazards, disasters, and vulnerabilities; and risk analysis. It also covers preparation of the Emergency Operations Plan (EOP), as well as staff safety and emergency preparation training. This chapter is available for free from www.nps.gov/ museum/publications/handbook.html.

Risk Management and Disaster Planning webpage
Published by the American Museum of Natural History (AMNH).

This webpage offers guidance for museums related to risk and disaster management. It covers risk assessment and management, offers a range of online resources, and provides information about common risks faced by cultural institutions. This site can be accessed at http://collections.paleo.amnh .org/9/risk-management-and-disaster-planning.

Chapter 9: Special Events in Cultural Institution Facilities

Event Safety Guidelines
Cambridge, MA: Massachusetts Institute of Technology (Environment, Health, and Safety), 2010.

Developed specifically for the Massachusetts Institute of Technology (MIT) campus, these guidelines offer museums and cultural institutions an example of thoroughly considered safety guidelines to reference as they compile their own guidelines. Elements addressed in the MIT guidelines include the types of events that require a safety plan, open-flame use, and slip, trip, and fall protection for special events. These guidelines are available from http://ehs.mit.edu/site/content/event-safety-guidelines.

Guide to Planning an Accessible Event
Ithaca, NY: Cornell University, n.d.

This guide was written to facilitate the planning of accessible events on the Cornell University campus; however, many of the pointers offered regarding making events accessible are also applicable to museums. Examples of topics covered include publicity and preregistration guidelines, location selection, staff awareness and sensitivity, and emergency procedures. This guide can be accessed online at http://sds.cornell.edu/Guide_to_Planning_an_Accessible_Event.pdf.

Special Events Contingency Planning Checklist
Washington, DC: The George Washington University (GWU) Office of Emergency Management, 2011.

The GWU *Special Events Contingency Planning Checklist* can serve as an example for cultural institutions that need help identifying safety and contingency planning considerations, especially for larger special events. Among the elements addressed are the organization of an event, the identification of responsible parties, the handling of event communications, and emergency response. This checklist is available from www.campusadvisories.gwu.edu/pdfs/2010/Special%20Events%20Planning%20Checklist.2010-2011.ForCampusAdvisoriesrtf.pdf.

Chapter 10: Training Cultural Facility Personnel

APPA, Leadership in Educational Facilities Training webpage
APPA offers training related to general administration, maintenance and operations, energy and utilities, and planning, design, and construction through in-person seminars and online webinars. More information about APPA training is available online at www.appa.org/training.

Cleaning Management Institute (CMI)

CMI is a professional society focusing on education, training, and career improvement for commercial cleaning professionals. CMI offers a variety of training programs including custodial supervisor certification, custodial technician, and "train the trainer" training. More information is available at www.cminstitue.net.

Emergency Management Institute webpage

Published by the Federal Energy Management Administration (FEMA).

FEMA offers seven interactive web-based courses related to emergency management in its Professional Development Series (PDS). These courses can be particularly helpful for facility managers who are responsible for leading their organizations through emergency management preparations. Course information is available online at http://training.fema.gov/IS/crslist.aspx.

International Facility Management Association (IMFA)

IFMA provides facility management education and globally recognized credentials. Facility professionals can earn Facility Management Professional (FMP), Sustainable Facility Professional (SFP), or Certified Facility Manager (CFM) credentials, or attend a verity of conferences related to facility management. Additional information can be found at www.ifma.org/professional-development.

National Association of Power Engineers
Educational Foundation (NAPEEF)

NAPEEF offers training on the operation and maintenance of commercial building properties. NAPEEF teaching professionals have a combination of knowledge, practical expertise, and operational expertise and focus on traditional and emerging building operations and maintenance. More information can be found at www.napeef.org/services.htm.

Operations and Maintenance Training webpage
Published by the U. S. Department of Energy (DOE).

This webpage describes strategies for training operations and maintenance staff to operate the facility, and the standards set for it during the commissioning process, particularly for facilities that have renewable energy systems. This page also describes the importance of formalizing training for facility management staff in a number of general areas, including basic operations, health and safety, emergency procedures, and troubleshooting. It can be accessed at www1.eere.energy.gov/femp/reconstructionguide/om_training.html.

BIBLIOGRAPHY

Chapter 1: An Introduction to Museum and Cultural Institution Facility Management

Alexander, Edward Porter, and Mary Alexander. 2008. *Museums in Motion: An Introduction to the History and Functions of Museums.* Lanham, MD: AltaMira.

American Alliance of Museums (AAM). 2009. Accessed July 18, 2012. "Median Annual Attendance for Different types of Museums (US)." Available at http://aam-us.org/about museums/abc.cfm#visitors.

"Botanical Garden." Accessed February 9, 2012. *Encyclopædia Britannica Online,* s.v. Available at www.britannica.com.

Burcaw, Ellis. 1997. *Introduction to Museum Work.* Walnut Creek, CA: AltaMira.

Crimm, Walter L., Martha Morris, and L. Carole Wharton. 2009. *Planning Successful Museum Building Projects.* Lanham, MD: AltaMira.

Davies, Daniel. 2010. Author's personal communication with Davies, zone manager of the Upper Northwest Zone of the Smithsonian Institution in Washington, DC. This account previously appeared in Angela Person and Judie Cooper, "A Work of Art: The Keeping of Cultural Facilities." *Facility Management Journal* (January–February 2011).

International Facility Management Association (IFMA). 2009. "Facility Management Staffing Report." Available at www.ifma.org.

———. 2012. "What Is FM? Definition of Facility Management." Available at www.ifma.org/resources/what-is-fm/default.htm.

Jellets, Christy. January 27, 2012. Author's personal communication with Jellets, facility operations manager at the Atlanta Botanical Garden in Atlanta, GA.

Merritt, Elizabeth E. 2005. *Covering Your Assets: Facilities and Risk Management in Museums.* Washington, DC: American Association of Museums.

Richardson, Lee. 2012. Author's personal communication with Richardson, assistant director of facilities and museum operations at the Experience Music Project in Seattle, WA.

Rodriguez, Angel. 2012. Author's personal communication with Rodriguez, zone manager of the West Mall Zone at the Smithsonian Institution in Washington, DC.

"Top 100 Art Museum Attendance: The Top 10." April 2013. *The Art Newspaper*, No. 223. Available at www.theartnewspaper.com/attfig/attfig10.pdf.

von Naredi-Rainer, Paul, and Oliver Hilger. 2004. *Museum Buildings: A Design Manual*. Basel: Birkhäuser.

"Zoos." *Encyclopædia Britannica Online*, s.v. Accessed February 9, 2012. Available at www .britannica.com.

Chapter 2: An Overview of Cultural Facility Management

American Alliance of Museums (AAM). Accessed April 16, 2012. "Characteristics of Excellence for Museums." Available at www.aam-us.org/resources/ethics-standards-and-best -practices/characteristics-of-excellence-for-u-s-museums.

Association of Zoos and Aquariums (AZA). Accessed May 9, 2013. "AZA Guide to Accreditation of Zoological Parks and Aquariums, 2013 edition," 34. Available at www.aza .org/uploadedFiles/Accreditation/Guide%20to%20Accreditation.pdf.

Clough, Wayne. September 2011. "The Top Ten Reasons I Get Excited about Facilities." *Smithsonian Torch*. Available at www.e-torch.org/from-the-secretary/september-2011.

Dirican, Alan. 2012. Author's personal communication with Dirican, deputy director for operations and capital planning at the Baltimore Museum of Art in Baltimore, MD.

Fried, Gil. 2005. *Managing Sport Facilities*. Champaign, IL: Human Kinetics.

Genoways, Hugh H., and Lynne M. Ireland. 2003. *Museum Administration: An Introduction*. Walnut Creek, CA: AltaMira.

International Facility Management Association (IFMA). 2012. "What Is FM? Definition of Facility Management." Available at www.ifma.org/resources/what-is-fm/default.htm.

Merritt, Elizabeth E. 2005. *Covering Your Assets: Facilities and Risk Management in Museums*. Washington, DC: American Association of Museums.

Wiggins, Jane M. 2010. *Facilities Manager's Desk Reference*. Chichester, UK: Wiley-Blackwell.

Wilcox, U. V. 1995. "Facility Management." In *Storage of Natural History Collections: A Preventive Conservation Approach*, ed. C. L. Rose, C. A. Hawks, and H. H. Genoways, 29–41. York, PA: Society for the Preservation of Natural History Collections.

Chapter 3: Cultural Facility Strategic Planning

Cooper, Judie, and Angela Person. April 11–13, 2012. "Facilities Best Practices Don't Have to Break the Bank." In *Proceedings of the International Facility Management Association's 2012 Facility Fusion Conference*, Chicago, IL.

Cotts, David G., Kathy O. Roper, and Richard P. Payant. 2010. *The Facility Management Handbook* (3rd ed.). New York: American Management Association.

Crimm, Walter L., Martha Morris, and L. Carole Wharton. 2009. *Planning Successful Museum Building Projects*. Lanham, MD: AltaMira.

Davies, Daniel. 2011. Author's personal communication with Davies, zone manager of the Upper Northwest Zone of the Smithsonian Institution in Washington, DC.

Erickess, Stephanie. 2012. Author's personal communication with Erickess, facility manager for The Seattle Public Library in Seattle, WA.

Jellets, Christy. 2012. Author's personal communication with Jellets, facility operations manager at the Atlanta Botanical Garden in Atlanta, GA.

Lord, Gail Dexter, and Kate Markert. 2007. *The Manual of Strategic Planning for Museums.* Lanham, MD: AltaMira.

Merritt, Elizabeth E. 2005. *Covering Your Assets: Facilities and Risk Management in Museums.* Washington, DC: American Association of Museums.

Office of Facilities Management and Reliability (OFMR), Smithsonian Institution. 2013. *2013–2017 Strategic Plan.* Washington, DC: Smithsonian Institution.

Person, Angela, and Judie Cooper. January–February 2011. "A Work of Art: The Keeping of Cultural Facilities." *Facility Management Journal*: 22–26. Available at www.ifma.org/publications/facility-management-journal.

Samec, David. 2012. Author's personal communication with Samec, chief of facilities management at the National Gallery of Art in Washington, DC.

Chapter 4: Managing Cultural Facility Systems

AIC (American Institute for Conservation) and IIC (International Institute for Conservation of Historic and Artistic Works). 2010. "The Plus/Minus Dilemma: The Way Forward in Environmental Guidelines." Available at www.iiconservation.org/dialogues/plus_minus_trans.pdf.

Anderson, Maxwell. April 2010. "Revising the Gold Standard of Environmental Control." *The Art Newspaper.* Available at www.theartnewspaper.com.

Brodrick, James. July 2011. "Can Museums Measure Up?" *Illuminating Engineering Society's Gateway Roundup.* Available at http://apps1.eere.energy.gov/buildings/publications/pdfs/ssl/gateway-roundup_7-11.pdf.

Cassar, May, and Jeremy Hutchings. 2000. *Relative Humidity and Temperature Pattern Book: A Guide to Understanding and Using Data on the Museum Environment.* London: Museums and Galleries Commission.

Cuttle, Christopher. 2007. *Light for Art's Sake: Lighting for Artworks and Museum Displays.* Amsterdam: Butterworth-Heinemann.

Dixon, Michael. Summer 2003. "Old Buildings, Old Systems and Older Books: Fighting Mold and Decay in the Twenty-First Century." *Papyrus: A Publication of the International Association of Museum Facility Administrators* 4(3): 29–31. Available at www.iamfa.org.

Druzik, James R. March 2010. Quoted in Dale Paul Krinkright, "Caution Urged When Considering LED Light Sources for Light-Sensitive Materials." *Conservation Online.* Available at http://cool.conservation-us.org/byform/mailing-lists/cdl/2010/0361.html.

Gardner, John W. 1961. *Excellence: Can We Be Equal and Excellent Too?* New York: Harper.

Humphrey, Vicki, and Julian Bickersteth. Winter 2011–2012. "Museum Environmental Standards in a Changing Environment." *Papyrus: A Publication of the International Association of Museum Facility Administrators* 12(3): 38–39. Available at www.iamfa.org.

Indianapolis Museum of Art (IMA). 2012. Accessed May 9, 2013. "Dashboard Series: Special Exhibitions Gallery Temperature and Humidity." Available at http://dashboard .imamuseum.org/series/Special+Exhibitions+Gallery+Temperature+and+Humidity.

International Association of Museum Facility Managers (IAMFA). May 2011. Proceedings of Washington, DC, chapter meeting, as noted by attendee Judie Cooper.

Johnson, Jessica S. 2006. "Museum Collections Environment." In National Park Service, *Museum Handbook*. Washington, DC: National Park Service. Available at www.nps.gov/museum/publications/handbook.html.

Kerschner, Richard L. 1992. "A Practical Approach to Environmental Requirements for Collections in Buildings." *Journal of the American Institute for Conservation* 31(1): 65.

"Lux." 2012. *Encyclopædia Britannica Online Academic Edition*. Available at www.britannica .com.

Michalski, Stefan. 2011a. "Incorrect Relative Humidity." *Canadian Conservation Institute*. Available at www.cci-icc.gc.ca.

———. 2011b. "Light, Ultraviolet and Infrared." *Canadian Conservation Institute*. Available at www.cci-icc.gc.ca.

Muller, Chris. Winter 2010–2011. "Air-Quality Standards for Preservation Environments: Considerations for Monitoring and Classification of Gaseous Pollutants." *Papyrus: A Publication of the International Association of Museum Facility Administrators* 11(2): 45–50. Available at www.iamfa.org.

"Optics." 2012. *Encyclopædia Britannica Online Academic Edition*. Available at www.britannica .com.

Royal Airforce Museum (RAM). June 2008. "The Royal Airforce Museum's Policy for Monitoring Relative Humidity and Temperature," RAFM/DCM/2/6/25/1. Available at www .rafmuseum.org.uk/about-us/policy-performance/collection-policies.aspx.

"Textile." 2012. *Encyclopædia Britannica Online Academic Edition*. Available at www.britannica .com.

Tung, Robin. May 16, 2012. "Museum of the Living Artist Swaps Halogens with LEDs." *San Diego Reader*. Available at www.sandiegoreader.com.

Chapter 5: Managing Cultural Facility Maintenance and Operations

Alten, Helen. Fall 1997. "Vacuums Put Power into Annual Cleaning." *Collection's Caretaker: A Publication of the Northern States Conservation Center* 1(2). Available at www.collection care.org/pubs/v1n2p1.html.

APPA, Leadership in Educational Facilities. 2013. Accessed May 6, 2013. "Financial Perspective: Facilities Condition Index." Available at www.appa.org/research/sam/facilities conditionindex.cfm/.

Bigger, Alan S., and Linda B. Bigger. May 2007. "Contract vs. In-House Staff: Finding the Right Source for Custodial and Maintenance Operations." *Association of College Unions International Bulletin* 73(3). Available at www.acui.org/publications/bulletin/article .aspx?issue=448&id=2298.

Brophy, Sarah S., and Elizabeth Wylie. 2008. *The Green Museum: A Primer on Environmental Practice*. Lanham, MD: AltaMira.

Camp, Robert C. 1989. *Benchmarking: The Search for Industry Best Practices That Lead to Superior Performance*. Milwaukee, WI: Quality Press.

Carroll, Sara. Fall 2011. "Meet Archie, the Four-Legged Pest Controller." *Papyrus: A Publication of the International Association of Museum Facility Administrators* 12(2): 18. Available at www.iamfa.org.

Cotts, David G., Kathy O. Roper, and Richard P. Payant. 2010. *The Facility Management Handbook*. New York: American Management Association.

Edson, Gary, and David Dean. 1994. *The Handbook for Museums*. London: Routledge.

Energy Star. 2010. "Energy Star Success Story: Mark Twain House & Museum." Available at www.energystar.gov/ia/business/entertainment/Success_Story_MarkTwainHouse_Museum.pdf.

———. 2012. Accessed May 9, 2013. "Guidelines for Energy Management: Assess Performance (Step 2.3: Benchmark)." Available at www.energystar.gov/index.cfm?c=assess_performance.benchmark.

Eppley Institute for Parks and Public Lands, Indiana University. 2013. Accessed May 6, 2013. "Facility Maintenance and Operations." Available at http://ets.eppley.org/fmss_foundations/course-content/asset-management-process-amp/facility-maintenance-and-operations.

Facilities Engineering Journal. May 2010. "Building a Facilities Team: A 'Family-Like' Atmosphere Is Key." Available at www.fmlink.com/article.cgi?type=Magazine&pub=AFE&id=30076&mode=source.

Facility Issues. 2011. "2011 IAMFA Benchmarking Survey Results and Trends." Available at www.facilityissues.com/Museums.

Genoways, Hugh H., and Lynne M. Ireland. 2003. *Museum Administration: An Introduction*. Walnut Creek, CA: AltaMira.

Glazner, Steve. 2011. *Operational Guidelines for Educational Facilities: Custodial*. Alexandria, VA: APPA.

Harding, Richard, and Edmond Richard. Summer 2002. "Black & McDonald, CMM, and Museums." *Papyrus: A Publication of the International Association of Museum Facility Administrators* (3)3: 16–18. Available at http://www.iamfa.org.

Hunt, Glenn. 2011. "Comprehensive Facility Operation & Maintenance Manual." In *Whole Building Design Guide*. Washington, DC: National Institute of Building Sciences. Available at www.wbdg.org/om/om_manual.php.

International Centre for the Study of the Preservation and Restoration of Cultural Property (ICCROM) and the United Nations Educational, Scientific and Cultural Organization (UNESCO). 2011. "ICCROM-UNESCO International Storage Survey 2011: Summary of Results." Available at www.re-org.info.

International Facility Management Association (IFMA). 2006. *An Inside Look at FM Outsourcing*. Research Report #27. Available at /www.ifma.org/publications/books-reports/an-inside-look-at-fm-outsourcing.

———. 2013. Accessed May 6, 2013. "Facility Condition Index (FCI)." Available at http://ifmacommunity.org/fmpedia/w/fmpedia/2459.aspx.

Jessup, Wendy. 1995. "Checklist for Pest Management in Collections Storage Facilities." In *Storage of Natural History Collections*, ed. Carolyn L. Rose, Catharine A. Hawks, and Hugh H. Genoways, 219–220. Washington, DC: Society for the Preservation of Natural History Collections.

Lambert, Simon. Winter 2011–2012. "Out of Sight, Out of Mind: Museum Collections in Storage at Serious Risk around the World." *Papyrus: A Publication of the International Association of Museum Facility Administrators* 12(3): 23. Available at www.iamfa.org.

Larocque, Guy. Fall–Winter 2006–2007. "Is Outsourcing Right for Your Organization?" *Papyrus: A Publication of the International Association of Museum Facility Administrators* 8(1): 16–17. Available at www.iamfa.org.

Lewis, Angela. Summer 2012. "Smithsonian National Air and Space Museum Welcomes Space Shuttle Discovery." *National Association of Power Engineers Bulletin*.

Lord, Barry, and Gail Dexter Lord. 1997. *The Manual of Museum Management*. London: The Stationery Office.

Mecklenburg, Marion F., and Alan Pride. Summer 2005. "Using Thermal Imaging to Diagnose Water Penetration and Condensation of the Walls at the Hirshhorn Museum." *Papyrus: A Publication of the International Association of Museum Facility Administrators* (6)2: 2–3. Available at www.iamfa.org.

Merritt, Elizabeth E. 2005. *Covering Your Assets: Facilities and Risk Management in Museums*. Washington, DC: American Association of Museums.

Missouri University of Science and Technology. Accessed May 6, 2013. "APPA Cleaning Standards." Available at http://custodial.mst.edu/appa.

National Aeronautics and Space Administration (NASA). 2000. *Reliability Centered Maintenance Guide for Facilities and Collateral Equipment*. Washington, DC: National Aeronautics and Space Administration. Available at www.hq.nasa.gov/office/codej/codejx/Assets/Docs/RCMGuideMar2000.pdf.

National Park Service (NPS). 1998. "Museum Housekeeping." In the *National Park Service Museum Handbook*. Washington, DC: National Park Service. Available at www.nps.gov/museum//publications/MHI/mushbkI.html.

National Research Council (NRC). 2012. *Predicting Outcomes of Investments in Maintenance and Repair of Federal Facilities*. Washington, DC: National Academies Press.

New South Wales Heritage Office. Accessed March 21, 2012. "The Maintenance Series: Information Sheet 1.1—Preparing a Maintenance Plan." Available at www.heritage.nsw.gov.au/docs/maintenance1-1_preparingplan.pdf.

Northern States Conservation Center (NSCC). August 21, 2012. "Pest ID Apps." *The Collections Caretaker e-Newsletter*. Available at www.collectioncare.org/pubs/Aug212012.html.

Office of Facilities Management and Reliability, Smithsonian Institution (OFMR). 2010. *OFMR Operations and Maintenance Manual*. Washington, DC: Smithsonian Institution.

———. 2012. "Facility Service Worker Assignment Sheet, National Museum of the American Indian." Washington, DC: Smithsonian Institution.

Samec, David. 2012. Author's personal communication with Samec, chief of facilities management at the National Gallery of Art in Washington, DC.

Smithsonian Institution, Museum Conservation Institute. 2006. "Integrated Pest Management Checklist." Available at www.si.edu/mci/downloads/articles/pests9.pdf.

United Nations Educational, Scientific and Cultural Organization (UNESCO). 2010. *Cultural Heritage Protection Handbook 5: Handling of Collections in Storage.* Available at http://unesdoc.unesco.org/images/0018/001879/187931e.pdf.

U.S. Department of Energy (DOE). 2010. *Operations & Maintenance Best Practices: A Guide to Achieving Operational Efficiency.* Available at www1.eere.energy.gov/femp/pdfs/omguide_complete.pdf.

Victoria and Albert Museum. 2003. "Conservation at the V&A: Glossary for Environmental Care." Available at www.vam.ac.uk.

Westerkamp, Thomas A. Summer–Fall 2009. "Lean Green Means Museum Restroom Sustainability and Savings." *Papyrus: A Publication of the International Association of Museum Facility Administrators* (10)2: 17–19. Available at www.iamfa.org.

Whalley, Rob. April 12, 2010. "BMS, CMMS, CAFM, IWMS, EMS . . . confused?" Available at http://cafm-tabs-fm.blogspot.com.

Wilcox, U. Vincent. 1995. "Pest Management," in *Storage of Natural History Collections*, ed. Carolyn L. Rose, Catharine A. Hawks, Hugh H. Genoways, and Amparo R. de Torres. Washington, DC: Society for the Preservation of Natural History Collections.

Chapter 6: Capital Improvement Planning and Implementation

American Society of Heating, Refrigerating, and Air-Conditioning Engineers (ASHRAE). 2005. *ASHRAE Guideline 0-2005, The Commissioning Process.* Atlanta, GA: ASHRAE.

Cable, John, and Jocelyn Davis. 2005. "Key Performance Indicators for Federal Facilities Portfolios." Washington, DC: Federal Facilities Council. Available at www.nap.edu/catalog/11226.html.

Center for Universal Design, North Carolina State University (CUD). April 1, 1997. "The Principles of Universal Design." Available at www.ncsu.edu/project/design-projects/udi/center-for-universal-design/the-principles-of-universal-design.

Cornell University. Accessed May 5, 2013. "Guide to Planning an Accessible Event." Available at http://sds.cornell.edu/Guide_to_Planning_an_Accessible_Event.pdf.

Cotts, David G., Kathy O. Roper, and Richard P. Payant. 2010. *The Facility Management Handbook* (3rd ed.). New York: American Management Association.

Crimm, Walter L., Martha Morris, and L. Carole Wharton. 2009. *Planning Successful Museum Building Projects.* Lanham, MD: AltaMira.

Dahl, P., M. Horman, T. Pohlman, and M. Pulaski. 2005. "Evaluating Design-Build-Operate-Maintain Delivery as a Tool for Sustainability." In *Proceedings of the 2005 Construction Research Congress*, San Diego, CA, 1–10.

Energy Star. 2013. Accessed May 30, 2013. "The Energy Star for Buildings and Manufacturing Plants." Available at www.energystar.gov/index.cfm?c=business.bus_bldgs&s=m.

Federal Facilities Council (FFC). 2002. *Learning from Our Buildings: A State-of-the-Practice Summary of Post-Occupancy Evaluation.* FFC Technical Report No. 145. Washington, DC: National Academies Press. Available at www.nap.edu/catalog/10288.html.

Fuller, Sieglinde. June 28, 2010. "Life-Cycle Cost Analysis," in *Whole Building Design Guide*. Washington, DC: National Institute of Building Sciences. Available at www.wbdg.org/resources/lcca.php.

Gonchar, Joann. January 2012. "Performance Puzzle: Museum Design Teams Juggle the Sometimes-Competing Demands for Preservation of Collections, Human Comfort, and Energy Conservation." In *Continuing Education*. New York: McGraw Hill Construction. Available at http://continuingeducation.construction.com/article.php?L=5&C=867&P=1.

Higher Education Funding Council for England (HEFCE). 2006. *Guide to Post Occupancy Evaluation*. Available at www.smg.ac.uk/documents/POEBrochureFinal06.pdf.

Historic Preservation Subcommittee of the *Whole Building Design Guide* (HPS). August 2, 2012. "Historic Preservation." In *Whole Building Design Guide*. Washington, DC: National Institute of Building Sciences. Available at www.wbdg.org/design/historic_pres.php.

International Facility Management Association (IFMA). Accessed May 6, 2013. "Facility Condition Index (FCI)." Available at http://ifmacommunity.org/fmpedia/w/fmpedia/2459.aspx.

Lord, Barry, Gail Dexter Lord, and Lindsay Martin. 2012. *Manual of Museum Planning: Sustainable Space, Facilities, and Operations*. Lanham, MD: AltaMira.

National Park Service (NPS). 1995. "Standards for the Treatment of Historic Properties." Available at www.nps.gov/history/local-law/arch_stnds_8_2.htm.

———. 2013. Accessed May 29, 2013. "Professional Qualifications Standards." Available at www.nps.gov/history/local-law/arch_stnds_9.htm.

Nonprofit Finance Fund (NFF). 2008. *Case Study: Appreciating Depreciation—Thinking Strategically about Fixed Assets, Boston Center for the Arts*. Available at http://nonprofitfinancefund.org/files/docs/BCACaseStudy102908.pdf.

Project Management Committee of the *Whole Building Design Guide* (PMC). June 11, 2012. "Building Commissioning." In *Whole Building Design Guide*. Washington, DC: National Institute of Building Sciences. Available at www.wbdg.org/project/plan_comm_process.php.

Robertson, Wayne. July 2011. "Retrocommissioning vs. Energy Audit." *Building Operating Management*. Available at www.facilitiesnet.com/energyefficiency/article/Retrocommissioning-vs-Energy-Audit--12569#.

Roper, Cathy, Jun Ha Kim, and Sang-Hoon Lee. 2009. *Strategic Facility Planning: A White Paper*. Houston, TX: International Facility Management Association. Available at www.ifma.org/docs/knowledge-base/sfp_whitepaper.pdf.

Salmen, J. P. S. 1998. *Everyone's Welcome: The Americans with Disabilities Act and Museums*. Washington, DC: American Association of Museums.

Smithsonian Institution. 2010. *OFMR Operations and Maintenance Manual*. Washington, DC: Smithsonian Institution.

Soper, Mary F. Spring 2005. "The Library of Parliament—Ready for a New Generation." *Papyrus: A Publication of the International Association of Museum Facility Administrators* (6) 1: 1–4.

Sullivan, G. P., R. Pugh, A. P. Melendez, and W. D. Hunt. August 2010. *Operations & Maintenance Best Practices: A Guide to Achieving Operational Efficiency*. Richland, WA: Pacific Northwest National Laboratory for the Federal Energy Management Program, U.S. Department of Energy. Available at www1.eere.energy.gov/femp/pdfs/omguide_complete.pdf.

U.S. General Services Administration (GSA). February 15, 2013. "Post Occupancy Evaluation." Available at www.gsa.gov/portal/content/103959.

U.S. Green Building Council (USGBC). 2013. Accessed May 30, 2013. "LEED Certification Process." Available at www.usgbc.org/leed/certification.

VFA. 2011. *The Seven Steps to Strategic Facilities Capital Planning and Management.* VFA, Inc. Available at www.nfmt.com/resources/EventDirectory/baltimore/VFA_Seven Steps%20_US.pdf.

Whole Building Design Guide, Aesthetics Subcommittee. November 5, 2012. "Engage the Integrated Design Process." In *Whole Building Design Guide.* Washington, DC: National Institute of Building Sciences. Available at www.wbdg.org/design/engage_process.php.

Zimmerman, Greg. September 2008. "LEED Points and Credits: What's the Difference?" *Building Operation Management.* Available at www.facilitiesnet.com/green/article/LEED -Points-and-Credits-Whats-the-Difference--9677#.

Zimmerman, Rachael. November 2006. "Universal Design Means Accessibility for One and All." *Building Operation Management.* Available at www.facilitiesnet.com/ada/article/ Accessibility-for-One-and-All--5573#.

Chapter 7: Sustainable Cultural Facility Management

Association of Zoos & Aquariums (AZA). April 29, 2011. "The Zoo & Aquarium Green Guide: Suggestions for Beginning or Expanding a Sustainability Program." Available at www.aza.org/sustainable-practices.

Boston Children's Museum (BCM-MA). 2013. Accessed May 9, 2013. "Green Facts." Available at www.bostonchildrensmuseum.org/newsroom/green-facts.

Bowdoin College Museum of Art (BCMA). Accessed May 9, 2013. "Sustainability Updates on Bowdoin College Museum of Art Renovations." Available at www.bowdoin.edu/ sustainability/buildings-grounds/green-buildings/bowdoin-college-museum-of-art.shtml.

Brooklyn Children's Museum (BCM-NY). 2013. Accessed May 9, 2013. "First 'Green' Museum in New York City." Available at www.brooklynkids.org/index.php/aboutus/ greenmuseum.

Brophy, Sarah S., and Elizabeth Wylie. 2008. *The Green Museum: A Primer on Environmental Practice.* Lanham, MD: AltaMira.

Canadian Museums Association (CMA). 2010. "Sustainable Development: How to Integrate Sustainable Development into Museum Operations?" Available at www.museums .ca/Sustainable_Development/Chapter_1_Sustainable_Development/3._How_to_inte grate_sustainable_development_into_museum_operations/?n=30-34-52.

Chandler, Nathan. July 27, 2009. "How Smart Power Strips Work." Available at http:// science.howstuffworks.com/environmental/green-tech/sustainable/smart-power-strip.htm.

Children's Museum of Pittsburgh (CMP). Accessed May 9, 2013. "Green Museum." Available at https://pittsburghkids.org/about/green-museum.

City of Houston Green Building Resource Center (GBRC). Accessed May 9, 2013. "Do-It-Yourself Home Energy Audit." Available at www.codegreenhouston.org/docman/home -energy-audit/view.htm.

Cleveland Metroparks Zoo (CMZ). 2012. "Sustainability, Recycling & Composting." Available at www.clemetzoo.com/conservation/environment.asp.

BIBLIOGRAPHY

Clough, Wayne. May 2012. "The Green Museum." *Smithsonian Magazine* 43(2). Available at www.smithsonianmag.com/arts-culture/Keeping-the-Smithsonian-Sustainable.html.

Coombs Bobenhausen, Catherine. July 21, 2010. "Sustainable O&M Practices." In *Whole Building Design Guide*. Washington, DC: National Institute of Building Sciences. Available at www.wbdg.org/resources/sustainableom.php.

Department of Environmental Quality, Montana (DEQ). March 25, 2013. "Integrated Waste Management Plan." Available at www.deq.mt.gov/recycle/intewastemanag.mcpx.

Deru, Michael P., Jim Kelsey, and Dick Pearson. 2011. *Procedures for Commercial Building Energy Audits*. Atlanta, GA: American Society of Heating, Refrigerating, and Air-Conditioning Engineers.

Dixon, Patrick. Spring–Summer 2011. "British Library: An Energy-Saving Case Study." *Papyrus: A Publication of the International Association of Museum Facility Administrators* (12)1: 17–18. Available at http://newiamfa.org/papyrus-spring-2011.php.

Duke University, Financial Services. Accessed May 9, 2013. "Environmentally Preferable Purchasing (EPP) Guidelines." Available at http://finance.duke.edu/procurement/green/epp.php.

EcoLogo. Accessed May 9, 2013. "About EcoLogo." Available at www.ecologo.org/en.

Energy Star. Accessed May 9, 2013. "Larger Opportunities: Lighting." Available at www.energystar.gov/index.cfm?c=sb_guidebook.sb_guidebook_lighting.

Executive Order 13423 (EO 13423) Steering Committee. March 29, 2007. "Instructions for Implementing Executive Order 13423." Available at www.fedcenter.gov/_kd/go.cfm?destination=ShowItem&Item_ID=6825.

Fairtrade International. Accessed May 9, 2013. "Buying Fairtrade." Available at www.fairtrade.net/buying_fairtrade.html.

Golisano Children's Museum of Naples. 2013. Accessed May 9, 2013. "History & Mission: C'mon Be Green." Available at www.cmon.org/museum-info/history-mission.

GreenCityBlueLake Institute of the Cleveland Museum of Natural History (GCBL). Accessed May 7, 2013. "Understanding How Much Energy We Use." Available at www.gcbl.org/live/home/efficiency/understanding-how-much-energy-we-use.

Green-e. Accessed May 9, 2013. "Find Green-e Certified." Available at www.green-e.org/gogreene.shtml.

GreenGuard. Accessed May 9, 2013. "GreenGuard Environmental Institute Product Guide." Available at www.greenguard.org/en/QuickSearch.aspx.

Green Seal. Accessed May 9, 2013. "Find Green Seal Products and Services." Available at www.greenseal.org.

Green Seal and Siemens, Inc. 2011. *Green Building Operations and Maintenance Manual: A Guide for Public Housing Authorities*. Available at www.greenseal.org/GreenBusiness/InstitutionalGreeningPrograms/GreenBuildingOperationsMaintenance.aspx.

Happy Hollow Park and Zoo. November 1, 2012. "Happy Hollow Green Tour (Map)." Available at www.hhpz.org/files/hhpz//documents/BeingGreen/HappyHollowGreenTour.pdf.

Harding, Richard. Summer 2006. "The Canadian War Museum—River Water for Sanitary Use: Trials and Tribulations." *Papyrus: A Publication of the International Association of Museum Facility Administrators* (7)2: 21–23. Available at http://newiamfa.org/papyrus-summer-2006.php.

Indianapolis Museum of Art. Accessed September 20, 2010. "Dashboard Series: Special Exhibitions Gallery Temperature and Humidity." Available at http://dashboard.imamuseum.org/series/Special+Exhibitions+Gallery+Temperature+and+Humidity.

Johannes, Laura. April 9, 2012. "The Positives and Negatives of Ionized Water." *The Wall Street Journal.* Available at http://online.wsj.com/article/SB100014240527023034047045 7314182468322256.html.

Keep America Beautiful (KAB). Accessed May 9, 2013. *Conducting a Waste Audit.* Available at www.kab.org/site/DocServer/WasteAudit.pdf.

Keith, Lauren, Lydia Gibson, Karin Scott, Ryan Rastok, and Renee Boyd. 2010. "Waste Audit of Wescoe, Strong, and the Spencer Museum of Art." Available at www.sustainability.ku.edu/students/CSA.shtml.

Kelsey, J., and D. Pearson. 2011. "Updated Procedures for Commercial Building Energy Audits." *ASHRAE Transactions* 117(Pt. 2): 374–381.

Kennedy, Mike. October 1, 2011. "Maintaining Sustainability for Green Schools." *American School & University Magazine.* Available at http://asumag.com/Maintenance/sustainable-maintenance-201110/index.html.

Koerner, Brendan. June 17, 2008. "Electric Hand Dryers vs. Paper Towels." *Slate.* Available at www.slate.com/articles/health_and_science/the_green_lantern/2008/06/electric_hand_dryers_vs_paper_towels.html.

Larocque, Guy, and Todd Keeley. Winter 2002. "Energy Management Improvements at the Canadian Museum of Civilization." *Papyrus: A Publication of the International Association of Museum Facility Administrators* (3)1: 10–11. Available at www.iamfa.org/PapyrusWinter02.pdf.

Lawrence Berkeley National Laboratory (LBNL). May 9, 2013. "Building Commissioning: What Is Commissioning?" Available at http://cx.lbl.gov/definition.html.

———. Accessed May 9, 2013. "Carbon Dioxide Measurement & People Counting for Demand Controlled Ventilation." Available at www.demandcontrolledventilation.lbl.gov/dcv.html.

Louisville Zoo. 2013. "ZooPoopyDoo Compost & Mulch Sale." Available at www.louisvillezoo.org/plants/events.htm.

Lutey, Tom. October 1, 2009. "High-Tech Parking Lot Helps Museum 'Go Green.'" *Billings Gazette.* Available at http://billingsgazette.com/news/local/high-tech-parking-lot-helps-museum-go-green/article_1d40f1a2-aeed-11de-92b2-001cc4c002e0.html.

Museum Conservation Institute, Smithsonian Institution (MCI). 2006. "Integrated Pest Management Checklist." Available at www.si.edu/mci/downloads/articles/pests9.pdf.

Museums Australia (MA). 2003. *Museums and Sustainability: Guidelines for Policy and Practice in Museums and Galleries.* Melbourne: Museums Australia. Available at www.museumsaustralia.org.au/userfiles/file/Policies/sustainability.pdf.

National Building Museum (NBM). October 2008. "Greening the National Building Museum." Available at www.nbm.org/about-us/national-building-museum-online/greening-the-museum-1.html.

National Museum of Science and Industry (NMSI). 2010. "NMSI Sustainable Development Policy." Available at www.sciencemuseum.org.uk/about_us/smg/~/~/media/52D60ABBA3154F71B2C88F826382E389.ashx.

Natural Resources Defense Council (NRDC). March 2009. "Water Efficiency Saves Energy: Reducing Global Warming Pollution through Water Use Strategies." Available at www.nrdc.org/water/files/energywater.pdf.

———. 2013. Accessed May 9, 2013. "Greening Advisor: Waste Audits." Available at www.nrdc.org/enterprise/greeningadvisor/wm-audits.asp.

New South Wales Environment & Heritage (NSW). February 27, 2011. "Developing a Sustainable Procurement Policy." Available at www.environment.nsw.gov.au/procurement/Developing.htm.

Office of Facilities Engineering and Operations, Smithsonian Institution (OFEO). November 16, 2012. "Smithsonian Institution Strategic Sustainability Performance Plan." Available at www.si.edu/About/Policies.

Peabody Museum of Archaeology and Ethnology, Harvard University (PMAE). 2013. Accessed May 8, 2013. "Integrated Pest Management (IPM)." Available at www.peabody.harvard.edu/node/275.

Pearson, Paul. May–June 2004. "A Children's Museum Goes Green." *Biodiversity*. Available at http://biodiversityllc.com/PDF/MayJun04-Full.pdf.

Petri, Alexandra. December 14, 2012. "The Paper Towel-Hand Dryer Wars Are Over." *Washington Post*. Available at www.washingtonpost.com/blogs/compost/wp/2012/12/14/the-paper-towel-hand-dryer-wars-are-over/.

Powell, Kevin. September 2012. *GSA Public Building Service Findings: Plug Load Control*. Available at www.gsa.gov/graphics/pbs/PlugLoadControl_508c.pdf.

Raman, Ravi. April 8, 2011. "Paper Towels Now Composted as a Part of AU's Zero Waste Policy." Available at www.american.edu/finance/sustainability/paper-composting.cfm.

Reid Park Zoo. 2013. August 13, 2009. "Conservation at Reid Park Zoo." Available at www.tucsonzoo.org/conservation/.

Rice University. May 9, 2013. "Sustainability Policies." Available at http://sustainability.rice.edu/sustainability-policies/.

Richardson, Lee. 2012. Author's personal communication with Richardson, assistant director of Facilities & Museum Operations at the Experience Music Project in Seattle, WA.

Rivas, Jessica. February 11, 2009. "Managing Plug Loads: Laptops & Chargers & Fans, Oh My!" Paper presented at the 2009 Climate Leaders Web Conference. Available at www.epa.gov/stateply/documents/events/11feb_plugloads.pdf.

Robertson, Wayne. July 2011. "Retrocommissioning vs. Energy Audit." *Building Operating Management*. Available at www.facilitiesnet.com/energyefficiency/article/Retrocommissioning-vs-Energy-Audit--12569#.

Royal British Columbia Museum (RBCM). 2008. "Environmental Sustainability Policy." Available at www.royalbcmuseum.bc.ca/Content_Files/Files/SustainabilityPolicyDecembe2008Final.doc.

Savitz, Andrew W., and Karl Weber. 2006. *The Triple Bottom Line: How Today's Best-Run Companies Are Achieving Economic, Social, and Environmental Success—and How You Can Too*. San Francisco, CA: Jossey-Bass.

Science Museum of Minnesota (SMM). June 6, 2012. "Science Museum of Minnesota Takes the Lead in Environmental Stewardship and Education with Brand New Project No Waste Initiative." Available at www.smm.org/media/projectnowaste.

Slaper, Timothy F., and Tanya J. Hall. Spring 2011. "The Triple Bottom Line: What Is It and How Does It Work?" *Indiana Business Review* (a publication of the Indiana University Kelley School of Business) (86)1: 4–8. Available at www.ibrc.indiana.edu/ibr/2011/spring/article2.html.

Smithsonian Institution. 2012. *Smithsonian Institution Strategic Sustainability Performance Plan*. Washington, DC: Smithsonian Institution. Available at www.si.edu/Content/Pdf/About/Smithsonian-Institution-Sustainability-Perf-Plan.pdf.

———. 2013. Accessed May 9, 2013. "Smithsonian Institution Summit on the Museum Preservation Environment." Available at www.si.edu/PreservationEnvironment.

South Dakota Municipal Electric Association (SCMEA). December 2011. "Member Highlight: Brookings Municipal Utilities." *Hometown Power* (1)11: 1. Available at www.sdmunicipalleague.org/vertical/sites/%7B2540DC39-A742-459F-8CAF-7839ECF21E89%7D/uploads/SDMEA_Hometown_Power_December_2011_Issue.pdf.

Stones River (SR). Accessed May 9, 2013. "Case Study: Ringling Museum of Art." Available at www.srcsolutionsonline.com/wp-content/uploads/case-studies/Ringling.pdf.

Sustainability Standards in Museums (SSM). Accessed May 7, 2013. "Sustainable Museums." Available at www.sustainablemuseum.com.

United Nations Global Marketplace (UNGM). 2010. "What Is Sustainable Procurement?" Available at www.ungm.org/sustainableprocurement/default.aspx.

U.S. Department of Energy (DOE). November 3, 2011. "Energy Service Companies." Available at www1.eere.energy.gov/femp/financing/espcs_companies.html.

———. May 31, 2012. "Honolulu Museum of Art Receives Largest Energy Efficiency Rebate." Available at http://apps1.eere.energy.gov/states/news_detail.cfm/news_id=18374.

U.S. Energy Information Administration (EIA). January 2, 2013. "How Much Energy Is Used in Buildings in the United States?" Available at www.eia.gov/tools/faqs/faq.cfm?id=86&t=1.

U.S. Environmental Protection Agency (EPA). October 2009. *Backyard Composting: It's Only Natural*. Brochure. Available at http://epa.gov/waste/conserve/tools/greenscapes/pubs/compost-guide.pdf.

———. March 6, 2012. "Water Trivia Facts." Available at http://water.epa.gov/learn/kids/drinkingwater/water_trivia_facts.cfm.

———. March 22, 2013. "After the Storm." Available at http://water.epa.gov/action/weatherchannel/stormwater.cfm.

U.S. Green Building Council (USGBC). 2010. *LEED Reference Guide for Green Building Operations and Maintenance*. Washington, DC: U.S. Green Building Council.

University of California, Davis, and California Collegiate Recycling Council (UCD–CCRC). Accessed May 9, 2013. *College and University Recycling Manual*. Available at sustainability.ucdavis.edu/local_resources/docs/recycling/manual.pdf.

University of North Carolina (UNC). 2009 "The University of North Carolina Sustainability Policy." Available at www.northcarolina.edu/policy/index.php?pg=vs&id=5606.

Vaughan, Adam. June 8, 2012. "LED Lightbulbs Can Save You Hundreds in Energy Bills." *The Guardian*. Available at www.guardian.co.uk/environment/2012/jun/08/led-lightbulbs-save-energy-bills.

Victoria and Albert Museum. Accessed May 9, 2013. "Sustainability at the V&A." Available at www.vam.ac.uk/content/articles/s/v-and-a-sustainability/.

Washington State University Energy Program. Accessed May 9, 2013. *Energy Audit Workbook*. Available at www.energy.wsu.edu/Documents/audit2.pdf.

WasteWise, U.S. Environmental Protection Agency. Accessed May 9, 2013. "WasteWise: Conserving Resources, Preventing Waste." Available at www.epa.gov/epawaste/conserve/smm/wastewise/index.htm.

Westerkamp, Thomas. Summer–Fall 2010. "Facility Managers Lead the Move to Green with Improvements in Energy Efficiency." *Papyrus: A Publication of the International Association of Museum Facility Administrators* 11(2): 33.

Wittig, Stacey. Fall–Winter 2008–2009. "Urban Bird Control: A Green Alternative." *Papyrus: A Publication of the International Association of Museum Facility Administrator* (9)3: 9–10. Available at http://iamfa.org/PapyrusWinter08.pdf.

Woodland Park Zoo (WPZ). Accessed May 9, 2013. "ZooDoo Compost." Available at www.zoo.org/page.aspx?pid=2001.

Wunschel, Andrew. January 15, 2013. "Integrated Pest Management in the Butterfly Haven." Peggy Notebaert Nature Museum. Available at www.naturemuseum.org/the-museum/blog/integrated-pest-management-in-the-butterfly-haven.

Chapter 8: Risk Management and Safety in Cultural Institution Facilities

Adams-Graf, Diane, and Claudia Nicholson. March 2000. "Thinking Ahead about Museum Protection: An Ounce of Prevention Is Worth a Pound of Cure." *Tech Talk* (a publication of the Minnesota Historical Society). Available at www.mnhs.org/about/publications/techtalk/TechTalkMarch2000.pdf.

American Museum of Natural History (AMNH). Accessed June 3, 2013. "Risk Management and Disaster Planning." Available at http://collections.paleo.amnh.org/9/risk-management-and-disaster-planning.

Beers, Meredith. October 2011. "Emergency Management Decision-Making under Pressure." *The International Association of Emergency Managers (IAEM) Bulletin* (26)10: 12. Available at www.iaem.com/documents/201110bulletinonline.pdf.

California Polytechnic State University. February 22, 2013. "Campus Administrative Policies—Policy vs. Procedure: A Guideline." Available at policy.calpoly.edu/cappolicy.htm.

Children's Museum & Theatre of Maine. Accessed June 7, 2013. "Health and Safety." Available at www.kitetails.org/about-us/health-and-safety.

Croft, Jim, and Alexander Sherman. 2005. "Avoid, Transfer, Assume, or Insure?" In Elizabeth Merritt, *Covering Your Assets: Facilities and Risk Management in Museums*. Washington, DC: American Association of Museums.

Cullen, Scott. June 11, 2012. "Risk Management." In *Whole Building Design Guide*. Washington, DC: National Institute of Building Sciences. Available at www.wbdg.org/project/riskmanage.php.

Dimas, Jennifer. July 19, 2007. "Colorado State's Morgan Library Marks 10 Years after Devastating Flood." Available at www.news.colostate.edu/release/print/958.

Dorge, Valerie, and Sharon L. Jones. 1999. *Building an Emergency Plan: A Guide for Museums and Other Cultural Institutions.* Los Angeles: Getty Conservation Institute.

Genoways, Hugh H., and Lynne M. Ireland. 2003. *Museum Administration: An Introduction.* Walnut Creek, CA: AltaMira.

Hankins, Roger. May 24, 2013. Author's personal communication with Hankins, supervisory safety manager of the Smithsonian Institution Office of Facilities Management and Reliability in Washington, DC.

Hansen, James. 2007. "1997 Flood: Logistics and Communication Challenges." In *Democracy's University—A History of Colorado State University, 1970–2003.* Fort Collins: University Press of Colorado. Available at www.colostate.edu/features/flood97-logistics.aspx.

Heritage Preservation. 2013. "Prepare for MayDay 2013." Available at www.heritagepreservation.org/PROGRAMS/TFlessons/MayDay2013/MayDayPress.pdf.

———. Accessed June 6, 2013. "Risk Evaluation and Planning Program." Available at www.heritagepreservation.org/REPP/docs/REPP_Walk-through_Checklist.pdf.

Miller, Paul. July 22, 2007. "10 Years after the Flood." *Denver Post.* Available at www.colostate.edu/features/flood97-damage.aspx.

Mitchell, Thomas. October 2011. "Emergency Management: A Continual Challenge and Opportunity for the Facility Management Professional." Paper presented at the 2011 International Facility Management Association World Workplace Conference, Phoenix, AZ.

O'Connor, Diane Vogt. 2006. "Emergency Planning." In *National Park Service Museum Handbook.* Washington, DC: National Park Service. Available at www.nps.gov/museum/publications/handbook.html.

Positive Promotions (PP). 2005. "Preventing Slips, Trips, and Falls (#828-SL)." Slide Guide Card. Available at http://www.positivepromotions.com/preventing-slips-trips-amp-falls-slideguide-with-personalization/p/828-s1.

Schindel, Terri. August 21, 2012. "Risk Assessment and Management." *The Collections Caretaker e-Newsletter* (a publication of the Northern States Conservation Center). Available at www.collectioncare.org/pubs/Aug212012.html.

Chapter 9: Special Events in Cultural Facilities

Artifax Event (a). Accessed May 9, 2013. *Artifax Event Brochure.* Available at http://us.artifax.net/files/Artifax%20Museum%20Brochure_12.pdf.

——— (b). Accessed May 9, 2013. "Smarter Event Management Software." Available at http://us.artifax.net/sectors/museums-a-galleries.

Bowers Museum. 2012. "Museum Rental Policies and Guidelines." Available at www.bowers.org/files/Rental_policies.pdf.

Cincinnati Art Museum (CAM). Accessed May 9, 2013. "Plan an Event." Available at www.cincinnatiartmuseum.org/visit/rent/plan-an-event.

Cornell University. Accessed May 5, 2013. *Guide to Planning an Accessible Event.* Available at http://sds.cornell.edu/Guide_to_Planning_an_Accessible_Event.pdf.

Denver Firefighters Museum (DFM). 2012. "Rental Brochure: Rental Contract." Available at www.denverfirefightersmuseum.org/downloads/documents/Rental%20Brochure.pdf.

Dirican, Alan. 2012. Author's personal communication with Dirican, deputy director for Operations and Capital Planning at the Baltimore Museum of Art in Baltimore, MD.

Genoways, Hugh H., and Lynne M. Ireland. 2003. *Museum Administration: An Introduction.* Walnut Creek, CA: AltaMira.

Humboldt Arts Council. Accessed May 9, 2013. "Humboldt Arts Council in the Morris Graves Museum of Art: Rental Policies." Available at http://humboldtarts.org/rentals.htm.

Jellets, Christy. 2012. Author's personal communication with Jellets, facility operations manager at the Atlanta Botanical Garden in Atlanta, GA.

Massachusetts Institute of Technology—Environment, Health, and Safety (MIT). March 25, 2010. "Event Safety Guidelines." Available at http://ehs.mit.edu/site/content/event -safety-guidelines.

Matagorda County Museum (MCM). Accessed May 9, 2013. "Renting our Facilities." Available at www.matagordamuseum.org/rentourfacilities.

Merritt, Elizabeth E. 2005. *Covering Your Assets: Facilities and Risk Management in Museums.* Washington, DC: American Association of Museums.

Morris Museum of Art (MMA). Accessed May 9, 2013. "Facility Rental Packet: Catering Checklist." Available at http://themorris.org/PDFS/rental_packet.pdf.

Museum of Chinese in America (MOCA). Accessed May 9, 2013. "Facility Rental." Available at www.mocanyc.org/about/facility_rental.

National Archives. Accessed May 9, 2013. "Space Use Guidelines." Available at www.archives .gov/nae/visit/host/space-use.html.

National Archives Southeast Region Facility. Accessed May 9, 2013. *Guidelines for Event Space Use at the National Archives Southeast Region Facility.* Available at www.archives.gov/ atlanta/public/event-space.pdf.

National Cowboy and Western Heritage Museum (NCWHM). 2011. "Facilities Rental Information." Available at www.nationalcowboymuseum.org/files/RentalPolicy.pdf.

Noyes Museum of Art. Accessed May 9, 2013. *Museum Rental Guidelines.* Available at http:// noyesmuseum.org/resources/rental_form_guidelines_policies.pdf.

Sam Noble Oklahoma Museum of Natural History (SNOMNH). November 2011. "Facility Rental Policy." Available at www.snomnh.ou.edu/events/documents/OURental_Guidelines .pdf.

Samec, David. 2012. Author's personal communication with Samec, chief of facilities management at the National Gallery of Art in Washington, DC.

San Diego History Center (SDHC). Accessed May 9, 2013. "Special Events and Wedding Rentals." Available at www.sandiegohistory.org/renting_our_sites.html.

Ungerboeck Software International (USI). Accessed May 9, 2013. "Event Management Software for Museums, Zoos, and Other Cultural Attractions." Available at http:// ungerboeck.com/software-solutions/Destinations_Attactions/event-management-soft ware-for-museums.aspx.

Warhawk Air Museum (WAM). Accessed May 9, 2013. "Facility Use Agreement: Checklist." Available at www.warhawkairmuseum.org/files/docs/facilityuseagreement.pdf.

Watson Hyatt, Glenda. May 2009. "How to Plan an Accessible Event." *Medical Meetings* (36)3: 5–6.

Zetcom. Accessed May 9, 2013. "Core Modules and Features of MuseumPlus." Available at www.zetcom.com/products/collection-management-software-museumplus/features/.

Chapter 10: Training Cultural Facility Personnel

Cupps, Stephen, and Kurt E. Olmosk. 2008. "Developing Effective Internships within Public Sector Organizations." *Public Personnel Management* 37(3): 303.

Trautman, Steve. 2007. *Teach What You Know: A Practical Leader's Guide to Knowledge Transfer Using Peer Mentoring*. Upper Saddle River, NJ: Prentice Hall.

INDEX

ABOUT THE AUTHORS

Angela Person-Harm holds a bachelor of science degree in environmental design and a master of science degree in museum studies, both from the University of Oklahoma. She works with the Office of Facilities Management and Reliability of the Smithsonian Institution to document and describe best practices in museum and cultural facility management. She has given presentations on facility management at the American Alliance of Museums and International Facility Management Association (IFMA) conferences, and has been awarded an "Editor's Pick" award for her work published in the *Facility Management Journal.* She is currently writing her dissertation about the architecture of the Hirshhorn Museum and Sculpture Garden in Washington, DC.

Judie Cooper is a facility management analyst in the Office of Facilities Management and Reliability of the Smithsonian Institution and is responsible for strategic initiatives, organizational development, benchmarking, research, staff professional development, and implementation of best practices. She is a certified facility manager, a past chairperson of the IFMA Capital Chapter Education Team, and the current president of the Museums/Cultural Institutional Council of IFMA. She is active in the International Association of Museum Facility Administrators, the American Society for Training and Development, and the Society for Human Resources Management.